AF615481

No. 1221
$14.95

How to Buy & Fly R/C Aircraft

by Edwin M. Moorman Jr.

TAB BOOKS Inc.
BLUE RIDGE SUMMIT, PA. 17214

FIRST EDITION

FIRST PRINTING

Printed in the United States of America

Library of Congress Cataloging in Publication Data

Moorman, Edwin M
How to buy and fly R/C aircraft.

Includes index.
1. Airplanes—Models—Radio control. I. Title.
TL770.M658 796.1'5 80-23599
ISBN 0-8306-9922-8
ISBN 0-8306-1221-1 (pbk.)

Preface

The sport/hobby of flying radio controlled (R/C) models is growing every year. The young and the old and men and women are discovering the challenge and the satisfaction of flying a R/C plane or helicopter. Professionals looking for a hobby where they can use their Knowledge, people wanting to fly but unable to go the real ones, former control-line or free-flight modelers, or just someone who saw or read about radio control are turning up at flying fields and club meetings wanting to know more about the hobby.

The usual R/C club, with two or three instructors, is finding itself caught short. Moreover, many instructors accustomed to teaching former modelers who already had a comprehensive knowledge of engine operation and building are discovering that their usual instructing techniques do not work with the person whose first model is an R/C plane or helicopter. Telling the student to "meet" me at the field with your plane and then giving him or her a few instructional and practice flights isn't enough. What is needed is a comprehensive, get-down-to-the-basics flight instruction course covering all phases of the hobby from selecting the plane and equipment to the point where the student is a competent pilot.

This book is for people involved in the instruction process, the R/C flight student and the R/C instructor. The first part of the book is aimed at the student. It is intended to be a basic reference and textbook that will give the student a working background for the hobby. The second part of the book is written for the instructor and it details a thoroughly tested flight instruction program complete with techniques and error analysis.

Edwin M. Moorman Jr.

Acknowledgements

I would like to thank the members of the Eglin Aero Modellers of the Eglin Air Force Base/Fort Walton Beach, Florida area for their help in the development and testing of the techniques detailed in this book. I would also like to mention Bob Violett, who kindly provided photographs of his planes, and John Dorman, whose many scale war planes are shown. A special thanks to my flying friends Herb Dickerson for the photography, Ken Stewart for many of the illustrations, and To Dr. Michael V. Tulloch of Systems Research Laboratories for his help on the subjects of human factors and perception. The book could not have been written without the unflagging help and assistance of my R/C flying wife, Phyllis, who edited and typed the manuscript.

Contents

Requirements Before Flight

As with full scale pilot training programs, there are some requirements that must be fulfilled before the student can begin training. These are an FCC radio license an, in most cases, membership in the Academy of Model Aeronautics.

FCC LICENSE

By law, every operator of a transmitter over 100 miliwatts is required to have a license issued by the Federal Communications Commission (FCC). Model radio control transmitters fall into this category since most are in the 500mw to 750mw range. The FCC has placed them in the citizen's band licensing area and the license is obtained in the same manner as you would obtain one for a CB radio for your car. Figures 1-1 and 1-2 show a copy of the FCC citizen's band license application form. You can get these from your hobby dealer selling radio control sets or any store, like Radio Shack, carrying CB radios. The R/C club secretary in your area should also have blank forms. It is a good idea to have the instructor help the student fill out the form and see that it is mailed off properly. Note that you check the block labeled "Class C, remote control of models." Citizen's band voice radio operators check the "Class D" block. These licenses are for their specific areas and one cannot be used for operating the other class of transmitter. If you already have a CB license, you still need to get an R/C one. The license is free. It is a requirement and you should have it before using your transmitter.

ACADEMY OF MODEL AERONAUTICS

The other requirement before flight, in most cases, is membership in the Academy of Model Aeronautics (AMA). Membership cost is currently $25. Since this seems a lot of money to spend

United States of America
Federal Communications Commission

Form Approved
GAO No. B-180227(R01 02)

FCC FORM 505

November 1976

APPLICATION FOR CLASS C OR D STATION LICENSE IN THE CITIZENS RADIO SERVICE

INSTRUCTIONS

A. Print clearly in capital letters or use a typewriter. Put one letter or number per box. Skip a box where a space would normally appear.

B. Enclose appropriate fee with application. Make check or money order payable to Federal Communications Commission. DO NOT SEND CASH. No fee is required of governmental entities. For additional fee details see FCC Form 76-K, or Subpart G of Part 1 of the FCC Rules and Regulations, or you may call any FCC Field Office.

C. Mail application to Federal Communications Commission, P.O. Box 1010, Gettysburg, Pa. 17326

NOTICE TO INDIVIDUALS REQUIRED BY PRIVACY ACT OF 1974

Sections 301, 303 and 308 of the Communications Act of 1934 and any amendments thereto (licensing powers) authorize the FCC to request the information on this application. The purpose of the information is to determine your eligibility for a license. The information will be used by FCC staff to evaluate the application, to determine station location, to provide information for enforcement and rulemaking proceedings and to maintain a current inventory of licensees. No license can be granted unless all information requested is provided.

1. Complete ONLY if license is for an Individual or Individual Doing Business AS

FIRST NAME **INIT** **LAST NAME**

2. DATE OF BIRTH

MONTH DAY YEAR

3. Complete ONLY if license is for a business, an organization, or Individual Doing Business AS

NAME OF BUSINESS OR ORGANIZATION

4. Mailing Address

4A. NUMBER AND STREET

4B. CITY **4C.** STATE **4D.** ZIP CODE

(See reverse side of this form, for filling in Item 4C.)

5. If you gave a P.O. Box No., RFD No., or General Delivery in Item 4A, you must also answer items 5A, 5B, and 5C

5A. *NUMBER AND STREET WHERE YOU OR YOUR PRINCIPLE STATION CAN BE FOUND*
(If your location can not be described by number and street, give other description, such as, on RT. 2, 3 mi., north of York)

5B. CITY

5C. STATE

(See reverse side of this form for filling in Item 5C.)

6. *Type of Applicant* **(Check Only One Box)**

- ☐ *Individual*
- ☐ *Association*
- ☐ *Corporation*
- ☐ *Business Partnership*
- ☐ *Governmental Entity*
- ☐ *Sole Proprietor or Individual/Doing Business As*
- ☐ *Other (Specify)* ______

7. *This application is for*

- ☐ *New License*
- ☐ *Renewal*
- ☐ *Increase in Number of Transmitters*

IMPORTANT
Give Official FCC Call Sign

8. *This application is for* **(Check Only One Box)**

- ☐ *Class C Station License (NON-VOICE—REMOTE CONTROL OF MODELS)*
- ☐ *Class D Station License (VOICE)*

9. *Indicate number of transmitters applicant will operate during the five year license period* **(Check Only One Box)**

- ☐ *1 to 5*
- ☐ *6 to 15*
- ☐ *16 or more (Specify No and attach statement justifying need.)*

10. CERTIFICATION I certify that:

- The applicant is not a foreign government or a representative thereof.
- The applicant has or has ordered a current copy of Part 95 of the Commission's rules governing the Citizens Radio Service. See reverse side for ordering information.
- The applicant will operate this transmitter in full compliance with the applicable law and current rules of the FCC and that his station will not be used for any purpose contrary to Federal, State, or local law or with greater power than authorized.
- The applicant waives any claim against the regulatory power of the United States relative to the use of a particular frequency or the use of the medium of transmission of radio waves because of any such previous use, whether licensed or unlicensed.

THIS APPLICATION WILL NOT BE PROCESSED UNLESS SIGNED AND DATED.

WILLFUL FALSE STATEMENTS MADE ON THIS FORM OR ATTACHMENTS ARE PUNISHABLE BY FINE AND IMPRISONMENT. U.S. CODE, TITLE 18, SECTION 1001.

11. SIGNATURE	12. DATE

Signature of: Individual applicant, partner, or authorized person on behalf of a governmental entity, or an officer of a corporation or association

Fig. 1-1. The front side of an FCC License Application.

just to fly a model airplane or helicopter, let me explain about the AMA and the services it provides to the modeler.

History

The original national model airplane organization was the Junior Division of the National Aeronautic Association, a full scale airplane organization. Like the present AMA, this body sanctioned contests, certified records and aided the growth of model aviation with its national newsletter and national championship contest. While there were dues, most of the services were actually provided and administered by the National Aeronautic Association. With the growth of modeling in the '30s, the task became larger than the NAA wanted to continue to perform. The leaders of the Junior Division were asked to form their own independent organization.

At the same time that the Junior Division of the NAA was in existence, there was also an organization called the Academy of Model Aeronautics. This was an honorary organization with elected membership. The candidates were selected from long-time modelers who had made contributions to the development of model aivation. When the Junior Division left the NAA, it simply reorganized under the name of the Academy of Model Aeronautics with the former elected members becoming essentially the senior advisors to the new national governing body. Since that time the AMA has become the largest sport aviation in the United States.

Services

Primary among the services provided by the AMA and the main reason, for all practical purposes, that membership is required by virtually every radio control club in the United States is the liability insurance coverage. Membership in AMA gives every R/C flier $1,000,000 in accident liability protection. Due to the prevalence of lawsuits in recent years, it is a rare property owner who will lease his land to an R/C club that doesn't require that all its members have AMA coverage.

Other services provided by AMA include a subscription to *Model Aviation*, a monthly magazine covering all areas of model flying. The magazine also prints informative articles, model plans and construction articles, a list of coming contests, rules changes and, of course, AMA news items.

The AMA sanctions contests and certifies the results or records set. As the U.S. representative to the FAI, or Federique

Aeronautique Internationale, the international aviation organization for both full scale and model airplanes, the AMA can have your record certified as an international record. They also sponsor teams to compete in international championship contests in R/C and control line and free flight as well.

The National Model Airplane Championship is sponsored by the AMA every year. The "Nats" is the largest contest in the country. It brings together modelers from all parts of the U.S. to compete in events covering all phases of the sport. The "Nats" is more than a contest. It is a gathering every year of modelers to compete, but it is also a chance to visit and exchange ideas. It is held in a different part of the country every year so everyone gets a chance to have one close to them.

For young modeler, the AMA provides several college scholarships every year. They also maintain a film library service. Clubs, schools and other organizations can rent professional quality films on every aspect of model aviation—at nominal fees.

AMA officers are elected from the membership. Each adult member has a vote. The president, secretary/treasurer, and the 11 district vice presidents all serve a two-year term. None of these are paid positions. There is also a full-time executive director who maintains an office at AMA Headquarters in Washington, D.C.

Figure 1-3 shows a copy of the AMA membership application form. Other applications can be obtained from the R/C club secretary or in *Model Aviation* magazine (sold in most hobby shops).

Check with your local club. They will undoubtedly have these requirements. So while you are reading you can get a headstart and send in for both your FCC license and your AMA membership.

FIELD AND LOCAL RULES

Every R/C flying field has some rules. They might be extensive and written or displayed at the field or they might be brief and verbally agreed on. But every field has them. Some of the more common ones are covered below.

Safety

Safety is usually the first area covered by field rules and restrictions. While many people consider radio controlled airplanes and helicopters to be toys, a 5- or 6-pound model going 75 miles per hour (or faster) has enough energy to possibly kill someone if it hits him. It is for this reason that virtually all R/Cers belong to AMA (for the insurance).

Sometimes it becomes necessary to return an application. By putting your name and address in the area below, you will enable us to return quickly any application which needs correction or clarification: 1) Put your name on the first line in regular order (for example, Joe Doe); 2) Put your number and street on the second line; 3) Put your city, state, and zip code on the third line.

If necessary, use abbreviations to stay within the guidemarks provided.

ORDERING PART 95 OF THE FCC RULES AND REGULATIONS

The 1976 edition of Part 95, Citizens Radio Service, is for sale at $1.50 per copy. Order from: Superintendent of Documents, U.S. Government Printing Office, Washington, D. C. 20402. Order by Stock Number: 004-000-00324-1 PLEASE NOTE: Part 95, Citizens Radio Service, is revised annually. The prices of government publications are subject to change without notice. Therefore, the price charged for 1977 and later editions may differ from that shown for the 1976 editions.

For Items 4C and 5C: use the two-letter state abbreviations below for filling in these items.

Alabama	AL	Kentucky	KY	Ohio	OH
Alaska	AK	Louisiana	LA	Oklahoma	OK
Arizona	AZ	Maine	ME	Oregon	OR
Arkansas	AR	Maryland	MD	Pennsylvania	PA
California	CA	Massachusetts	MA	Puerto Rico	PR
Colorado	CO	Michigan	MI	Rhode Island	RI
Connecticut	CT	Minnesota	MN	South Carolina	SC
Delaware	DE	Mississippi	MS	South Dakota	SD
District of Columbia	DC	Missouri	MO	Tennessee	TN
Florida	FL	Montana	MT	Texas	TX
Georgia	GA	Nebraska	NB	Utah	UT
Guam	GU	Nevada	NV	Vermont	VT
Hawaii	HI	New Hampshire	NH	Virginia	VA
Idaho	ID	New Jersey	NJ	Virgin Islands	VI
Illinois	IL	New Mexico	NM	Washington	WA
Indiana	IN	New York	NY	West Virginia	WV
Iowa	IA	North Carolina	NC	Wisconsin	WI
Kansas	KS	North Dakota	ND	Wyoming	WY

TEMPORARY PERMIT

(Do not use for license renewals)

If you will use a Temporary Permit, FCC Form 555-B, complete the following:

I hereby request a temporary permit pursuant to my certification on FCC Form 555-B.
My temporary call sign will be [K] [ ] [ ]   [ ] [ ] [ ] [ ] [ ]

Fig. 1-2. The back side of an FCC License Application.

APPLICATION—1980 A.M.A. MEMBERSHIP
Academy of Model Aeronautics
815 Fifteenth St., N.W., Washington, D.C. 20005
(1980 Membership Expires December 31, 1980)

For Those 19 or Over by July 1, 1980

☐ OPEN FULL MEMBERSHIP $25.00
Includes all membership and competition privileges, liability and accident/medical insurance, and subscription to monthly Model Aviation magazine.

SPECIAL FAMILY RATE. . . . . . . See Back Side

SPECIAL SENIOR CITIZEN RATE . See Back Side

FOR ALL AGES

MAIN INTEREST (check one)
☐ CL ☐ FF ☐ RC ☐ Indoor ☐ Scale ☐ All

FAI STAMP (see other side) ☐ $5.00 ☐ $1.00

For Those Not 19 by July 1, 1980
Fill in Date of Birth: MONTH ☐☐ DAY ☐☐ YEAR ☐☐

For Those Not 15 by July 1, 1980—*Check One Only!*

☐ JUNIOR FULL MEMBERSHIP. $13.00
Same privileges as Open Full Member.

☐ JUNIOR LIMITED MEMBERSHIP. $5.00
Same as above but no magazine.

For Those 15 But Not 19 by July 1, 1980—*Check One Only!*

☐ SENIOR FULL MEMBERSHIP. $15.50
Same privileges as Open Full Member.

☐ SENIOR LIMITED MEMBERSHIP. $7.50
Same as above but no magazine.

INSTRUCTIONS: PRINT CLEARLY IN CAPITAL LETTERS. PUT ONE LETTER OR NUMBER PER BOX. SKIP A BOX WHERE SPACE WOULD NORMALLY APPEAR. REQUESTED INFORMATION MUST FIT WITHIN THE NUMBER OF BOXES PROVIDED. ABBREVIATE IF NECESSARY FOR FITTING.

FIRST NAME INIT. LAST NAME

MAILING ADDRESS (TYPICALLY NUMBER AND STREET)

MAILING ADDRESS CONTINUATION (USE ONLY IF REQUIRED FOR YOUR ADDRESS)

CITY STATE ZIP CODE

☐ VISA ACCOUNT NO. ☐ MASTER CHARGE ACCOUNT NO.

Total: $ ________ ☐ Enclosed ☐ Charged*

*Only Visa or Master Charge

EXPIRATION DATE OF CREDIT CARD

☐ New ☐ Renewal (number ________)

HQ USE ONLY
AMA NO.
PUB
C1
C2
C7

Fig. 1-3. Academy of Model Aeronautics membership form.

Each club will have their specific unsafe areas where it is forbidden to fly. Common one are: over the *pit* area (the area used for setting up and getting the planes ready), over roads and buildings, and over spectator areas. You should fully understand the area restrictions before you fly.

Solo Qualification

Many clubs have a set of rules governing solo qualification. Fledgling R/Cers must meet certain proficiency requirements before they are allowed to fly without a supervising instructor. Some clubs tend to be very lax in this area and leave solo qualification entirely at the discretion of the instructor. Other clubs have specific flight maneuvers which must be accomplished. Sometimes these must be witnessed by another instructor before solo qualification is granted.

The attainment of solo proficiency, "earning your wings," is a big event for an R/C pilot. Many clubs present the new flier with an award such as a certificate or patch. Figure 1-4 shows a sample solo certificate used by one club. Other clubs use antenna flags to designate classes of pilots: pre-solo, solo and instructor.

Frequency Control

A third area covered by local rules in every club is frequency. Improper frequency control can result in the loss of a plane. This is always a monetary loss and it can pose a safety problem as well. For this reason, it is important to be thoroughly familiar with the frequency control measures in your local club.

The frequency control problem results from the fact that two aircraft cannot operate on the same frequency at the same time. For example, suppose pilot A turns on his radio receiver and transmitter which is operating on 72.24 MHz. He starts his engines, taxis out and takes off. Now suppose pilot B, also with a transmitter on 72.24 MHz, turns his radio on. The receiver in A-plane, tuned to receive 72.24 MHz, now picks up two transmitters, each with different commands. These interfering commands can wreak havoc with the receiver and servos in the plane and cause the servos to drive to a limit. This results in a spin or a spiral and a crash. For this reason, every club has some type of control to insure that only one transmitter on each frequency operates at a time.

There are two main methods of frequency control and both usually involve colored clothes pins. The colors indicate the specific frequency. The clothes pin, clipped on a transmitter an-

Table 1-1. R/C Frequencies and Color Codes.

27 MHz Band	72-76 MHz Band
26.995 - Brown	72.08 - White and Brown
27.045 - Red	72.16 - White and Blue
27.095 - Orange	72.24 - White and Red
27.145 - Yellow	72.32 - White and Violet
27.195 - Green	72.40 - White and Orange
27.225 - Blue	72.96 - White and Yellow
	75.64 - White and Green

53 MHz Band (Amateur License Required)
53.1 - Black and Brown
53.2 - Black and Red
53.3 - Black and Orange
53.4 - Black and Yellow
53.5 - Black and Green

tenna or on a frequency control board, indicates who is operating on that frequency. That is frequency control in a nutshell. Since it is such an important part of R/C flying, I'll go into it in greater detail.

The AMA has assigned each one of the FCC-allocated model radio control frequencies a color code. Table 1-1 shows a chart of the respective colors and their frequencies. These colors are required to be displayed on transmitters by most clubs in the form of ribbons or flags attached to the transmitter antenna. This allows quick identification of the frequency any transmitter is operating on. By checking the color of the ribbons on the transmitters, it is easy to tell if anyone is operating on the same frequency you have. If another flier is using your frequency, you must wait until he lands and turns his transmitter off before you turn yours on.

About 90 percent of the R/C clubs control frequencies with a control board and colored clothes pins. Figure 1-5 shows a frequency control board used by one club. The control board can be used two ways.

Club Frequency Pins. In the first way, clothes pins are painted colors matching the frequency colors. These are then placed on the board until a flier is ready to fly. Before turning on his transmitter, the flier goes to the frequency control board and gets the proper color pin and clips it to his transmitter antenna. Figure 1-6 shows this procedure. After flying he turns his transmitter off and returns the pin to the control board for another flier on that frequency to use. *In no case* does he turn his transmitter on without having the proper frequency pin. For proper frequency control this rule must be inviolate: *do not turn on without the proper frequency pin.*

Individual Frequency Pins. Another popular type of control, although not as widely-used as the first method, also uses a control board and colored clothes pins. In this case, each flier has his own pin, which in addition to having the proper frequency colors on it, also has his name written on it. When the flier is ready to turn on his transmitter, he goes to the frequency control board and checks his frequency. If there is no pin clipped to that frequency, he assumes no one is operating on it. He clips his own pin on, turns on his radio, and flies. Conversely, if another pin is on that frequency, he knows that someone else is using that frequency and he cannot turn on. A check of the pin also tells him the name of the flier. Figure 1-7 shows the frequency control board with three fliers using frequencies.

There are advantages and disadvantages to both methods. In the case of the club-pin method, a flier can inadvertently take a pin home with him and leave a blank spot on the control board. In the case of the second method, a flier can forget to bring his pin. The second method also requires the flier to have a different pin for each frequency he has a transmitter on. Both methods work well if they are used properly. Again, the golden rule: *never turn on without the pin*.

Impounds. While it is not a separate method of frequency control, many clubs, in addition to one of the above methods, also require impounding of transmitters when they are not being used. This consists of placing your transmitter on a designated table or rack when you do not have the frequency pin. The theory behind transmitter impound is that "if you don't have it, you can't turn it on when you aren't supposed to." Essentially, if you do not have the frequency pin (or have your pin clipped to your frequency on the control board), you can't turn your transmitter on. If you can't turn it on, it might as well be in the impound area. This might sound extreme, but it works very well in preventing frequency conflicts. Most clubs have in their constitutions a monetary liability clause in case of frequency conflict. The person responsible for the conflict is obligated to pay for the damaged plane, engine and radio. This could, in some cases, be several hundred dollars. Responsible use of frequency control is well worth the minor effort it takes.

Hours of Operation

It is common for clubs with flying fields near residential areas to have restrictions on the times flying is allowed. Some clubs limit flying to after 9 a.m. on weekends or after noon on Sundays if they are near a church. Some clubs, flying from a military or reserve base, are restricted to flying on weekends only. Whatever the restrictions, there are good reasons for them. Take the time to become familiar with the rules.

Muffler Requirements

Everyone will agree that an unmuffled model airplane engine is loud when it is close by. However, when the actual decibel level is checked with a decibel meter it does not turn out to be as loud as it seems. At any distance, a model engine is not as loud as a power lawn mower. What causes all the complaints about R/C engine noise? It turns out to be the pitch of the sound and not the loudness. Like a two-stroke motorcycle, a model engine has a high pitched sound that not only carries a long distance, it is in a frequency that is particularly annoying to the human ear.

In an effort to keep their good public images and minimize complaints, nearly every club has some sort of muffler requirement. These vary from club to club. For example, most clubs allow the very small .049- or .10-sized engines to be run unmuffled, but require mufflers on anything larger. Other clubs have a higher cutoff such as at .25-sized engines. Some clubs specify a certain type of muffler. For example, usually a quieter, closed-front type versus an open-front design. And of course, many clubs don't have a formal muffler rule, but it's *understood* that you just don't bring out a .60-sized engine and run it without a muffler.

Type of Aircraft Restrictions

Another type of restriction many clubs have is on aircraft types. Some types of planes, particularly when flown from a small field, are not compatible. For instance, it is common for clubs to restrict race planes from flying at the same time as sport or acrobatic planes. This is desirable from an instructor/student standpoint as it can be quite disconcerting to the student to have a race plane going 150 mph to 175 mph flying back and forth in front of him while he is still trying to master a level turn with a 50-mph trainer.

Some clubs do not allow sailplanes to mix with sport and acrobatic planes. This is usually due to conflicts over time allotments on the frequencies rather than a speed problem. A sailplane in a thermal or updraft can easily stay aloft for 30 minutes or more to the delight of the sailplaner, but to the annoyance of perhaps several powered aircraft pilots who fly on that same frequency. In addition, the launch tow line used by the sailplane can pose somewhat of a hazard to a powered plane if the sailplane is launched into or across the powered plane flying area.

Obviously, helicopters have different runway and taxiway needs than powered planes. A helicopter can be flown from a much smaller area than a plane can. However, having a helicopter lift off, hover and set down again can tie up a runway or taxiway and cause conflicts with the conventional aircraft fliers. For this reason, some clubs require that helicopters be flown from a special area or at special times.

Engine Run-Up Restrictions

Many clubs, especially those in the areas of the country where the soil is sandy or where they fly from grass fields, have restrictions on the direction you point your plane when you run the engine up to full power. This is to keep your propeller blast from blowing sand, grass and other debris onto other people's planes. It is a logical and courteous rule, but one that is easily overlooked unless you're aware of it. In most clubs you point your plane perpendicular to the pits when you run up. That is, if your pit area runs east-west, point the nose of your plane either north or south when you start or rev the engine to high power. It'll save you a lot of dirty looks from your neighbors in the pits.

Engine Break-in Restrictions

An engine runs cooler without a muffler. For this reason, many people want to break a plane in without a muffler. Not using a muffler means a lot of noise. Even clubs that don't have formal muffler requirements balk at having someone run a .60-sized engine in the pits unmuffled for 30 minutes or so to break it in. So before you bring out your brand new 2-horsepower marvel, bolt it to a test stand and fire it up, check on the local rules. And by the way, modern ringed engines, unlike those of 10 or 15 years ago, are set up at the factory pretty loose and need very little break-in other than a few flights with the needle valve set on the rich side.

Emergency Calls

Every club has emergency calls. This might be an agreement to shout, "Look out!" if you are having trouble with your plane and a crash is imminent or it might be an elaborate set of calls. In addition, there are also courtesy calls that are nice if you use them. (Some clubs make them mandatory.)

The need for a call-out system stems from the way an R/C aircraft is flown. At any distance away, an R/C plane is a very small object in the sky. Once you take your eyes off it, it might be extremely difficult to reacquire it. This is especially true for the faster planes that can travel from one sector of the sky to another in a very short time—even seconds. It is also true for the student who does not have the experience to know where or how to look for his plane once he has lost sight of it. Since the R/C pilot looks only at his plane, he cannot see what is going on around him. His peripheral vision or a quick glance around will allow him to see if someone walks up beside him and he will also see another plane if it crosses through his field of view. But this is about all he'll see of other R/C activities while he's flying. Therefore, it is important for the flier having the emergency to call out the nature of his problem or what is going to happen to alert both the spectators in the pits and the other fliers as well.

Heads Up. A shout of "heads up" or "look out" is the most commonly required call. This is given when a crash or collision is imminent and everyone should be prepared to get out of the way of an uncontrolled aircraft. At this time, everyone—fliers included, should quickly locate the aircraft in trouble and be ready to duck or dodge if it's necessary. This doesn't have to be a radio or structural problem; it can be a student on his early landing practice who gave a wrong control input and is heading for the pits. A loud, "heads up!" gets everyone's attention so they can prepare to take evasive action or protect their planes.

I Haven't Got It. "I haven't got it," means that the flier does not have control of his plane. It is a clear statement of radio or perhaps control linkage problems. It tells everyone that an uncontrolled plane or helicopter is in the area. Experienced members will know that the next call is usually, "heads up!" They will spot the plane in trouble and be ready in case it heads towards the pit area.

Dead Stick. This is a call copied from the jargon of full scale fliers of the '20s and '30s. Landing dead stick meant that they landed with an engine failure. A call of "dead stick" means the same thing in virtually ever R/C club; a landing with the engine out. This call also requires other R/C pilots to take certain actions. At a "Dead stick" call all other fliers should clear the landing approach area and give way to the plane with the engine failure. Planes on final approach should add power and go around and planes in the traffic pattern should stay clear of the approach end of the runway. Planes on the runway should clear it as soon as they can and planes waiting for take-off should not taxi on to the runway. The pilot with the engine out is making a forced landing. He might not judge his descent or turns perfectly and he might land on any part of the runway. Since he cannot go around or extend his approach, it is imperative that all other planes yield to him. Those on the ground who do not clear the runway face a definite collision hazard.

Courtesy Calls

Whether or not they are required by your club, calling your intentions when you are near the runway is considerate and helpful to those flying. Calls of, "taking off," "landing," and "making a low pass," let the other fliers know what you are doing when your plane is close to them.

There might also be other restrictions in your club. In many cases, following them is vital to the club's continued use of its flying field. And since the single most serious problem in the R/C world today is getting and keeping flying sites, it pays to be aware of the rules and abide by them.

The Radio

The heart of any radio controlled aircraft is, of course, the radio. Unless it is properly installed, maintained and cared for, R/C flying can become nothing more than a series of hassles and crashes. Since it is so critical a part of the R/C flight system, it deserves a closer look.

HOW IT WORKS

The radio sets in use today are digital, proportional control systems. Figure 2-1 shows a typical set. The transmitter sends out a constant frequency signal that is divided up into different *pulses* (or channels). First, a *reset* (or synchronizing pulse) is sent. This is followed by four or more pulses or channels containing information placed on them by an encoder. Then the cycle repeats. Figure 2-2 shows these pulses.

The long sync pulse is received by the receiver in the airplane and resets the decoder to start taking information from the signal—starting with channel 1. The information channels can vary from 1 to 2 milliseconds in length. This length is determined by how far you move the control stick. Roughly speaking, the decoder measures the length of the pulse and moves the control arm on a servo an amount corresponding to the amount you moved the transmitter stick. Figure 2-3 shows two servos. The servo on the left has the control arm in the neutral position. The other servo has the control arm at full deflection.

This is a very basic description of radio operation and little more in this area would be necessary were it not for the only moving electronic part in the airborne part of the system, the *potentiometer* (or pot, for short). Since the pot can cause the need for some periodic minor maintenance, you might want to know a little about its functioning.

Going back to the information sent to the receiver, recall that the decoder picks off the information for each channel and sends it to a servo. This information is in the form of a voltage or a change in the base voltage. A very small amplifier in the servo amplifies the voltage and the signal turns on battery power to a small electric motor in the servo (see Fig. 2-4). This motor, through a gear train, drives the servo control arm. On the other end of the shaft that the servo arm is on is the potentiometer, a special type of variable resistor. The signal voltage from the amplifier that turned on the battery power to the motor goes through the pot. As the motor and gear train move the servo arm, they also move the pot. As the pot moves, the resistance changes. This reduces the increased voltage back to the preset level. This, in turn, cuts off the signal sending the battery power to the motor.

Since the pot has a moving part, it can wear. This is where minor problems can crop up and cause chattering controls and poor centering. Do not think that this is a major problem. Today's radio sets are remarkably reliable. They usually require only annual check-ups to maintain perfect operation. The very active flier will wear the pots on his frequently used servos—usually the aileron and elevator—and to save himself some money, he might choose to replace or clean them himself.

COMPONENTS OF THE RADIO SYSTEM

The radio set consists of the transmitter, receiver, one or more servos, a battery pack, switch harness and a battery charger.

Fig. 2-1. Typical radio set.

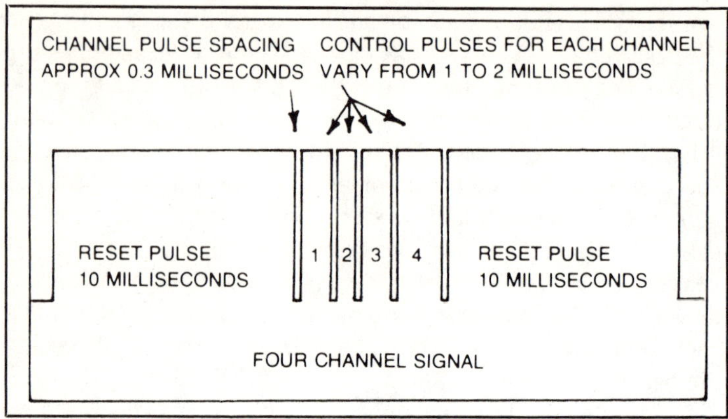

Fig. 2-2. Pulse train showing sync or reset pulse and channel pulses.

The sets available today are made by both American and foreign manufacturers and all of them will give good reliable service if cared for properly. Since there are many different phases of R/C flying, the radio set manufacturers have produced specialized sets that are more suitable for a specific area of flying than the standard set. For example, some manufacturers offer a set specifically designed for helicopter operation. It contains a mixing circuit that allows the operator to set the system to add a small amount of tail rotor change when power is added to the main rotors. This gives an automatic compensation for the torque of the main rotor.

Some manufacturers will even custom tailor the set to your personal requirements. These specialized and custom sets are naturally quite expensive and most fliers use a standard set. Even within the "standard" realm, however, sets come in different transmitter modes and different servo and battery sizes. It is in this area, transmitter mode, battery and servo size, that a beginner can make a choice that can help or hinder his rate of learning and his final proficiency.

A student should know the various options available before making a purchase of a radio set. The choice should be based on personal desires, the type of plane he will learn to fly on and on a certain amount of human factors engineering.

I personally caution students against an instructor who is biased in favor or against one particular name brand or transmitter mode. All of the different brands of radio sets are good. If they weren't, they wouldn't be selling. Bear in mind that in a hobby that requires you to make an investment of about $200 minimum just for

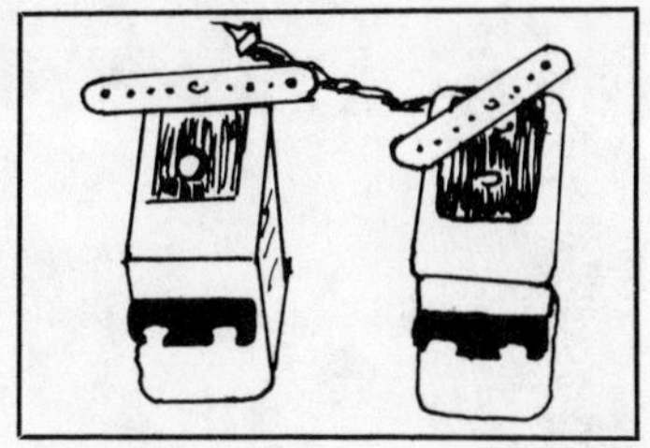

Fig. 2-3. Two servos. The left servo has the control arm in neutral position and the right servo has the control arm at full deflection.

the control system, buyers can be very fickle and discriminating. A poorly made and unreliable radio set will be known nationwide in a short time and sales will drop immediately. It has happened to several companies. Of greater consideration when choosing a brand is the proximity of the service center. You'll find that, more than likely, the most popular radio in your club is the one with the closest service center and the quickest service. Ask one of the fliers in your club about the repair of the brand you contemplate buying. If the service center is in California and you live on the East Coast, you might want to consider another brand.

THE TRANSMITTER

Transmitters come in various sizes and stick modes. This allows the potential flier to pick the one best suited for the type of flying he will do and to his physiology. It's unfortunate, but most beginning R/Cers walk into a hobby shop and buy a set on the recommendation of a friend or the salesman. Usually this works out all right but at times it can be a problem. Consider the stick modes available and some human factors and you'll see what I mean.

Two-stick Transmitter—Mode II

The most popular form of transmitter is the two-stick in Mode II. Figure 2-5 shows a transmitter of this type. The Mode II

Fig. 2-4. The servo opened up showing the servo motor and other components.

Fig. 2-5. Two-stick Mode II transmitter.

configuration has the *roll* (aileron) and *pitch* (elevator) controls on the right stick. You fly this stick exactly the same way you would fly a full-scale plane with a stick. The left stick is for the *yaw* (rudder and nosewheel steering) and for the throttle. You can see that all your steering on the ground, taxi, take off roll and landing roll, will be done with your left hand with this mode. More on that feature later.

Two-stick Transmitter—Mode I

Another two-stick mode, although not nearly as popular as Mode II, is Mode I. Outwardly it looks like a Mode II transmitter, but the functions are on different sticks. Mode I has the rudder and aileron functions reversed. The elevator and the rudder functions

Fig. 2-6. The single-stick transmitter.

are on the right stick and the aileron and throttle functions are on the left stick. This was the first stick set up used on these type sets. The configuration came from older radio sets that used tuned reeds for control. The flier would move a toggle switch to give the plane commands. There were individual toggle switches for each of the aileron, elevator, rudder and throttle functions.

Since a flier usually wants to use aileron and elevator simultaneously, the toggles for these were placed on separate sides of the transmitter so you could operate one with each hand. When the modern digital proportional sets became available, most fliers wanted the same set up that they knew how to fly—aileron on the left and elevator on the right—even though it in no way matched the controls of the full scale aircraft. Mode I is still popular on the West Coast.

Single Stick Transmitter

A third type of transmitter set up is single stick. Figures 2-6 and 2-7 show the front and side of a single stick transmitter. The single stick transmitter uses one stick to perform the functions of the two sticks on the Modes I and II transmitters. The large stick

Fig. 2-7. Single-stick transmitter with side throttle which is controlled with the left index finger. Landing gear retraction switch is the silver toggle switch near the second finger.

Fig. 2-8. Single stick transmitter with top throttle controlled by thumb. Landing gear retraction switch is the toggle switch on the extreme upper right corner of the case.

on the transmitter is a three-axis stick. That is, it has three functions instead of two. The basic stick moves exactly the same as a Mode II transmitter with left and right stick movements for aileron or roll control and forward and backward movements for elevator or pitch control. The difference is the large knob on top of the stick. This knob controls the rudder and nosewheel steering.

With a single stick transmitter, all of the steering is done with your right hand. The throttle on a single stick transmitter is either on the side, as shown in Figure 2-6, or on the top—depending on the brand of radio set. The toggle switch on the side of the transmitter in Figure 2-6 is for retractable landing gear. With the side throttle, you control engine power with your left index finger (Fig. 2-7). With a top throttle, you use your thumb (Fig. 2-8).

What About Extra Channels?

In discussing transmitters, I have mentioned the four primary functions: aileron, elevator, rudder and throttle. These are what the four channels on a transmitter are used for. In addition to the four main channels, many transmitters have from one to as many as four extra channels. As a matter of fact, the most common transmitter is the five-channel. What is the fifth channel used for?

Actually, it can be used for anything the flier wants, but most commonly it controls retractable landing gear.

Five-channel transmitters that are primarily set up for retracts have a toggle switch for the fifth channel. The retract switch, as it is called, is located on the upper left side on two-stick transmitters (Fig. 2-9). It is on the right side of single stick transmitters. Look at Fig. 2-7 for a view of the retract switch on a single stick transmitter.

Other transmitters have the fifth channel as a variable switch on the front of the transmitter. This type channel can be used for flaps or other functions that have more than two positions, open and closed, like the retractable landing gear.

The sixth, seventh and eighth channels, if the transmitter has them, are located in various spots on the face of the transmitter. These give the expert flier a great deal of flexibility in what he can do with his plane. Most competitors use these extra channels, while the sport flier rarely does.

You can imagine what a scale flier can do with a model of a four-engine bomber. Bombay doors can open and close, bombs drop, turrets, lights and flaps operate. Many acrobatic competitors also use the extra channels. A championship plane will have retractable landing gear, flaps or spoilers (or both) and mixture control on the engine (in addition to the normal throttle). Each of these functions requires an extra channel. The student pilot will never need these extra functions during his instruction, but if you have a specific goal in mind it might be a good idea to plan ahead.

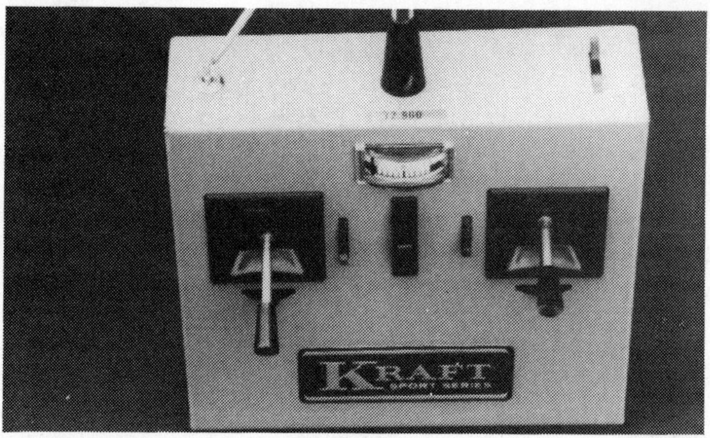

Fig. 2-9. Two-stick transmitter. Landing gear retraction switch is the toggle switch in the upper left.

Transmitters With Fewer Than Four Channels

In addition to the transmitters I've already discussed, there are several configurations for the sets that have fewer than the usual four channels or functions of aileron, elevator, rudder and throttle. These sets are sold either for specialized phases of R/C flying or as a cheaper set for the beginner. Some fliers, like those who fly sailplanes or old timers (explained later), as well as R/C boat and car fanciers, need only two or three functions. Many manufacturers design special sets for these fliers. Other two-and three-channel sets are sold as inexpensive versions of the "full house" sets.

Two-channel sets come in both one- and two-stick configurations. In the single stick version, you get one-half of a Mode II set, or one stick assemble. The two stick version is essentially a Mode I variation. Each stick controls one function. The right stick moves forward and back and is used for the elevator function. The left stick moves right and left and is used for turning the plane. With a two-channel plane you have no throttle control. These transmitters are quite common among sailplane fliers where no throttle is needed since there is no engine. Two-channel sets are also sold for the small .049-powered planes. These small engines run full-power until they run out of fuel. The pilot then glides the plane in for a landing.

Three-channel sets are sold to many beginners for trainers. Many trainer type planes do not have ailerons and need only three channels. The configuration of the three-channel sets is always a single stick like the right stick in a Mode II transmitter with one other control for the throttle. This throttle control can be a variable switch on the face or side of the transmitter or, in the more expensive three-channel sets, a second stick, but with only one function—up and down for the throttle. These transmitters are the "full house" sets with the extra electronics left out. Some of them have the advantage of being convertible to four channels (or greater) later on.

CHOOSING YOUR TRANSMITTER

Now that you know the difference between the transmitter modes, let's see how that can help you make a wise choice of a radio set. You'll find that a large percentage of fliers use a two-stick transmitter. While that fact sometimes leads beginners to assume it's because they are the best type, the actual reason is cost. The more inexpensive sets are two-stick sets. The large majority of fliers started out with this mode and just stuck with it. For you as the potential flier, however, there are considerations other than cost that you should be aware of when making your choice. These other considerations involve a knowledge of human factors.

My introduction to human factors in R/C came when I was teaching my wife to fly. She learned to fly well in the air, and to land, but her taxiing and her take off roll were erratic. These are two of the easier skills to master in R/C, so it left me perplexed. A discussion with a local human factors engineer revealed some useful facts. First, she probably has a condition known as mirror image transference. She moved the stick backwards in a mirror image to the direction it was supposed to go.

As a general background, R/C flying, unlike full scale flying, is a hand-eye coordination function. The pilot doesn't have a feel for the plane like he would if he were actually sitting in it. You have to look at the plane, interpret its attitude, decide on the correct input and move the control stick in the proper direction. You can have a physical problem in two areas, either in the perception of the plane's attitude, or in actually moving the sticks. Perception will be covered in a later chapter. The other area, stick movement, is where knowledge of human factors can help in transmitter selection.

When you talk about R/C stick movement, you must consider the person's non-dominant hand. For most people, the non-dominant hand is the left one. Your dominant hand is the one you learn to do most things with; to write, throw a ball, etc. It's when you try to do things with your other, non-dominant hand that you can run into trouble.

Some people can do things equally with their non-dominant hand. These people are ambidextrous. Next we have a large group of average people who can use their non-dominant hand for some functions, but not nearly as well as their dominant one. Finally, we have a very small group of people who are very right (or left) handed. These are the ones who'll say, "I just can't do anything with my left hand." These are the people, like my wife, who probably need a single-stick radio.

For two-stick flying, you learn to use your non-dominant hand first through what is called *transference.* This is the ability to learn something with one hand and transfer the skill to the other hand. When you first learn to fly, your instructor will take your plane off and demonstrate the controls. He will do a turn, then ask you to try one. You look at the plane, perceive its attitude and decide to turn left. Your brain says "push left" and sends a signal to your hand to move the stick left.

You will have mastered this pretty well by the time you get to try taking off and landing. When you have to steer with your left hand, the knowledge "push left to go left" will easily transfer to that hand. That is, for most people. With some people, the transfer circuit doesn't work too well and they have to essentially learn it all over again with the left hand. In a few, like my wife, the transfer circuit works fine, but the directions get reversed in the process. She was seeing a need to go left, but the stick would move right.

As you might guess, I arranged for her to fly with a single stick radio and her performance on take off roll and landing roll out showed marked improvement. I have since recommended a single stick transmitter to other students who were having this type of problem. If you are the sort of person who is very one handed, find a single stick flier at your club's field or try one at a hobby shop and see how it feels to you. As human factors experts say, "Don't make a man change to fit the machine, change the machine to fit the man." Remember this when you pick your transmitter.

Another item to consider in choosing a transmitter style is the number of channels. Generally speaking, the more channels, the more cost. What you must consider is the ultimate cost to you of the hobby. Check around your club flying field and more than likely 95 percent of the fliers will have sets with four or more channels. That is, of course, unless yours is a sailplane club. These multi-channel sets are the ones that experienced fliers buy and then use for several years. Starting off with an inexpensive two or three-channel radio set might be fine while you learn to fly, but how about a few months down the road when you want that next airplane or a helicopter that requires four channels? Now you're stuck with buying a four or more channel set in addition to your original one.

Since most people fly with four or more channels, there is also very little resale market for these sets with fewer channels. It's almost invariably cheaper in the long run to start out with a four- or five-channel set. Even if you learn on a three-function trainer, your next plane will need four functions and that fourth channel will be there waiting.

You're probably thinking about those three channel sets that are expandable to four channels. This can be a good idea, but it is more expensive than starting out with four channels. Adding that fourth channel requires not only parts, but a lot of expensive hand labor. Your original set and the original four channel set were probably machine assembled and wave soldered. Adding an extra channel is done by hand and is more costly. Fortunately, the most competition for sales and the best buys are in the four- and five-channel sets.

To sum it all up, first determine whether or not you need a single-stick transmitter. Are you extremely one-handed? If so, you'd be better off going this way. Second, find out which is the most popular brand of radio set at your field and why. It is more than likely the availability of service. Finally, decide how many channels you need in a set for now and for the future.

Now you're ready to check hobby shop and magazine ads. Several of the giant discount houses run specials every month on radios. You will probably find the one you want listed. Always compare the discount house price to the total package your local hobby shop offers. Many hobby dealers will teach you to fly on a shop-owned trainer if you buy a radio from them. This can make the higher price of the radio well worth it.

HOW ABOUT A KIT?

A discussion of transmitters and components of the radio system is not complete without mention of a radio kit. If you have electronic experience or if you are a confirmed do-it-yourselfer, you might want to build your own radio control set. The kits available are quality systems of proven reliability. They all come with detailed instructions on how to construct, tune and care for the radio. They all maintain a full-time staff to help you with any problems you might encounter or to make repairs that you aren't able to make yourself.

Most notable of the R/C kit manufacturers is the Heathkit Company. Their name is synonomous with quality kits and clear instructions. Heathkit radios come in either two-stick or a single-stick configuration. The two-stick model can, of course, be built as either a Mode I or a Mode II set. A feature that Heathkit radios have in common with only the very expensive sets of other manufacturers is a plug-in module that lets you change your frequency in a matter of a few seconds at the flying field. This feature can be worth its weight in gold at a crowded field when several other fliers are on the same frequency as you. You have the capability to just find out the frequency with the least fliers, arrange your time with the others, pop in that module, and fly.

Other kit manufacturers are Ace R/C and Royal Electronics. The Ace kit line is noted for its variety of servos, down to the

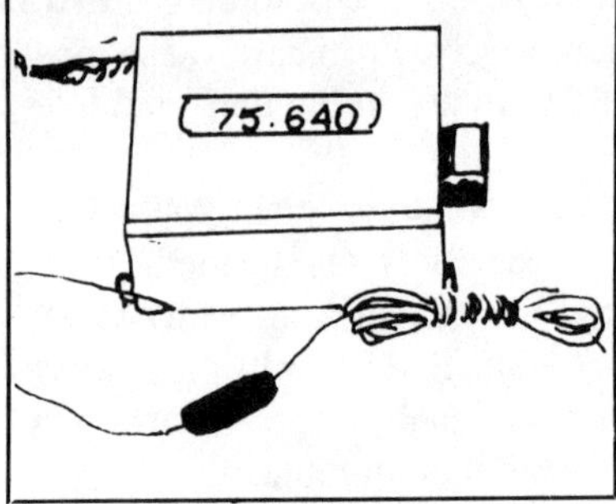

Fig. 2-10. Standard size receiver made by Kraft Systems.

smallest, or micro, size. These kits are especially popular with fliers who want to save a little money and have two airplanes to fly. They build only the airborne portion (all components in the Ace line are available separately) and use their original transmitter for both units. Like the Heathkit, Ace radios are available in single- and two-stick configurations.

Royal Electronics sells a kit version and a ready-to-fly version. They also market an extensive line of components for the flier who's in the market for a second airborne pack. Probably the most popular item in the Royal Line is their miniature receiver. It can be constructed in two, four or even more channels and it is small enough to fit in even the tiniest R/C plane.

The availability of kits should be taken into consideration before you make your final choice of radios. Many people have as much fun building the kit as they do flying. However, you will notice that the kits tend to be expensive. Modern day machine construction, in addition to the competition of foreign made radios, has driven the price of the standard four-and five-channel sets down until they are available for, in many cases, less than the price of a kit. Check the prices of all units available and unless you insist on building a kit, I'm sure you'll find a quality ready-to-fly set at a lower price.

A RECEIVER

The second major component of the radio system is the receiver. Figure 2-10 shows a receiver manufactured by Kraft Systems. Unlike the transmitter, there is very little to choose from in receivers. Some manufacturers offer different size and shaped receivers with their standard radio sets and others don't. Your only concern is whether it will fit into the plane you plan to fly and this is only a minor concern.

If you are planning to learn on a very small trainer or on a sailplane, then you'll want to get one of the smaller receivers. Check the components list from the radio manufacturers to see if they make a small receiver. Better yet, ask your instructor or hobby dealer which size they recommend. If you are going to fly the small R/C aircraft, the receiver size will influence which radio to buy. Figure 2-11 shows the Royal miniature receiver compared to the Kraft standard size receiver.

Another type of receiver is the dual conversion receiver. It was designed with two intermediate frequencies and, therefore a high noise and interference rejection ability. Many clubs that fly in an area of high electronic interference use these type receivers almost exclusively. They are an expensive, special order item. But compared to having interference cause a crash and the cost and time of rebuilding a new plane, they can be well worth the extra expense involved. Again, check with your local club members or hobby dealers. They'll know if you live in an area that warrants the use of a dual conversion receiver.

Servos

In servos you have a lot of choices. Most R/C manufacturers offer several different types and some offer as many as eight different sizes and configurations. Generally speaking, there are standard size servos (although these might be in two or three different sizes), micro sized servos (very small ones for the small planes), heavy duty servos (large and strong servos for the newer giant sized aircraft or for other applications that require a lot of oomph), and retract servos (strong servos with double the amount of servo arm travel for raising and lowering landing gear).

Fig. 2-11. Comparison of the Royal miniature receiver to the Kraft Systems standard sized unit.

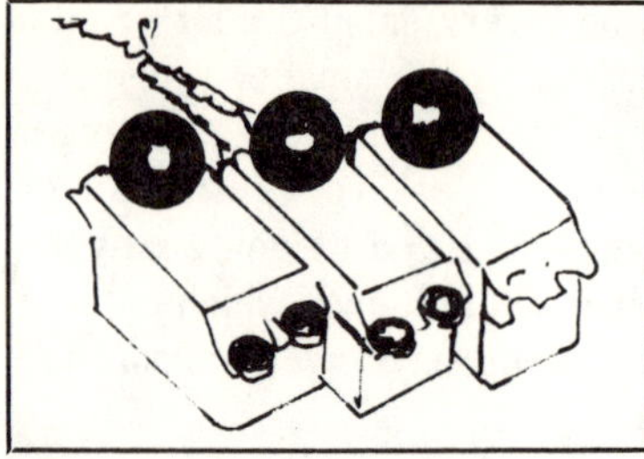

Fig. 2-12. Three standard size servos made by Kraft Systems.

Standard Sized Servos

These are the servos that come with every R/C radio set unless you specify differently and perhaps pay a little more. It's actually hard to call these servos "standard" since none of the servos from the various manufacturers are the same size. These are merely the general-purpose servos not made for a specific application. Figure 2-12 shows standard servos. Notice the difference in sizes. Some manufacturers will sell their sets with the most popular servo and charge a slightly higher price for a different, even though still a standard, servo.

Micro Servos

In the past few years, radio sets—in particular the airborne portion—have grown smaller. This has allowed the smaller planes to really come into their own. The main item in shrinking the radio size has been the advent of the *micro servo*. Compare the micro servo in Figure 2-13 with the standard size servo next to it. These new micro servos are not only small, they also draw less current. A smaller and lighter battery pack can be carried in the plane and this will reduce the weight even more.

Micro servos are normally available as a special order item with the radio and also as individual servos from various manufacturers. Ace R/C and Royal Electronics both produce micro servos and servo kits. These are extremely popular with sailplane and small R/C plane enthusiasts. Generally, they do not have the thrust or torque available at the servo arm to be used in the larger planes. However, more power can be obtained from them by substituting a different gear set for the original set. If you are planning to fly from a confined area and use small planes, then these are your servos.

Heavy Duty Servos

One look at Figure 2-14 to compare the heavy duty servo with a standard size one and you can tell that the "big boy" has some

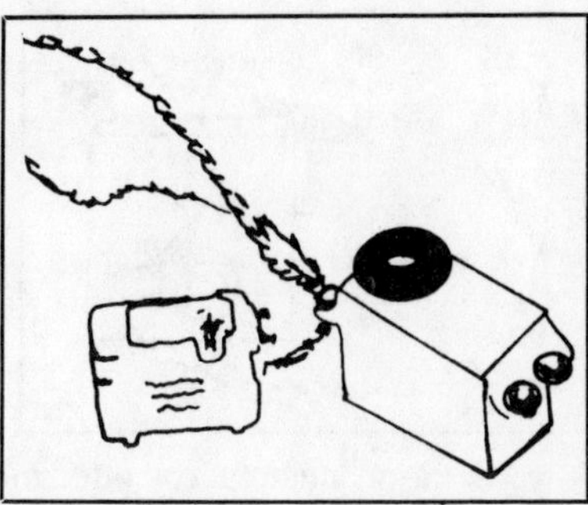

Fig. 2-13. Midget servo compared to a standard servo.

power. This servo, the Chevron servo sold by Royal Electronics, is extremely powerful. It is very popular with the giant aircraft (R/C models ⅓ to ¼ the size of the real aircraft). These heavy duty servos are made by a few other companies, too, with more companies tooling up as the popularity of the larger R/C planes grows. At the time of this writing the heavy duty servos are not offered as an option with radio sets, but only sold as individual items. The beginner generally does not need this type of servo.

Retract Servos

Every manufacturer of radio sets offers a special servo for retracting landing gear. It is virtually always a standard sized servo with a gearing change to make it more powerful (sometimes accompanied by a change to a more powerful motor) and a change to allow the servo arm throw to increase to 180 degrees. This increased servo throw is to match the servo movement to that required by the gear retracting mechanism. Figure 2-15 shows a retract servo with a special control arm for use in retracting all three gear. These servos are, of necessity, powerful, but they have sacrificed speed of operation for power. Speed is not a vital quality in retracting landing gear.

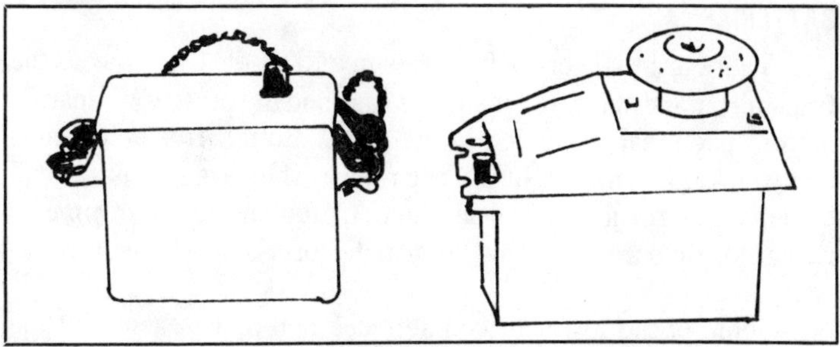

Fig. 2-14. Heavy duty Chevron compared to a standard servo.

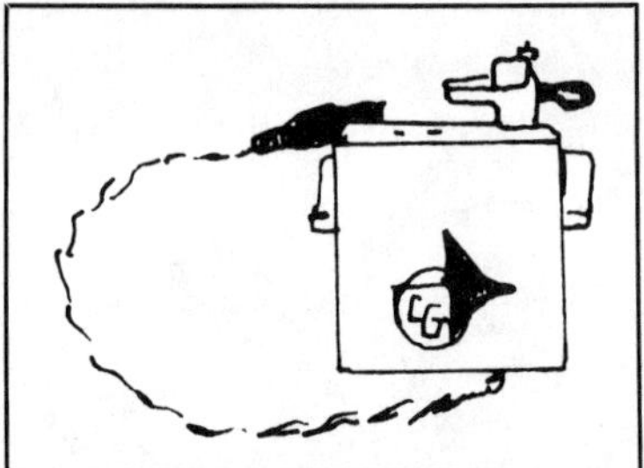

Fig. 2-15. Landing gear retraction servo showing the special control arm for retracting all three landing gear.

Some manufacturers offer more than one size retract servo, but many don't. Generally speaking, the planes that have retractable gear are the larger ones where servo size doesn't matter greatly. Exceptions to this are the various retractable landing gear designed for the smaller planes. These, however, do not use a special retract servo. Instead the gear are designed for a shorter retracting movement and they use a micro servo without the throw increased to 180 degrees.

Choosing Your Servos

There is not nearly as much to decide when picking your servos compared to choosing the correct transmitter. By and large, your choice will be the standard servos. If you do plan to fly the smaller planes, you'll want to special order the micro servos. The standard ones might be too large and heavy. Conversely, if you intend to become a buff of large R/C planes, you might consider starting off with the large, powerful, heavy-duty servos.

It's rare for an R/C set to come with a retract servo. As a student, you'll have your hands full without having to worry about retracting landing gear. When you learn to fly and move on to your second or third plane, that's the time to begin thinking about retracts and to get that retract servo.

BATTERIES

There are two sets of batteries in a R/C set. One powers the transmitter and is located inside its case and the other is a separate battery pack that is carried in the plane. Both batteries are normally nickel-cadmium (NiCad) and rechargable. Your radio set will come with a recharger and instructions for the length of time to recharge. Be sure to follow the manufacturer's directions carefully.

Some of the lower-priced sets use non-rechargable alkaline batteries in the transmitter. The companies that market these sets will also sell a kit to convert the transmitter to NiCad battery power. I don't recommend the alkaline battery because the R/Cer will invariably convert to NiCads. In the long run, it is cheaper to start with them.

The battery pack that is carried in the plane, also called the *airborne pack*, powers the receiver and the servos. It is this battery pack that I'll discuss since you usually have a choice of sizes.

Standard-Size Batteries

Like servos, radio manufacturers usually have a standard size—depending on the set. For the four and more channel sets, the 500-milliampere hour capacity battery is the standard. Five hundred milliampere hours, usually written 500 mah or 500 ma, is the capacity of the battery. That is, it will power something requiring a current of 500 milliamperes for one hour or for any combination of time and current whose product is 500. This standard, "500 mil pack" as we normally say it, might be actually any capacity from 475 mah to 550 mah. It depends on the specific type of batteries used, but the airborne packs of standard size are all around 500 mah. Figure 2-16 shows two configurations of the 500-mah battery.

Miniature Batteries

The two, and sometimes the three channel sets, normally are equipped with a smaller capacity battery pack of 225 mah. Since servoes draw considerably more power than the receiver, the lesser number of servos with these sets means that you can make do with the smaller battery pack. Smaller capacity battery packs are also physically smaller in size and weigh less than the larger capacity ones.

Compare the sizes of the two in Figure 2-17. The smaller battery pack is very popular with sailplane fliers where its lightness is a definite plus. It is also popular with fliers of extra small

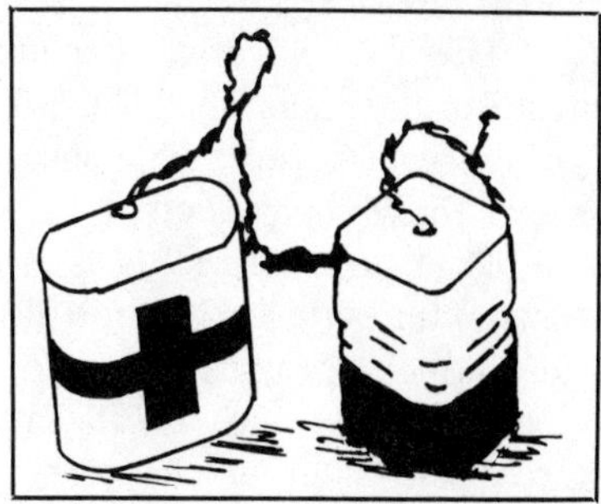

Fig. 2-16. Two configurations of the 500-milliampere hour battery pack.

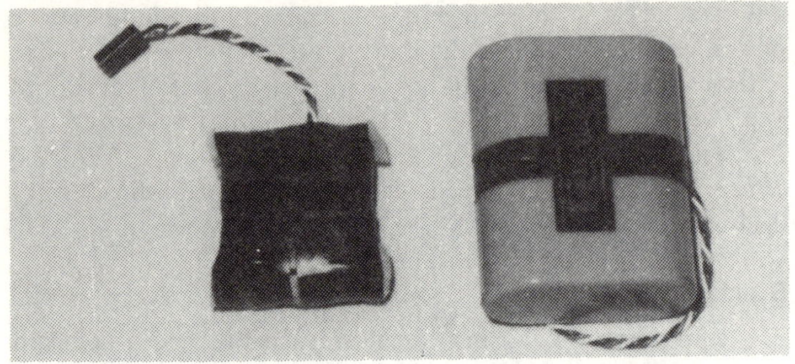

Fig. 2-17. Miniature battery pack compared to the 500-mah pack.

aircraft who demand not only light weight but also small size. The 225-mah battery is not the limit on small size. Batteries are also available in 175 and 100 mah sizes. These last two are extremely small, but work quite well in a plane with two micro servos. These batteries are usually only available as a special order item or from the companies who specialize in extra radio components like Ace R/C and Royal Electronics.

Heavy Duty Batteries

These big batteries are used when a lot of power is needed and the weight of the battery pack doesn't matter. Heavy-duty batteries are of the 1000-mah or 1-amp hour capacity. These are normally not sold made up, but are put together by the flier from C- or D-size NiCad cells. Some of the giant R/C aircraft that use many extra servos, such as two servos for aileron control, (one for each aileron) might require the extra capacity of the heavy-duty battery pack. Of course, with these aircraft the additional weight of the larger battery pack is a negligible factor.

OTHER RADIO SET COMPONENTS

There are several other minor, but very important components of the radio set. These include the battery charger, the switch harness, servo trays and additional servo arms. Figure 2-18 shows these components.

The battery charger is used to simultaneously charge both the transmitter batteries and the airborne battery pack. It is a small transformer type unit similar to those used to recharge many other electronic items such as calculators. Different radio set manufacturers use different charge rates and most of them specify a minimum and a maximum time to charge batteries. Be sure to read your instructions carefully so you won't inadvertently damage your NiCads.

The switch harness is used to connect the parts of the airborne unit. It consists of an on-off switch, a recharging jack, and connectors for the battery and receiver. The servos plug directly into the receiver. The on-off switch will be mounted in a convenient spot on your plane. Preferably it should be placed on the side opposite to the engine exhaust so that oil won't get in it. The recharging jack on some sets also mounts on the plane, but on other sets it is simply tucked away inside the fuselage while you are flying.

Having the recharging jack mounted on the plane is a convenience. You can check your battery voltage, recharge at the field with a special field charger or recharge at home without having to take the wing off the plane. The other two leads to the switch harness connect the battery and the receiver to the system. This makes the electrical circuit complete.

Every radio set comes with one or more servo trays. These plastic items are used to mount the rudder, elevator and throttle servos in the fuselage and provide double insulation from vibration. The servos are mounted on rubber grommets to the tray and the tray is mounted on rubber grommets to the mount rails in the fuselage of the plane. Some sets provide different servo arrangements, usually three abreast and two abreast and one across

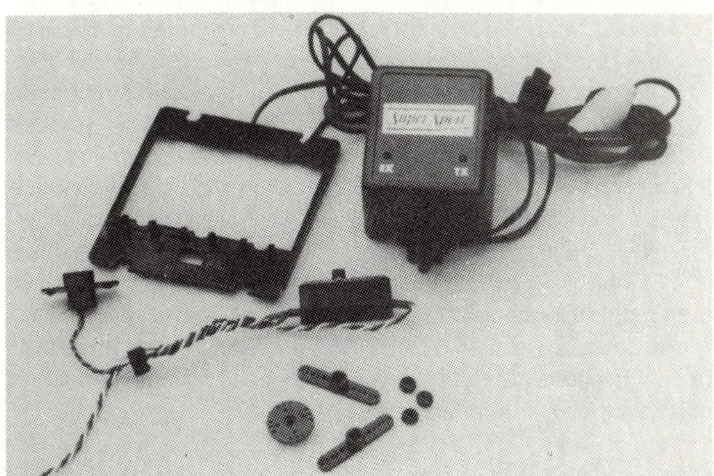

Fig. 2-18. Radio set accessories standard with most sets. These are the rectangular servo tray/holder, battery charger, switch and harness, and extra control arms.

(2 × 1), as well as a single servo tray for the aileron servo—which is mounted in the wing. The 2 × 1 configuration is very popular because it allows the servos to be mounted in a narrower, sleeker fuselage or in a smaller plane.

Although all servos come with a servo arm attached, it is nice to have additional arms and output wheels. With these extra arms of different sizes, you can tailor the servo output throw to any necessary aircraft control movement. These are one of the little extras that good manufacturers supply with their sets.

YOUR FINAL CHOICE OF RADIO

You can see that there are many variables and items to choose from when picking a radio. Most people don't know that these options exist, much less take advantage of them. They end up flying, usually, just as well as if they had completely tailored their radio set to their individual needs. Actually, if you are going to learn to fly on one of the popular trainers using a .35-to .40-sized engine, the standard sized everything is the best bet. Only if you are going to one extreme or the other, to very large or very small aircraft, do you need to worry very much about the optional sized equipment. But in those cases you need to be very much concerned.

Your absolute major concern should be the transmitter configuration. Ask yourself if you are skillful with your left or right hand. Do you think you can steer your plane at about 30 mph down the runway with your "off" hand? Go out to your club's field and borrow a single-stick transmitter for a minute or two to get the feel of it. The extra time taken in deciding on a transmitter configuration can pay big dividends later on. Although I personally fly a two-stick radio, I have seen too many students struggle to learn this system when they would have been much better off with the single-stick version.

Next, check for the popular brand at your field. Check the availability of service. Also, check how other owners feel about their radios in terms of reliability. Finally, check with your instructor, to get his recommendations. This is especially true if you plan to fly helicopters. Give all of these factors good consideration, then make your choice of radio sets—the right choice.

RADIO INSTALLATION

Although it's impossible to cover all individual cases, some mention must be made of radio installation because the beginner might find this a baffling chore. Just about every manufacturer includes instructions on how to install the radio. Unfortunately, the instructions tend to be in generalities because every case is different and the manufacturer does not know what type plane you are putting the radio in or even it it's going in a plane at all—you might have a boat or a car. Let's look at some of the basics of radio installation and list a few hints that might make it easier.

Servo Trays

Every radio set I know of comes with one or more servo trays. If your set did not, I suggest that you buy one. The tray gives your servos double isolation from vibration. Use one. The most popular tray is the 2 by 1 (2 × 1) tray that places two servos side by side and one across at the end. This allows a narrower installation than a three side-by-side tray.

Mounting The Servo Tray

The servo tray should be mounted on two hard wood or plywood beams running across the fuselage. The wood should be in the one-fourth inch range, and plywood, three-sixteenth or heavier. Usually you mount the servos in the rear of the fuselage radio compartment under the wing. The receiver and battery will go forward of them. Check the plans and instructions that came with your plane or helicopter to see if the manufacturer recom-

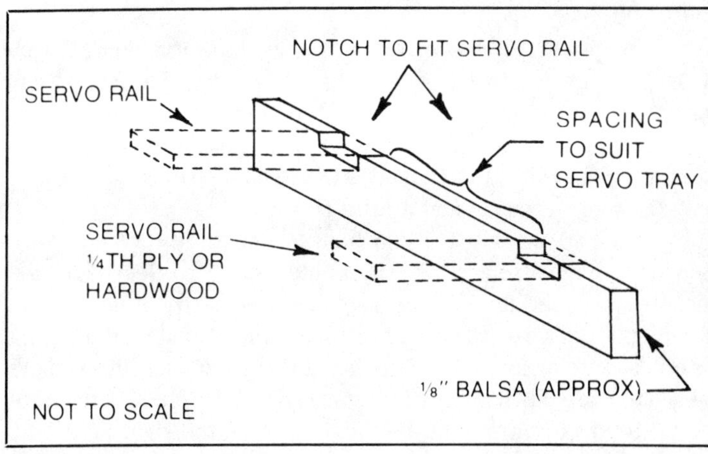

Fig. 2-19. Notched positioning bar for locating hardwood rails on which the servo tray is mounted. These positioning bars are glued to the sides of the fuselage.

mends any specific location. You can use the location of the servos and battery to help balance the plane by changing their placement forward or back.

Cut two beams that fill fit snugly between the fuselage sides in the radio compartment. Lay the servo tray across the beams and mark where the servos will go. Drill pilot holes and screw the tray to the beams. Put one servo in the tray, then pre-fit the beams in place. This lets you get the height correct so that the servos don't hit bottom because you put the beams in too low. Mark where you want the beams, remove them, then glue them in place with epoxy glue used liberally. This type installation, beams glued directly to the fuselage, is used by most fliers. A neater, much stronger installation can be made by using notched positioning bars. See Figure 2-19.

The positioning bars are cut from hard one-eighth inch balsa or light plywood. Mark the notches for the cross beams with the servo beams screwed to the tray. Cut out the shallow notches, then measure the height of the servo beams like you did in the other method. This time, epoxy the positioning bar in place so that the notches are under the places you marked for the beams. The positioning bars are then glued to each side of the fuselage and the beams are glued in place across between them—secure in the notches. You can see that this installation has a lot more surface glued to the fuselage. Therefore, it is much stronger.

Servo Arrangement

The idea in *servo arrangement* is to get the servo doing the job closest to the control it is moving. This gives the neatest and shortest pushrod arrangement. As a bad example, you wouldn't put the throttle servo in the back of the plane and the elevator servo near the nose. Of course not; you would do the reverse. But let's look at servo arrangement a little closer.

There are actually four functions for the three servos that are mounted in the fuselage to perform: elevator, throttle, rudder and nosewheel steering. Your arrangement needs to optimize these functions. Let's assume you have a high wing trainer and the wing is off. You are looking down into the radio compartment at an empty servo tray as shown in Fig. 2-20. An engine is mounted in the nose and the throttle arm is in the usual place on the right side. The closest servo mount to the engine, assuming we're using the 2 × 1 tray, is the across one. This is where you should put the throttle servo.

Fig. 2-20. Radio compartment with servo tray in place.

In addition, the servo should be turned in the tray so that the output arm or wheel is closest to the right side. This will make it as straight a shot as possible from the servo arm to the throttle arm on the engine. Wait a minute now before you just drop a servo in the hole and start screwing it in place. You need to check which way the servo moves. Hook up your radio and switch it on. Place the servo on the throttle channel in the same position it is in when it is permanently mounted.

Now advance the throttle to the high position. The side of the servo arm nearest to the side of the plane should make a pushing action so that when you have a cable pushrod hooked to the servo and the engine throttle arm, the throttle will be pushed open. By the way, pushing the throttle stick toward the top of the transmitter is high throttle on a two-stick and pushing the switch toward the top, or face of the transmitter, is high throttle on a single-stick transmitter. See Fig. 2-21. The pushrod will go through a guide tube that is glued to the side of the fuselage inside. You can tell from the illustration that your servo has to move counterclockwise for high throttle. If it does, you're OK. If not, change that servo for another one and try it. Usually you will have two servos that go one direction and two that go the other, or three and one. When you have found the servo that goes the correct direction, mark it for the throttle.

Next let's check the aileron servo. I know it isn't in the group that goes in the tray, but you don't want to go ahead and choose those and then be left with an aileron servo that goes the wrong way. Your aileron servo will be upside down (on a high wing plane)

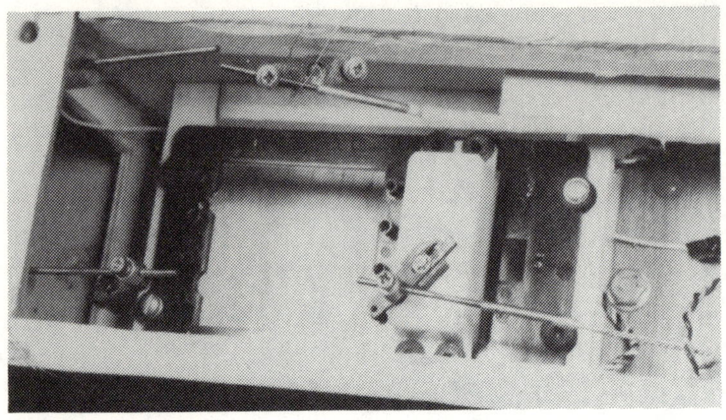

Fig. 2-21. The throttle servo in place and throttle pushrod in place running through a guide tube.

when the wing is in place, so be careful to consider that in your selection. When you move the aileron stick to the *right* you want a counterclockwise movement. You can hold the servo upside down and visualize the positions of the control horns on the underside of the wing and you'll see that a counterclockwise movement gives a push on the right aileron and moves it to produce a right roll. Find a servo that goes the correct direction, mark it for the aileron, and lay it aside.

All that's left now is to select and position the rudder and elevator servos. The rudder servo does double duty, controlling both the rudder and the nosewheel steering, so let's pick it and let the one left over be the elevator servo. Check your plans and see which side of the plane they call for the nosewheel steering pushrod (or cable) to be placed on. I normally run it down the opposite side from the throttle cable, but some people put it on the same side.

No matter which side it runs down, you will need the servo arm next to the fuselage side just as it is for the throttle. Figure 2-22 shows a radio installation with an arrow indicating the rudder-nosewheel steering servo. Notice that the nosewheel steering pushrod comes off the servo output arm on the side next to the fuselage. Generally speaking, you use the other side of the servo arm for the rudder output and locate the control horn on the side of the rudder that gives you the correct rudder direction.

Before you do this, however, check the direction of the elevator servo. A high wing trainer normally has the control horn on the top of the elevator (Fig. 2-23). This requires a pull for up

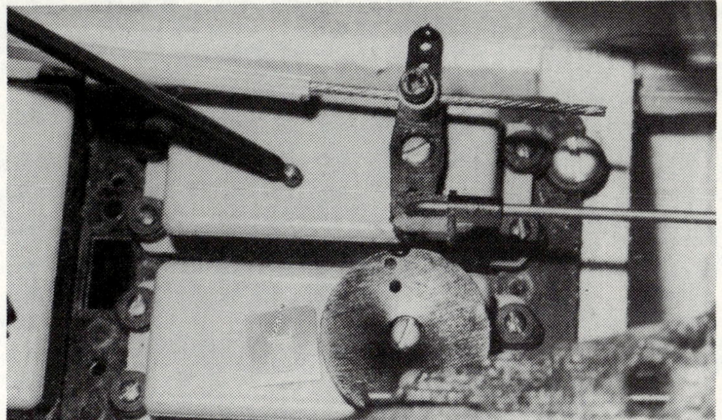

Fig. 2-22. Servo with rudder and nosewheel steering pushrods connected.

elevator. Check which side of the servo gives you a pull. If it is the side of the servo near the fuselage side, then use the arrangement mentioned earlier—nosewheel steering and rudder pushrods from different sides of the servo.

On the other hand, if a pull movement on your elevator servo requires you to have the pushrod near the center of the fuselage rather than along the side, you might want to put the two pushrods on the rudder servo on the same side. This will give you more clearance and eliminate any possible interference. Check Fig. 2-24 and you'll see what I mean. Figure 2-25 shows the same arrangement, but with the nosewheel steering and throttle pushrods on the same sides.

Installing The Other Components

So far I have discussed only servo installation, but there are several other components of the radio set that must be considered.

Fig. 2-23. Control horn on top elevator on a trainer.

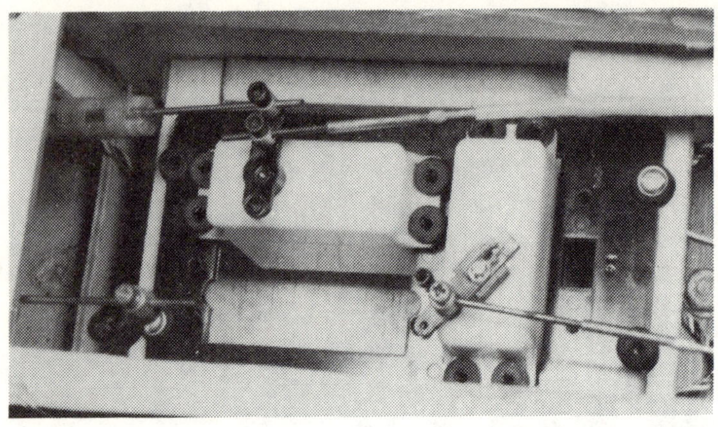

Fig. 2-24. Servo arrangement showing the rudder and nosewheel steering pushrods on the same side of the control arm. Compare it to Fig. 2-22.

The receiver must be wrapped in foam. Most radio manufacturers ask for an inch. If you have a small radio and a large plane you might make it. Most of us use half-inch foam rubber in a loose pack. Put a couple of strips of tape around the foam to hold it in place and lay the receiver in the fuselage. It will usually fit forward of the servos. Don't forget it has to be close enough to connect to the servo leads. Route the antenna wire out the side of the fuselage through a small hole drilled in the plane near where the receiver is.

The idea here is to get the antenna away from the servo leads and other wires as soon as you can to prevent any possible interference. To dress up the hole you drilled in the fuselage, insert a

Fig. 2-25. Servo arrangement with the nosewheel steering and throttle pushrods on the same side.

Fig. 2-26. Du Bro push/pull switch attachment.

rubber grommet or epoxy in a short length of plastic pushrod guide. Attach the antenna to the vertical tail. A good way to attach it is to tie a rubber band to it and loop the rubber band through the vertical fin-rudder joint. The rubber band will provide some stretch and "give" when you snag the antenna wire. This could save you a repair bill.

The battery is also wrapped in foam and usually goes forward, either under the tank or next to the forward bulkhead. If you are going to put it under the tank, drop it, foam and all, into the plastic sandwich bag and tape it closed with only the lead hanging out. This is a safety measure, just in case a fuel line or the tank breaks.

Don't forget the switch harness. You should mount the switch and the charge plug (if your set has one) on the fuselage. First, always mount these two on the side opposite to the engine exhaust. This is understandable, since you don't want sticky exhaust residue fouling the switch contacts.

Next, you might mount your switch directly to the fuselage or buy a commercial push-pull switch from your hobby dealer. If your fuselage sides are thicker than one-eight of an inch, the slide switch will not protrude past the installation plate when you mount it to the outside of the fuselage. You'll have to move it with your fingernail or a screwdriver. You can instead use a commercial push-pull switch that your slide mounts in. These will work on any thickness fuselage. See Fig. 2-26.

If you use this type of switch, I recommend that you set it up to pull for "on" and push for "off." If it is set up for push "on", there is always the chance that it might be accidently bumped on and run your batteries down or allow another flier's transmitter to drive your servos past their limits since his transmitter isn't likely to be tuned exactly like yours.

The installation of a radio can be perplexing the first time. Look your plans over and see what they recommend, then lay it out using the guides I've given you. You'll find it will go quicker than you thought at first glance.

Engine Theory and Components

If the radio is the heart of your R/C aircraft system, the engine is the muscle that pulls it along. The moden airplane engine is a marvel of reliability and longevity. It is a simple machine — there are only three moving parts—and practically foolproof. Virtually all of these engines on the market today will give good, dependable service.

In many cases, there is little reason to choose between two engines other than personal preference. Even so, there are different types of engines and accessories that you are sure to hear about. The differences are mainly internal configuration, but they can affect your choice of engine. The purpose of this chapter is to explain a little bit about the various types of engines, carburetors and other engine related equipment. Also covered is the operation and adjustment of your engine and recommendations for which size engine to start your R/C flying with.

PARTS OF THE ENGINE

The model airplane engine is made up of a crankcase (in one or two parts), a crankshaft, a connecting rod, wrist pin, piston, cylinder, cylinder head, glow plug, rear cover and carburetor. There are also bearings (either ball, roller or bronze bushings), a thrust washer, prop washer, nut, gaskets and screws. Figure 3-1 shows a disassembled engine. This particular engine has a two-piece crankcase with a removable front housing. Notice that the two ball bearings that support the crankshaft go into the front and rear of the front housing. Figure 3-2 shows another engine. This one has a one-piece crankcase.

The materials used in the manufacturing of model engines varies only slightly from company to company. The crankcase, cylinder head, rear cover and front housing of the engine are usually pressure cast aluminum. However, a few engines have

Fig. 3-1. Disassembled OS .40 engine featuring a two piece crankcase. The removable front housing through which the crankshaft passes holds two ball bearings.

cylinder heads machined from bar stock. Connecting rods are generally made from forged aluminum and might have bronze bushings. The crankshaft is always made from very high quality hardened steel. The cylinder in most engines is steel and the bore might be chrome plated. A few engines have a special alloy brass cylinder with chrome plating. This type will be discussed in more detail later. Soft iron is the material of choice for pistons in the smaller engines and aluminum with a ring or rings is used in the larger ones. The wrist pin, like the crankshaft, is made from hardened steel.

HOW IT WORKS

By far, the largest majority of R/C engines are glow plug engines that run on a fuel of methanol, nitromethane and oil. There are a couple of diesels on the market, but these have yet to achieve any popularity. The giant R/C aircraft use converted chain saw or industrial engines that run on gasoline. A few fliers use the old style ignition engines on replicas of vintage model aircraft, but the vast majority of all R/C planes and helicopters will use a modern, powerful glow plug engine.

The actual operation of a two-stroke cycle engine is shown in Figs. 3-3A and 3-3B. Starting with the ignition of the fuel by the

Fig. 3-2. Disassembled Fox .45 engine. This engine features a one-piece crankcase.

glow plug, the piston is forced down, turning the crankshaft and the prop which is bolted to it. At the same time that the burned mixture is expanding in the combustion chamber, the fresh fuel-air mixture in the crankcase is being compressed. The crankcase in a two-stroke engine is sealed. A four-stroke engine is vented. As the piston moves down, it first uncovers the exhause port. At that time, the hot expanding gasses start to leave the combustion chamber. The piston continues down, and the bypass port opens, allowing the compressed fuel-air mixture in the crankcase to enter the combustion chamber on the opposite side from the exhaust.

Notice that this fuel-air mixture goes around, or bypasses the piston, hence the name *bypass port*. You will also notice that part of the time the exhaust and bypass ports are open at the same time. This is called the overlap and is very important to the power output of your engine. During the overlap period, the fresh fuel-air charge being forced into the cylinder by the descending piston helps to force the old burned gases out the exhaust. Some of the fresh charge also goes out the exhaust, so some fuel economy has been sacrificed for power. This method of forcing the old gases out with the new ones is called *scavenging*. In a later section, several different scavenging methods will be discussed.

As the piston reaches bottom dead center and starts up again, the intake port in the hollow crankshaft opens. The vacuum in the crankcase caused by the rising piston sucks a fresh charge of fuel and air through the carburetor. The piston continues upward, closing first the bypass port, then the exhaust port. Now the new fuel-air charge in the combustion chamber is compressed, ignited by the glow plug, and the process repeats itself.

PISTON-CYLINDER TYPES

Before going into the scavenging methods, there are a few terms that you need to know relating to piston and cylinder types. These relate directly to some of the different scavenging methods.

Lapped Piston. The term *lapped piston* refers to an engine that has a steel cylinder and an iron piston that has been machined to fit tightly, then finally lapped with an abrasive compound to a close tolerance. Lapped pistons are seldom used in engines with displacements above .36 cubic inches because the heavy iron piston causes excessive vibration in larger engines. Lapped piston

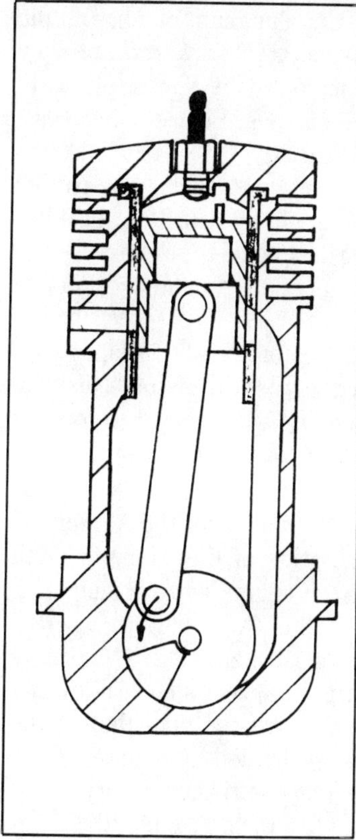

Fig. 3-3A. Operation of the two-stroke model engine.

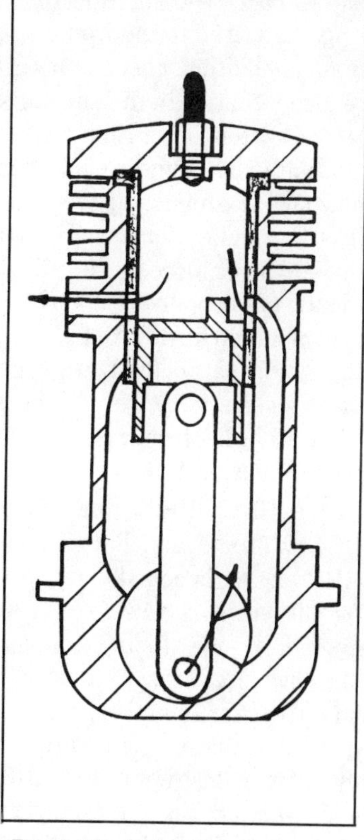

Fig. 3-3B. Operation of the two-stroke model engine.

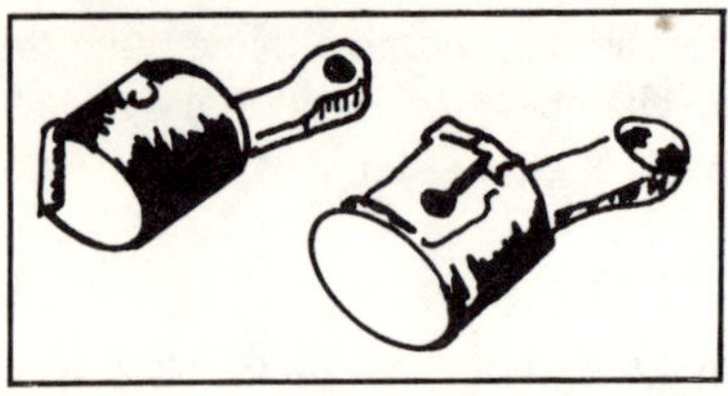

Fig. 3-4. Two model engine pistons. The left piston is an iron lapped piston. The right one is aluminum with an iron ring.

engines generally require a longer break-in than a ringed engine, but if broken in carefully they will give long and reliable service.

Ringed Engine. Virtually all engines above .36 cubic inch displacement are ringed engines. They have aluminum pistons with one or two iron rings running in a steel cylinder. The cylinder might be chrome plated. These engines require little break-in, only two or three inch runs in most cases, before they can be flown at full power. It is rare to see a small displacement ringed engine due to cost. The additional cost of the aluminum piston and the ring, compared to the iron piston, is too great to warrant production. In addition, there is no great need for the lighter piston to reduce vibration in the smaller sized engines. Figure 3-4 shows a lapped piston and a ringed piston.

Although some ringed engines have two rings, one ring is much more common. The single ring might wear faster, but it has less drag on the cylinder. This allows the engine to rev up more and this produces more power. Single rings can be mounted just below the top of the piston or a *Dykes* ring can be used. A Dykes ring is a ring mounted flush with the top of the piston. It is "L" shaped with the bottom part of the L fitting into a groove in the piston. This type of ring seals very well as the expanding gasses tend to force it outward against the cylinder wall. The K&B .40, a popular sport engine, uses a Dykes ring.

ABC Cylinder and Piston. ABC stands for the Aluminum-Brass-Chrome metallurgical configuration of these engines. An ABC engine is actually a lapped piston engine with an aluminum piston, but it is never referred to in this way—only as an ABC engine. Along with its aluminum piston lacking a ring, it also has a chrome plated brass cylinder. The brass is a very special alloy that has a coefficient of expansion slightly greater than that of the aluminum piston. The chrome plating hardens the bore of the cylinder against wear. The ABC configuration is generally used on a high-performance or racing engine. In a racing engine, the different expansion rates of the cylinder and piston are a distinct advantage. A lean, hot run will cause the brass cylinder to expand more and save the engine from seizing and probable ruining itself. Figure 3-5 shows the piston and cylinder of an ABC engine.

ABCD Configuration. The Super Tigre company of Italy, one of the world's leading manufacturers of model airplane engines, has recently come out with an arrangement that tries to capture the best features of both the ringed and ABC configurations. This is an ABC engine with a Dykes ring. Their idea is to take the ABC features and technology that have been so successful on their racing engines and use them on a high performance R/C engine designed to pull the present day sport and acrobatic planes. The idea behind the addition of the Dykes ring is to increase the longevity of the engine because the unringed aluminum piston of ABC engines has a much faster wear rate than that of a ringed engine.

SCAVENGING METHODS

The beginning R/C flier actually does not need the technical details of what type of scavenging a certain engines uses, or for that matter, what it's piston configuration is. Many engines, however, are advertised as being a certain type or perhaps a manufacturer will have two or even three different engines of the same displacement with different scavenging methods at different prices. In order to be able to distinguish between these types and make a judgement as to which one to buy, knowing a certain amount of technical details becomes necessary.

Model airplane engines are *loop scavenged* engines. The incoming fuel makes a loop, or turn through the cylinder, forcing the burned exhaust gasses out. The actual scavenging types I'll describe are variations on the basic loop scavenging scheme.

Fig. 3-5. ABC cylinder and piston. This set up features an aluminum piston running in a chrome-plated brass cylinder.

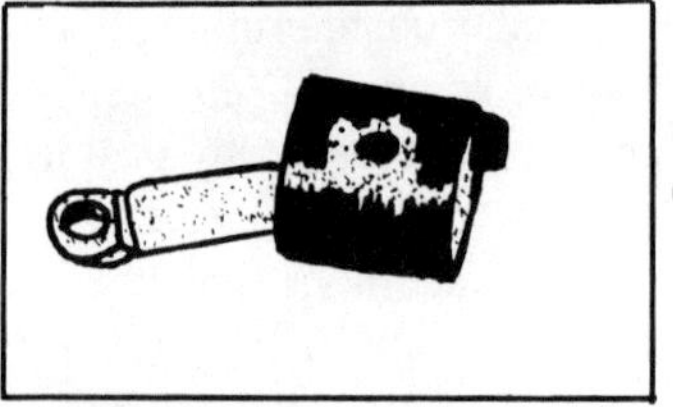

Fig. 3-6. Cross flow piston showing the deflector on top.

Cross Flow

Cross flow engines are the old standards that have been around model aviation for years. These engines were the only type of engine until the 1960s, when control line speed fliers began trying other scavenging ideas. At the time, these exotics were hand-built specials.

The cross flow engine, as shown in Fig. 3-6, uses a deflictor on top of the piston to turn the incoming fuel-air charge upward so that it makes a more efficient loop through the cylinder. These engines take fewer machining operations on the cylinder and the crankcase is easier to cast than their more exotic cousins. Therefore, they are much less expensive. Despite the fact that they are less powerful, for the beginner and sport flier, these engines are the best buy on the market.

Schnuerle

Schnuerle ported engines are the most powerful ones on the market today. They are also the most expensive. Invented in the 1930s, this scavengine method was not used on R/C model engines until they had become popular with control line speed fliers. Figure 3-7 shows a Schnuerle ported cylinder and the flat-topped, deflectorless piston used with it. In Fig. 3-7, the port which appears higher is a Schnuerle port and the lower one is the boost port.

Hidden from view are a second Schnuerle port and the exhaust port. Figure 3-8 dipicts the gas flow in the Schnuerle engine. The two Schnuerle ports, front and rear in a side exhaust engine, are machined so that they direct the incoming fuel-air charge away from the exhaust port. The boost port, machined at an upward angle, directs more fuel-air charge in an upward loop to scavenge the upper part of the cylinder. As you can see, the Schnuerle engine with its hugh bypass ports can transfer a large quantity of fuel-air mixture to the cylinder. This is the reason for its tremendous power output. You do pay the price for all this power, however, in terms of fuel economy and purchase price. The Schnuerle engine is

Fig. 3-7. Schnuerle piston and cylinder. Note the angled Schnuerle ports.

definitely a gas hog. In fact, fuel tank manufacturers have had to make new, larger sizes so that competetion acrobatic pilots can carry enough fuel to complete the required maneuvers. It is not unusual for a .40 sized Schnuerle engine to need a tank the same size as a more economical cross flow .60. Schnuerle engines also cost more.

The different bypass ports, each cut through the cylinder at a different angle, are more time consuming and costly to machine. The crankcase, with the channels leading to these ports is also more difficult and costly to cast. All of this leads to a much higher purchase price. One manufacturer, Fox Manufacturing Company, of Fort Smith, Arkansas, has come up with a novel method of reducing the cost of casting the crankcase. Their engines have the

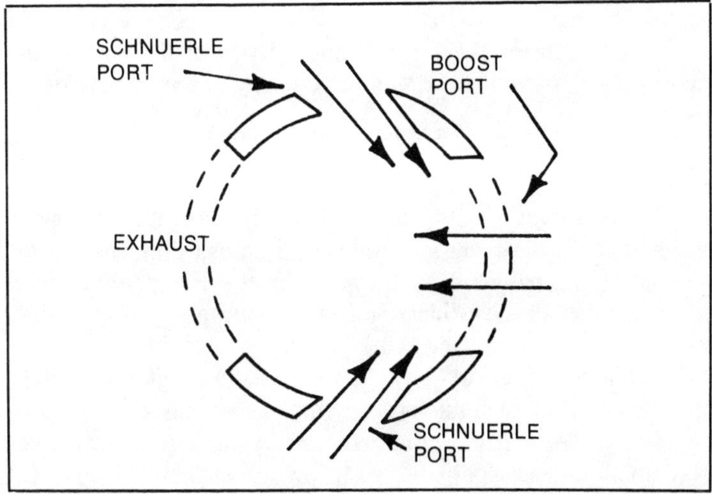

Fig. 3-8. Gas flow in a Schnuerle engine. Note how the ports shown in the top and bottom position angle the fuel away from the exhaust. The port opposite the exhaust, the boost port, is angled upwards.

Fig. 3-9. Fox .45 engine showing the large rear cover with the transfer area for the rear Schnuerle port cast into the upper portion.

channel for the rear Schnuerle port included in a very tall rear cover (Fig. 3-9). This patented feature has allowed them to produce a powerful Schnuerle engine at much less cost than other manufacturers.

Despite the disadvantage of high fuel consumption and high price, Schnuerle ported engines are the most popular type sold today. Competition fliers would not be without them and many sport fliers also will spend the extra money to buy the increased power.

PDP

Perry Directional Porting, or PDP, is a modification of the conventional scavenging method used in cross flow engines for years. It is a patented modification by the Perry Aeromotive Company that adds considerable power to these engines. In some cases it makes the engine equal to Schnuerle engines.

While working with cross flow engines in an effort to extract more power and keep them from being pushed into obsolescense by the more expensive Schnuerles, Perry discovered what was essentially a dead spot in the cross flow scavenging. He found that after the incoming fuel-air mixture loops around the top of the cylinder, it makes a smooth flow that curves from its downward flow out toward the exhaust (Fig. 3-10).

Fig. 3-10. Dead spot on the exhaust side of the piston deflector where very little scavenging occurs.

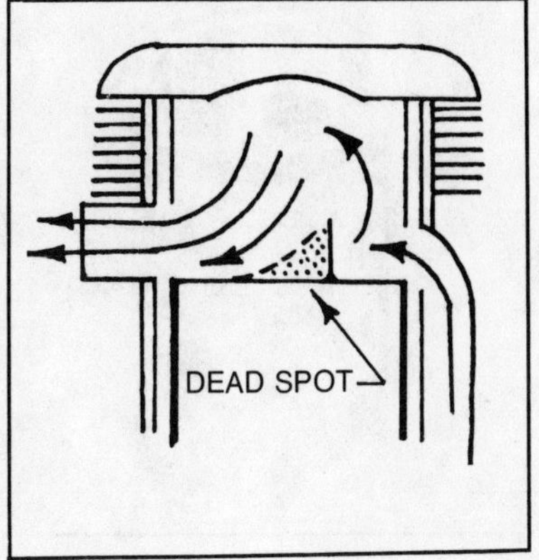

Notice that as the fuel-air mixture flows toward the exhaust it leaves a small triangular area adjacent to the deflector unscavenged. It was this area that Perry began working on. His solution was to machine two small ports, each directed toward the deflector, at the edge of the bypass area. Figure 3-11 shows a top

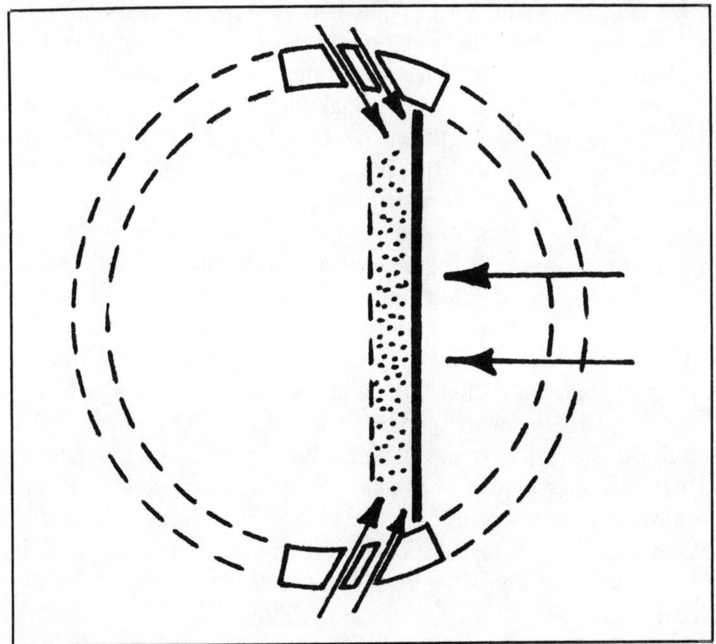

Fig. 3-11. Perry directional porting gas flow. Notice how the Perry ports direct the flow of the incoming fuel-air mixture into the formerly unscavenged are for increased engine power.

Fig. 3-12. Super Tigre G-60 cylinder showing the two small Perry ports. The exhaust is on the left. Note how the Perry ports angle fuel away from it.

view of the cylinder and bypass area. He enlarged the bypass channel at the edges so that the fuel-air mixture could get to the new "Perry" ports and the modification was complete.

After demonstrating the success of the PDP modification, Perry licensed several manufacturers to use his method. Notable among these were the Super Tigre Company of Italy and the Bavarian Precision Products Company of West Germany, makers of HB engines. Engines from both of these companies, as well as custom engines with the PDP mod compete very successfully with the Schnuerles. HB has yet to make a Schnuerle. While Super Tigre makes both types, their G-60 Blue Head continues to be one of their best sellers due to the increased power from the PDP mod. Figure 3-12 shows a G-60 cylinder with the two small Perry ports.

ABC normally refers to the aluminum-brass-chrome cylinder/piston configuration. However, when speaking of a special version of the Super Tigre G-60, it refers also to a porting scheme that is used exclusively by that company. It is a cross flow scavenging method that uses an upward angle cut through the thick brass cylinder along with a flat topped piston rather than a square cut bypass and a piston with a deflector on it. Figure 3-13 shows a cross section of the cylinders and pistons of both type cross flow engines. This particular engine was never very popular except for the control line speed version, due to the high wear rate of the aluminum piston. It would not merit mentioning in this book were it not for the adaptation of the Perry Directional Porting made for this specific engine.

ABC-PDP

The ABC upward angled bypass Super Tigre G-60 proved to be only marginally more powerful than the normal ringed version.

The latest version, which has Perry porting, has an output horsepower equal to or greater than many Schnuerles. Look at the top view of the ABC-PDP engine in Fig. 3-14 and compare it to the Schnuerle porting scheme. You'll notice that the flow pattern is the same: two ports front and back angled away from the exhaust and an upward angled side port.

In the Schnuerle engine, they are the front and rear Schnuerle ports and the side boost port. In the ABC-PDP engine, they are the two Perry ports and the normal upward angled cross flow bypass. The only difference is the relative size of the ports. The Schnuerle has the large Schnuerle ports compared to the ABC-PDP's small Perry Ports.

The ABC-PDP is, in effect, a Schnuerle engine with a hugh boost port. It is a "poor man's Schnuerle" with the same power output at a lower price. The latest model even has a modification to the crankcase casting that allows for larger Perry ports. This model is also the engine with the ABCD configuration. It incorporates a Dykes ring to eliminate the only complaint about the engine—rapid wear of the unringed piston. It should actually be called an ABCD-PDP engine. All this might sound like "alphabet soup," but with any name it's a great engine.

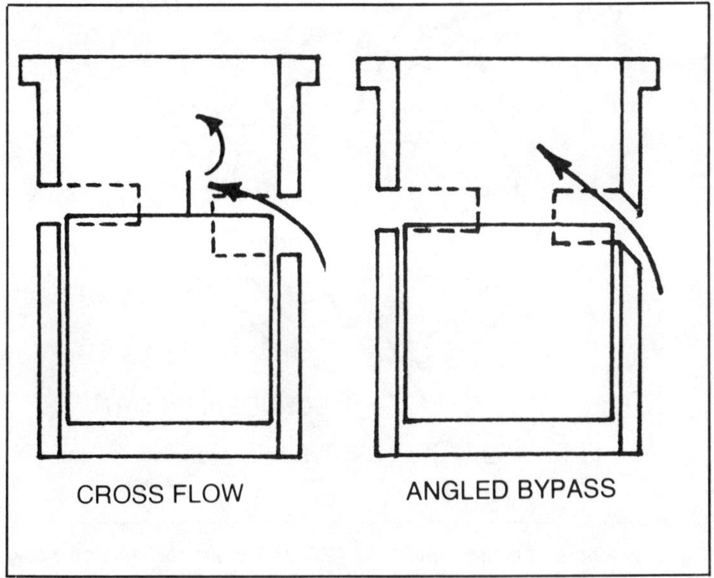

Fig. 3-13. Cross sections of the deflector piston cross flow cylinder and the Super Tigre ABC angled bypass engine cylinder.

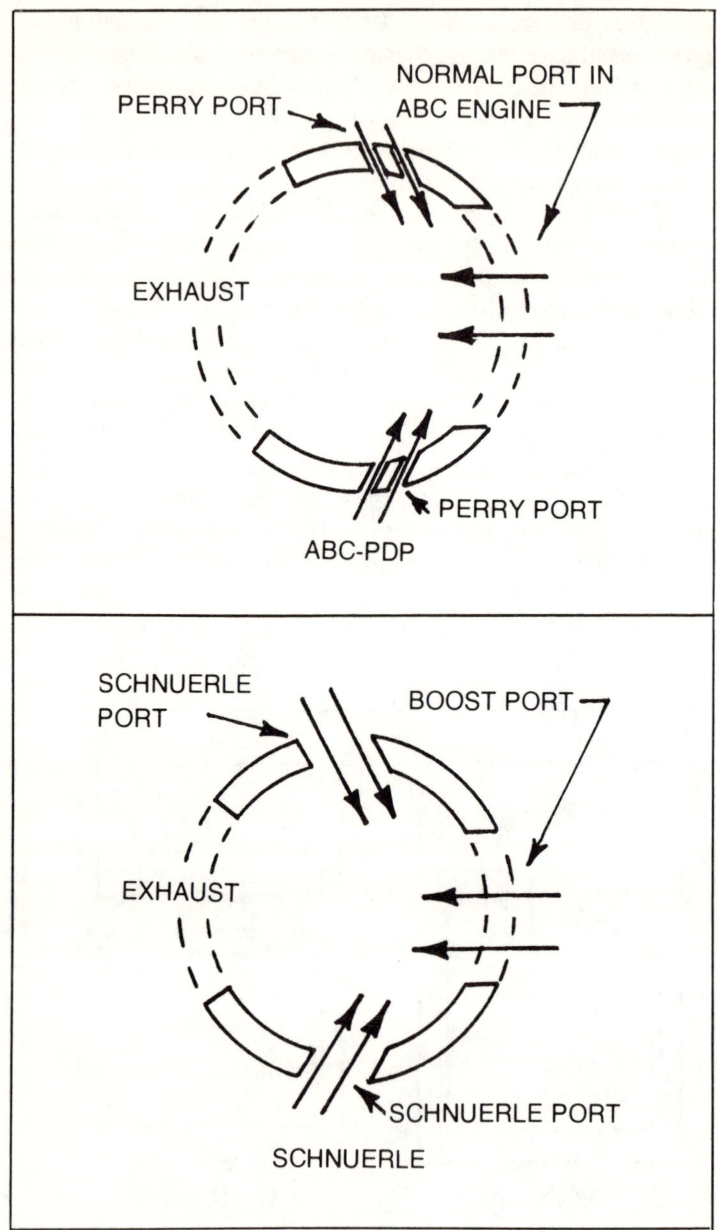

Fig. 3 .14. Gas flow in the Super Tigre ABC-PDP engine. Note how the flow pattern is very similar to that of a Schnuerle engine. This porting scheme actually has very small Schnuerle ports (the Perry ports) and a large boost port (the normal angled bypass ports).

THE CARBURETOR

The item that separates R/C engines from model engines used in other phases of modeling is the carburetor. Control line and free flight modelers, with the exception of the control line Navy Carrier and perhaps Scale events, use a simple venturi carburetor that allows the engine to run only at full power. Nowhere in control line and free flight, except in those two events already mentioned above, is a full variable range of power needed like it is in R/C. With few exceptions, virtually every R/C take off and landing is made just like a full scale one. The engine is started, the plane is taxied out, it is run up to full power and then it takes off. After flying for a time, the pilot throttles back, descends, lands and taxis the plane back to the pit area. All of this requires an engine with a full range of power. In the R/C engine, like full scale engines, this variation of power is performed by the carburetor.

Early Carburetors

One of the first, and very rudimentary R/C carburetors, was a venturi with two spray bars and two jets. Each one had a standard control line needle valve. With only one needle valve metering fuel, the engine ran at full power. When the second one opened, more fuel was added and the engine ran over-rich and slower. This was, naturally, only a two-speed carburetor.

Later R/C carburetors had a drum that rotated in the carb body. As the drum rotated, the size of the air inlet was reduced. This caused the engine to run richer and slower. Figure 3-15 shows a carburetor of this type with the drum removed. The disadvantage of this type of carb was that at very low speed the engine ran exceptionally rich and would sometimes quit. The carburetor that solved this problem, the *air bleed carburetor*, is still very much in use today.

The Air Bleed Carburetor

The rotating drum carb, while it had variable speed, lacked one essential item to be the R/C carb—a good idle. The mixture

Fig. 3-15. Early type of carburetor with the drum removed.

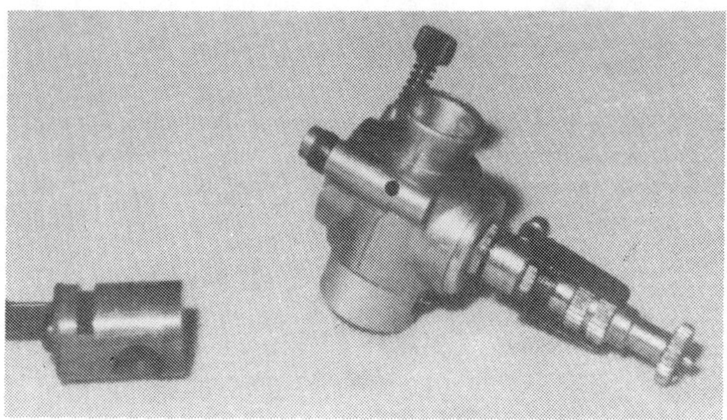

Fig. 3-16. An air-bleed carburetor showing the small air-bleed hole.

was just too rich at the low end. This was solved by placing an adjustable air bleed hole in the carburetor body that is open at idle and allows more air into the engine for a leaner mixture at low speed. Figure 3-16 shows an air bleed carb with the air bleed hole in the front. The small screw on the right adjusts the size of the hole (adjusting the idle mixture). Figure 3-17 shows a cross section of this carb. At the top, the rotating drum is at the full power position and the air bleed hole is closed. At the bottom, in the idle position, the air bleed hole is aligned with the opening in the rotating drum and additional air is allowed to enter the crankcase.

You can see that the air bleed carb is accurately adjusted only at full throttle or at idle and you might not think that this is a good situation. In practice, however, it works quite well. The engine does run rich in the mid-range, but this area is not used very much; most R/Cers use idle or full throttle most of the time. The fact that the engine is running rich is actually not a large concern. What R/C fliers tend to be concerned about is that they have variable power. The air bleed carb certainly delivers that. The only drawback to this carburetor is that it usually has a slow acceleration to full power from idle while the engine goes through the rich area. Once you get used to this feature, it is hardly noticeable and certainly not a detraction.

The Fuel Metering Carburetor

The final improvement to the R/C carburetor was to make it fully variable with linear response by varying not only the air coming into the engine, but also the fuel. The problem in doing this with an R/C carb is twofold: technical difficulty and cost are the sticky points. In the first place, the carburetor for any aerobatic aircraft, R/C or full scale, must work under a variety of very severe conditions. It must function upright and inverted, on either side, and under high positive and negative conditions. This means that any type of float system similar to the carburetor on a car will not work.

Cost is another factor in any new development. In a competetive market, it can be the one overriding factor. This means that a super-sophisticated new carb, despite the fact that it outperforms

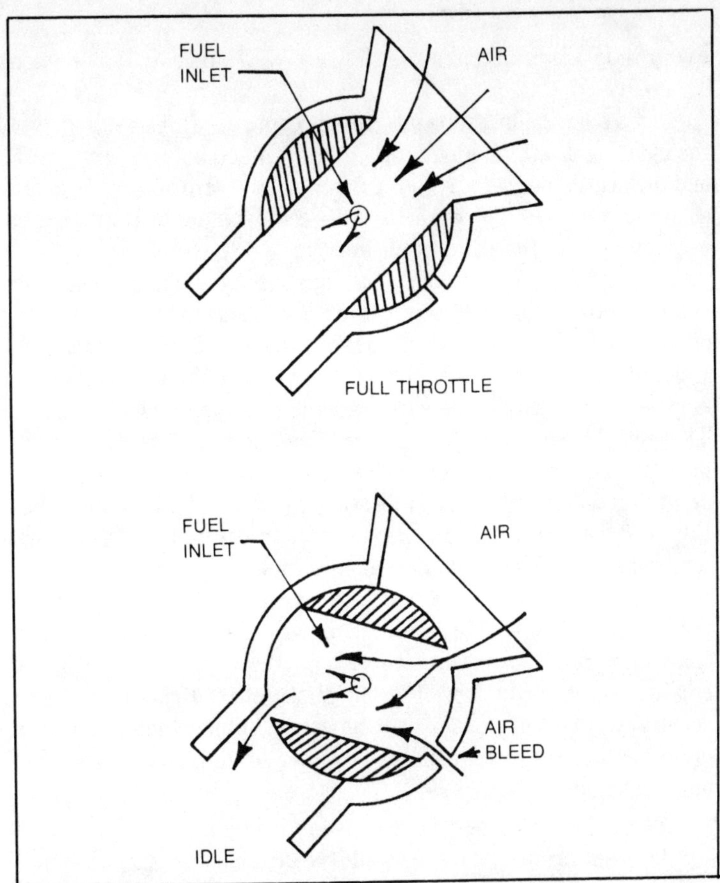

Fig. 3-17. Operation of an air-bleed carburetor. When the drum is rotated to the idle position, the air flow is restricted but not the fuel flow. At full idle, the opening in the drum coincides with the small air bleed hole. This allows more air to enter and keeping the mixture from becoming too rich.

Fig. 3-18. Modern carburetor with an angled cam groove in the drum.

everything else, might not sell very well since it will be too expensive.

The solution most manufacturers came up with was to modify the rotating drum, air bleed carb. The air bleed hole was removed, and the drum, instead of rotating flushly in the carb body, was given a cam action or a slight spiral in-and-out movement by the means of a groove cut in the rotating drum (Fig. 3-18).

A screw in the carb body fits into the groove and causes the drum to move in and out as it rotates. As the drum moves, either a needle or an adjustable sleeve covers a slit in the spray bar through which the fuel flows. This meters the amount of fuel going into the engine. The adjustable needle or sleeve sets the idle fuel mixture. The high-speed needle valve is retained and is adjusted as in all previous carburetor designs. The cam action of the drum is preset at the factory to give fuel metering for the average mid-range. Figure 3-19 shows the underside of a typical fuel metering carb with a moveable sleeve to meter the fuel.

In practice, these carburetors work extremely well. They give a low, dependable idle, full power and also a rapid, lean transition from one to the other. They also give a more linear engine response compared to radio stick setting than the air bleed carb. They are more expensive, however, so many manufacturers only use fuel metering type carburetors on their larger (.40 and up), higher priced engines.

Other manufacturers have chosen to implement fuel metering in a different manner, but the results were the same: good idle, full power and lean transition. Notable among these are Fox and Perry.

Fox was actually one of the first to have a fuel metering carburetor. His three-needle valve fuel metering carb was available on Fox engines when most other manufacturers were still using

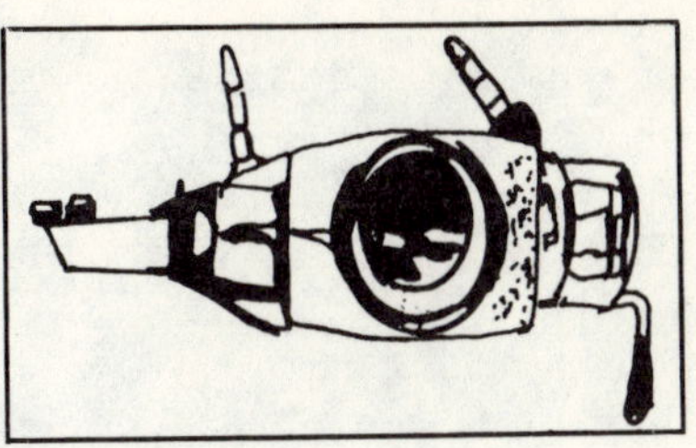

Fig. 3-19. The underside of a modern carburetor showing the moveable sleeve partially covering the slit in the incoming fuel line.

air bleed carbs. But it was not well accepted by modelers since it was complicated to adjust. The later Fox two-needle carb adjusts in approximately the same way as do other carburetors.

Instead of a drum, however, Fox uses a rotating butterfly or air valve similar to the ones used in an automobile carburetor—except that the fuel passes through the air valve. As fuel goes from the carb body to the air valve, it passes through a "V" shaped groove of varying depth that meters it depending on the angle of the air valve. Figure 3-20 shows the Fox carburetor with the air valve removed. Note the V groove on the side nearest the adjustable high speed needle. This carb has very linear response and excellent fuel draw.

The Perry carburetor is a variation of the rotating drum carb, but uses a metering slit to a fuel reservoir in the carb body rather than cam action to meter the fuel. Perry carburetors were first manufactured as a replacement for other original equipment air bleed carburetors.

This made them extremely popular and in many cases they became the standard against which other fuel metering carbs were

Fig. 3-20. Fox carburetor with the air valve removed. Note the small V-groove running from the right hole in the air valve.

Fig. 3-21. Perry Carburetor. This is a large throat pump carburetor for high power.

judged. Perry carburetors are now offered as original equipment on several brands of engines. Perry also manufactures a special large intake carburetor to be used in conjunction with the fuel pump (to be discussed in a later section). The combination of these two can give an engine as much as a 20 percent power increase. This combination is very popular with competition fliers. Figure 3-21 shows a Perry carburetor.

THE GLOW PLUG

Virtually all model aircraft engines are glow-plug engines. The glow plug engine is actually a semidiesel engine. It uses a battery to cause a platinum coil in the plug to glow for starting. After the engine is started and adjusted, the battery can be disconnected and the engine will continue to run. It uses the residual heat of the coil and the catalytic action of the platinum to ignite the fuel-air mixture. This is the beauty of these engines. There is no coil, no condenser and no points to worry about or adjust. There are no heavy magnets, electronic ignition or engine-related batteries to carry around. Your only concerns are the fuel mixture and the adjustments on the carb.

There are several types of glow plugs. The "standard" type will usually have no identifying word or phrase on the package; just the manufacturer's name and *glow plug*. It will probably state

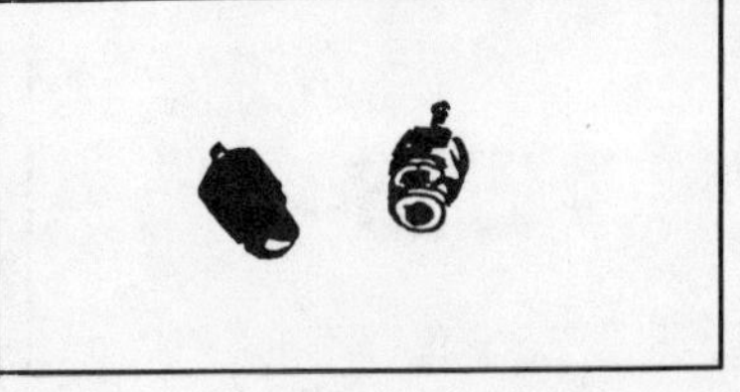

Fig. 3-22. Standard and idle bar glow plugs.

whether it is a "short," meaning a *short reach glow plug* that is used in the smaller engines with thinner cylinder heads or a "long" for *long reach glow plug* that is used for larger engines (usually .19s and larger). These plugs are normally used for control line engines that do not have to idle.

Glow plugs normally used in R/C engines have what is called an *idle bar* and are marked *R/C Long* or *R/C Short* on the package. A look at Fig. 3-22 will show you both a standard and an R/C idle bar type glow plug. Note the idle bar across the base of the plug on the left.

The model aircraft engine continues to run after the battery is disconnected because of the residual heat of the platinum coil which is continually being reheated by the combustion process and because of the catalytic action of the platinum. When the engine is throttled back to idle, it runs cooler. It is so cool that the glow plug is on the verge of being extinguished by the incoming charge of fuel-air mixture.

The solution to this problem was twofold. First tried was an exhaust baffle that closed off part of the exhaust at idle to keep heat in the cylinder. This has since been supplanted by mufflers that increase the back pressure and raise the temperature. Even more effective was the addition of a shield over the element of the glow plug so that the incoming mixture could not directly hit the coil. Later it was found that a small bar across the cavity where the platinum coil is located is sufficient, hence the term *idle bar*.

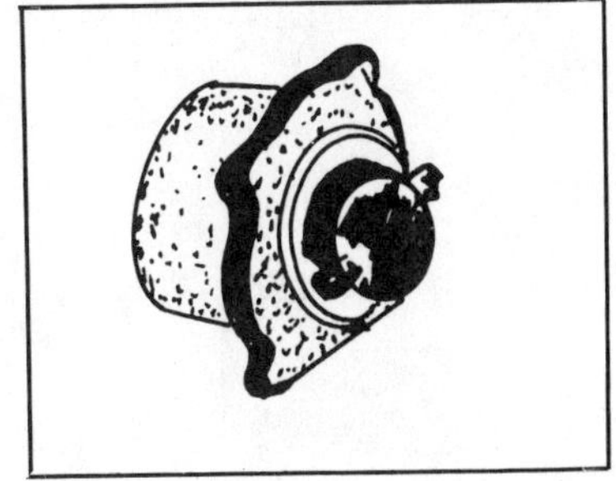

Fig. 3-23. The Perry fuel pump that replaces the rear cover of the engine. This one is for an OS .60 FSR.

Fig. 3-24. Robart diaphram fuel pump.

FUEL PUMPS

Perry manufactures a fuel pump to be used with his special, large intake carburetor. This pump is a diaphram-operated pump containing a fuel regulator. It is sold in a housing so that it replaces the normal engine rear cover. See Fig. 3-23

Large throat carburetors, like the Perry pump carb, have a venturi so large that they are not able to generate a low enough pressure in the throat to draw fuel from the tank. The fuel pump was designed to eliminate this problem and to allow the use of these large carburetors. In addition to the Perry pump, which must be made in different specific sizes since they replace the engine back plate, Robart also makes a pump. The Robart pump is connected to the engine in a less permanent fashion and can be used on any engine. Its main drawback is that it doesn't have a regulator. Figure 3-24 shows a Robart pump.

Both the Perry and Robart pumps allow the use of extra large carburetors and the placement of the fuel tank an extended distance from the engine. They both supply fuel under very adverse conditions. The Perry, due to its regulator, maintains a steadier needle valve setting, but is more costly than the Robart. It is also only available for the more popular .60-sized engines and for the K&B .40.

Engine Accessories and Operation

Now that we've looked at engine theory and components, let's take a look at what accessories go with the engine and how to start and adjust the engine.

MUFFLERS AND PIPES

Virtually every engine sold today comes with a muffler. The use of larger, noisier engines and the location of most R/C flying sites near residential areas has made their use almost universal. While early mufflers were noted for their power consumption, present ones take away very little power. In the case of tuned exhaust pipes, they actually add power. In addition to the mufflers manufactured by the engine makers, there are several types of mufflers available from specialty manufacturers.

Expansion Type Mufflers

The usual original equipment muffler is the expansion type. This type muffler is essentially a large chamber bolted over the engine exhaust with a small hole in the back. Figure 4-1 shows examples of expansion mufflers.

In operation, the hot exhaust gasses enter the chamber, turn, and pass out the rear hole. They are slowed down and cooled in the process and lose their high pitched wail and considerable noise. These mufflers create some back pressure that helps the idle, but also takes away some power. Five hundred rpm from a top of 14,000 rpm is an average loss I have noted in testing mufflers. Not a very large amount compared to the peak rpm.

Venturi Mufflers

Another type of muffler is the *venturi* or *flow-through* muffler. Figure 4-2 shows a venturi muffler. Notice the hole in front. This

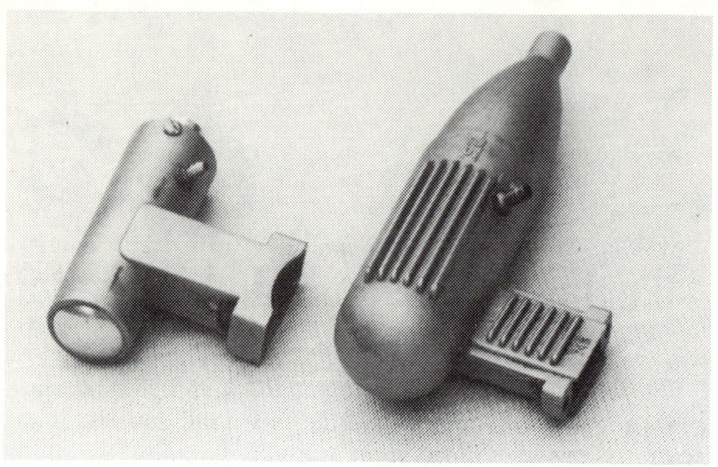

Fig. 4-1. Two examples of expansion mufflers.

muffler is actually in two sections. It has an outer section with a ring cross-section and the inner venturi. Refer to Fig. 4-3. The exhaust from the engine enters the outer ring and expands and cools as it goes. This action is similar to the expansion muffler. The difference is in the final extraction of the exhaust gasses.

In the expansion muffler, they exit the hole in the rear by the force of their own expansion. In the venturi muffler, they are *pulled out*. The ring section of the muffler has a series of small holes drilled through it so that the exhaust gasses can flow out into the inner venturi tube. From the side cross section in Fig. 4-3 you can see how this happens. As the plane flies, air enters the front of the venturi tube. Just like a carburetor, as the cross section gets smaller the pressure is lowered and this draws the exhaust out through the small holes drilled in the wall of the tube.

Venturi mufflers are quite effective in terms of reducing power loss that's associated with muffling an engine. I have recorded losses as low as only 200 rpm on the ground. On the ground, venturi tube is not as effective as it is when the plane is at top speed. Some manufacturers claim no power loss in the air or a slight gain in rpm due to better scavenging. There is no accurate way to check this, but in view of the principles the muffler operates under, it seems possible. Venturi mufflers, however, are not as quiet as the expansion type. They muffle much of the high-pitched bark of the engine, but are still loud compared to some other types. For this reason, some clubs only allow a closed-front muffler. This rules out the open-ended venturi muffler.

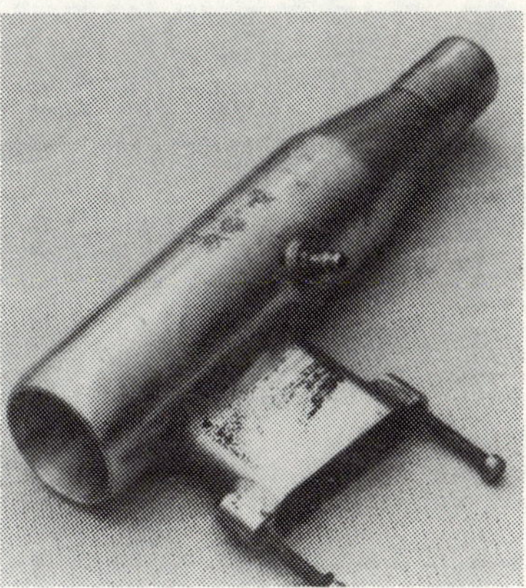

Fig. 4-2. Venturi muffler. Notice the opening in the front on the left.

Tuned Exhaust Pipes

Tuned exhaust pipes were used on two-cycle engines in racing boats and motorcycles for several years before they were used on model airplane engines. The first work of note on this type exhaust system for model engines was done by Bill Wiznewski several years ago. He used the tuned exhaust for his control line speed engines. It was not until the 1970s that they were used on R/C planes.

Tuned exhausts on R/C planes came about as a result of the muffler requirement on FAI (international class) acrobatic planes. The stiff noise reduction requirements dictated a very restrictive muffler that robbed the engine of a lot of power. If a tuned exhaust system could give the power back and also be quiet, it seemed like the way to go. Figure 4-4 shows two examples of *tuned exhaust pipes*. They are normally called tuned pipes or just a pipe for short.

The tuned pipe works two ways. It aids scavengine, like the venturi muffler, and it also helps to pack the new fuel-air mixture in—sort of a supercharging effect. Look at a cross section of the

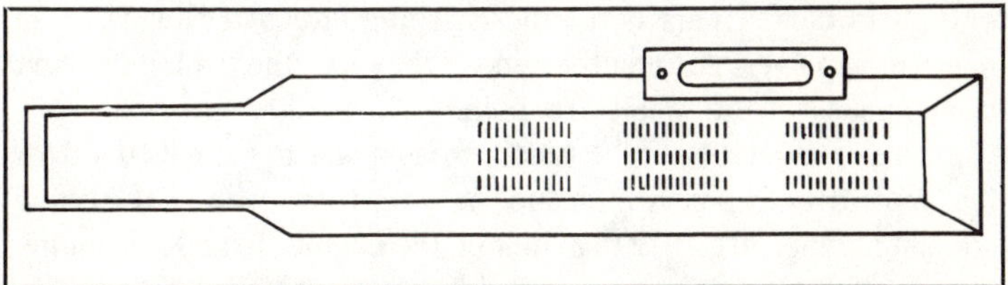

Fig. 4-3. Cross section of a venturi muffler. The exhaust enters the outer chamber. Air flows through the narrowed down center hole, creating a low pressure, and draws the exhaust out through the perforations.

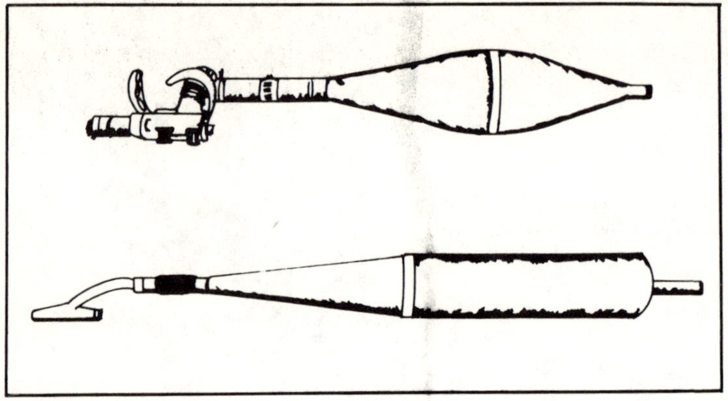

Fig. 4-4. Two examples of tuned exhaust pipes. The upper short pipe is tuned for a racing engine. The longer pipe is broad range tuned for competition acrobatics.

tuned pipe in Fig. 4-5. When the exhaust port opens, the hot, high-speed gasses enter the pipe and a pressure wave is formed. These gasses expand and cool through the diverging section of the chamber. As they do, the pressure behind the pressure wave is lower than the pressure in front of it. This causes additional exhaust gasses to be sucked out of the cylinder. The exhaust gasses cool further as the pressure wave passes through the converging section of the chamber. At the end of the converging section, the pressure wave is reflected and it heads back toward the exhaust port.

The length of the pipe is critical. It is chosen so that the pressure wave arrives back at the exhaust port just as the new fuel-air mixture has completed its scavenging and is beginning to go out the exhaust. The pressure wave hits this new mixture and stuffs it back into the cylinder. The fuel-air mixture is pushed from the other side by the normal action of the engine. The result is a higher pressure mixture being trapped when the exhaust and intake ports close. This is a supercharging effect and leads to an increase in power. At the other end of the pipe, the cooled exhaust gasses pass out the small exit hole.

The original idea of the tuned exhaust was to have it tuned for one rpm—usually a very high one. At other rpm settings, the tuned exhaust hampered rather than helped the engine. In an R/C engine with variable rpm requirements, this could not be tolerated. The pipes were re-designed for a lower rpm and a much broader range. Many of the successful tuned pipes only improve the engine rpm

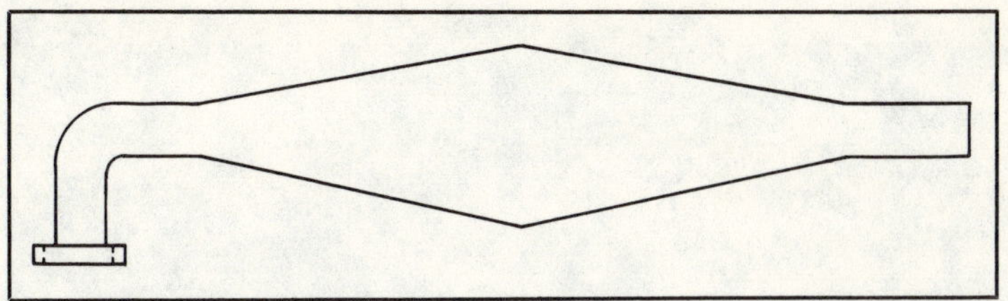

Fig. 4-5. The cross section of a tuned exhaust pipe. As the exhaust opens, a pressure wave is formed. The hot gasses expand and the wave travels down the diverging section. They cool and contract along the converging section. Then the wave reflects back toward the exhaust and keeps a fresh fuel-air mixture from being drawn out after the burned gasses.

marginally over the open exhaust rpm, but they do it very quietly. Therefore, they are becoming very popular.

It has also been found that modifying the engine's exhaust timing by increasing the time the exhaust port stays open will give an increase of power with a tuned pipe. For this reason, some of the .60-sized engines normally used for competition acrobatic planes come either pipe or non-pipe tuned. The pipe-tuned engine has the modified exhaust timing. If you intend to buy one of these engines, be sure to find out which type it is. The pipe-tuned engine does not run as well as the regular engine on a standard muffler.

Other Mufflers

There are several other mufflers and most are made for specialty applications. One example is the Heloball muffler. It is

Fig. 4-6. A Heloball muffler.

Fig. 4-7. An unobtrusive Slim Line brand muffler on a scale Skybolt biplane.

made by Mac's Mufflers for helicopter use (Fig. 4-6). Other planes, scale planes in particular, have need of mufflers that are unobtrusive rather than especially quiet. Both Slim Line and DuBro offer a flat, small muffler. The DuBro muffler is relatively quiet, but the Slim Line tends to be noisy. They both blend in with the model better than other types. This is shown by the Slim Line muffler on the author's scale model of a Steen Skybolt acrobatic biplane in Fig. 4-7.

ENGINE MOUNTS

Your engine mount does more than just hold the engine to the plane. Certainly it must be adequate to do that, but it should also dampen some of the vibration from the engine so that vibrations won't be transferred to the radio. The mount should also allow you to make thrust adjustments easily to trim your airplane. There are two ways of mounting the engine, or more specifically, two types of mounts: *beam mounts* and *radial mounts*. Each of them has its peculiarities and its advantages and disadvantages. Let's look at each type.

Beam Mounts

The former control line flier will recall that the only mount in that type of flying is the beam mount. In most cases, the engine is bolted directly to two hardwood beams, hence the name beam mount. The procedure is the same in R/C planes. The hardwood, or in some cases plywood, beams are built into the nose of the plane and the engine is bolted to them. The wood has the advantage of being an excellent absorber of vibration and wood mounts are very inexpensive compared to a radial mount. While wood mounts are not as popular in balsa kits as they used to be, many kits with fiberglass fuselages come with a motor mount of heavy plywood already molded in. This is a distinct time and money saver.

On the disadvantage side, wood acts as an insulator and does not help cool the engine as do metal radial mounts. They also tend to be damaged by the combination of heat from the engine and oil in the fuel. No matter what type of finish you put on the wood, heat from direct contact with the engine mounting lugs invariably breaks it down and oil gets in.

Radial Mounts

The more common type of engine mount on R/C planes today is the radial mount. The mount is actually a beam/radial mount since the engine mounts on beams through its mounting lugs, but then the entire engine and motor mount assembly is radially mounted to a heavy plywood firewall. Figure 4-8 shows examples of radial engine mounts.

Radial engine mounts are made from various materials. The most common are aluminum and fiberglass filled nylon. Others are made from magnesium and sheet aluminum. Aluminum mounts are either cast and machine finished or milled from extruded aluminum

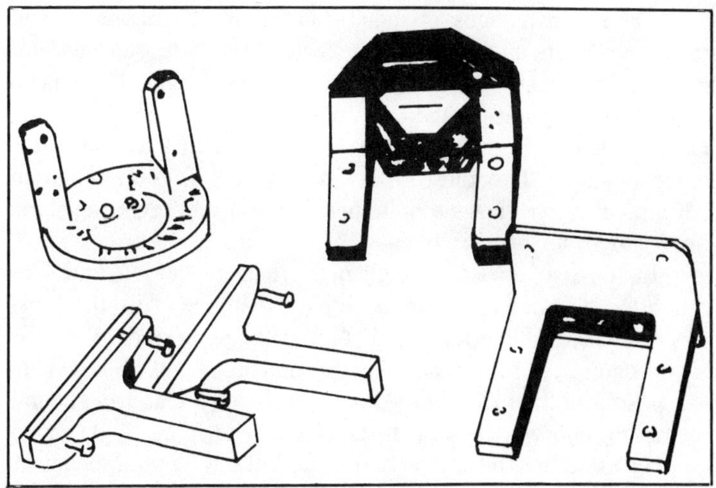

Fig. 4-8. Several examples of radial engine mounts.

stock. The filled nylon mounts are injection molded from hard, high-quality materials.

Advantages of the radial type mount are thrustline adjustment and cooling. Nothing can be more aggravating than to find that your new acrobatic creation needs some side thrust and you have to re-drill your wood mounts. With a radial mount, you remove the bolts holding it to the firewall, put washers in the proper place for the side thrust, replace the bolts and go try it. This is a much easier process. This is not a necessary thing for the beginner. But to many experienced fliers, being able to make quick and easy thrust adjustments is well worth the small extra cost (in the $5 to $7 range) of the radial mount.

Metal motor mounts also help to cool the engine. Heat is transferred through the mounting lugs to the mount. This gives a much larger area through which to dissipate the heat. The fiber-filled nylon mounts do not, of course, have this advantage.

The final advantage of the radial mount that can be useful to many modelers is that of engine interchangeability. Even though various brands of engines have different mounting lug widths and spacings, the radial mount of the same brand will have the same bolt pattern for bolting it into the plane. This allows you to remove one brand of engine and replace it with one with a wholly different lug bolt pattern. You simply remove the entire engine and mount assembly and replace it with the new engine and mount. For this reason, many modelers choose one brand of mount and stick with it no matter what engine they use.

The disadvantages of radial mounts are cost, weight and mounting the engine. Radial mounts, with their casting and machining, naturally cost more than two pieces of hardwood. There is no way to get around it. In addition, radial mounts, especially for the larger .40- and .60-sized engines, weigh more than a comparable wood mount. While this is often a problem, it is at times an advantage. Many planes tend to be tail-heavy and requiring some nose weight for proper balance.

In this case, the extra weight of the radial mount is useful. The other disadvantage comes in mounting the engine. With the wood mounts, you drill four holes and bolt the engine in place. With the radial mount, you must accurately drill and then tap the holes. This can pose a problem to the beginner, but every club has several members who will be glad to help out. The filled nylon radial mounts can either be drilled and tapped like the metal mount or drilled for self-tapping screws.

PROPELLERS

The engine has to have a propeller and there are dozens of sizes and types to choose from. Finding the best one for your engine is most easily done by checking what props other modelers at the flying field use on a similar size engine. Aside from the basic size requirements, there are several other areas concerning propellers that the beginner should be familiar with. These are prop terminology, what types of materials props are made of (and the advantages and disadvantages of each material), how to balance a prop and why, and most important, safety considerations.

Terminology

You've probably already heard someone using prop terminology. If you've heard, "Get a 10-6," or some other size, like 6-3 or 11-7, you've been introduced to prop terms. Let's look at these numbers and what they mean. The first number is the *diameter*, or length of the prop. A 10-6, and it's said *10 six*, not *10 dash six*, is 10 inches long, or the diameter of the circle it makes when it spins is 10 inches. The second number is the pitch. This is a measure of the angle of the blade. It means that if the prop were 100 percent efficient in the air, it would move forward 6 inches in one revolution. Of course, props aren't 100 percent efficient, but this is the standard way of measuring the blade angle.

Different size and pitch props can have a great effect on your plane's performance. A long, low-pitch prop, for example, will give it more acceleration and pulling power when the plane is slow. A short, high-pitch prop will give it a higher speed, but slower acceleration.

You might be familiar with similar pitch-diameter trade-offs with boat props. Suppose that you have a .40-powered trainer. You'll probably use a 10-6 prop. That is a very popular size for .40-sized sport engines. Another person with the same type .40 engine in a race plane may run a 9-7 or even an 8-7 or 8-7½ prop for greater speed. Notice that as you go up in pitch you have to go down in diameter. This is to keep the engine turning at its best rpm for maximum horsepower. Naturally, you can't just increase the pitch and keep the diameter the same. This would put an increased load on the engine and slow it down below its best rpm.

As you can guess, the ultimate prop is the variable pitch prop. This is what full-scale planes use. The pilot sets a low pitch for take-off to get the acceleration he needs. The low pitch is also good

Table 4-1. Recommended Prop Sizes.

Engine Displacement	Props
	5 ¼-4, 6-3
.049	6-4, 7-4
.09-.10	7-6, 8-4
.15	8-6, 9-4
.19-.25 and 3.5 cc	9-6
.29-.30	9-6, 10-6,
.35-.36	9-7, 10-6, 11-6
.40-.45 (6.5 cc)	11-7, 11-7 ½,
.60	11-8, 12-6

for climb. After leveling off the pilot sets a higher pitch, keeping the rpm at its best cruise setting, and enjoys greater speed than the lower take-off and climb pitch would have given him. A variable pitch prop for R/C planes has recently come on to the market. This first version is expensive, but it could be the prop of the future. Table 4-1 shows some recommended prop sizes for sport engines.

Materials

About 20 to 25 years ago, all props were made of wood. In the 50s, injection molded nylon props came along. Now props are made not only from these materials, but from Space-Age materials like epoxy, graphite fibers and fiberglass.

Despite these advances, wood props are still the standard in R/C. Nylon props, which were enthusiastically accepted in control line, were popular in R/C until the advent of the larger, .60-sized engines. These engines had enough power to literally sling the blades off nylon props. This was a serious enough hazard to cause many clubs to ban the use of nylon props on large engines.

Wood props, made from hardrock maple, hold together under the highest rpm. They also have another advantage: a lack of flexibility. The wooden prop maintains its pitch and the tips track true, while its nylon counterpart tends to lose pitch in flight and wobble at the tip under high rpm conditions. Both of these faults result in deteriorated climb and speed performance, so wood props are very much preferred. Figure 4-9 shows wood and nylon props.

Although wood props dominate the scene today at most flying fields, advances in prop materials are beginning to change the industry. Props made from fiberglass-filled nylon are now on the market. These tend to be much stiffer than the unfilled ones and their price compared to maple props is making them more attractive every day. Many competition acrobatic fliers are reporting

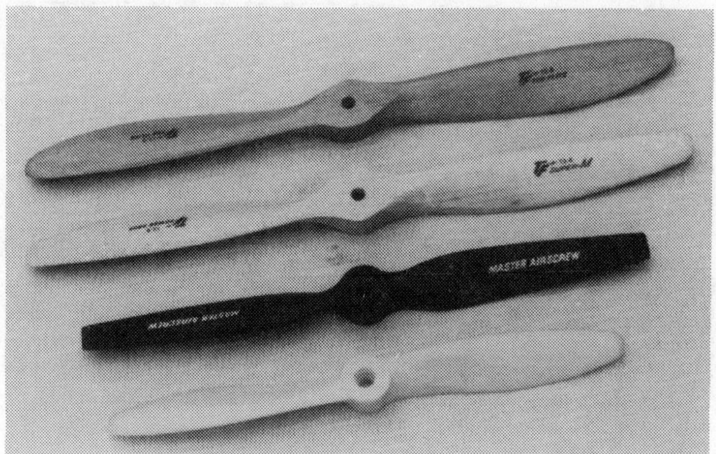

Fig. 4-9. Two wood props on the top contrast with a black fiberglass filled nylon prop and an unfilled nylon prop.

that they can tell no difference between the better filled-nylon props and wood ones. Notice the black color of the filled-nylon props in Fig. 4-10 compared to the white or yellow unfilled ones.

Materials that are more exotic than fiberglass-filled nylon are also available. They result in a thin, stiff, fantastically strong prop. These are the epoxy props that are made from epoxy resin with either graphite or fiberglass strands for strength. These props can easily withstand any rpm possible with a model engine. At present,

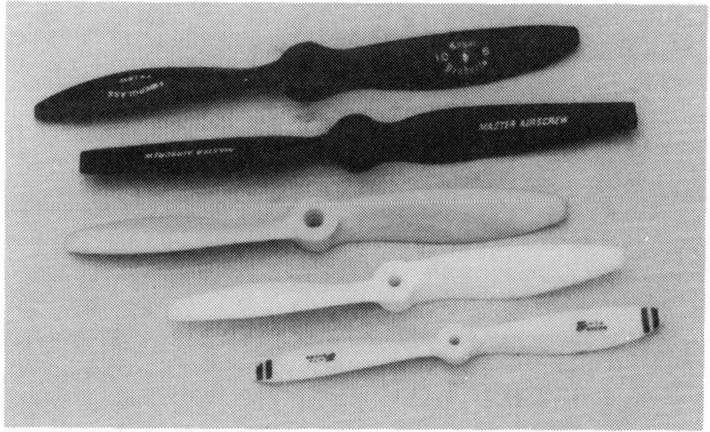

Fig. 4-10. The black Royal and Master Airscrew props are fiberglass filled nylon, while the three lighter colored props are Tornado and Top Flite unfilled nylon.

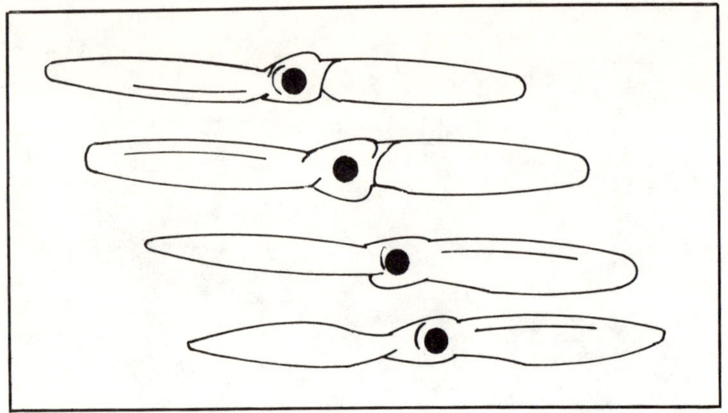

Fig. 4-11. Props.

they are hand made and expensive. They cost from $3.50 to $8 and up per prop. This pretty well takes them out of the price range for sport fliers, but for the race pilot, they are well worth the price. Figure 4-11 shows examples of graphite-epoxy props on the left and fiberglass-epoxy props on the right.

Balancing Your Prop

Many R/C fliers just take a prop out of their field box, bolt it on the engine, and go fly. Never a thought is given to balancing and the effects of an unbalanced prop on the engine, plane and radio. This usually works out, because most high quality *wood* props are fairly well balanced when they come from the manufacturer. On the other hand, if you read the instructions that come with your radio set very carefully, you'll invariably find that the manufacturer cautions about the damage that can occur due to excessive vibration from an unbalanced prop. Vibration damage is insidious. It often isn't readily visible, but it's a real problem.

Let's face it, it takes a severely unbalanced prop to do any serious damage to a radio set, right? Well, the problem is that the long-term cumulative effects of vibration can shorten the life of certain components. This is particularly true for batteries and servo potentiometers. Maintenance costs will be lower in the long run if you take the time to balance your props.

Balancing a prop takes an inexpensive balancer and some fine sandpaper. Figure 4-12 shows two balancers. One is made by DuBro and the other is made by Prather Products. The DuBro balancer is used by screwing the knob into one side of the prop and

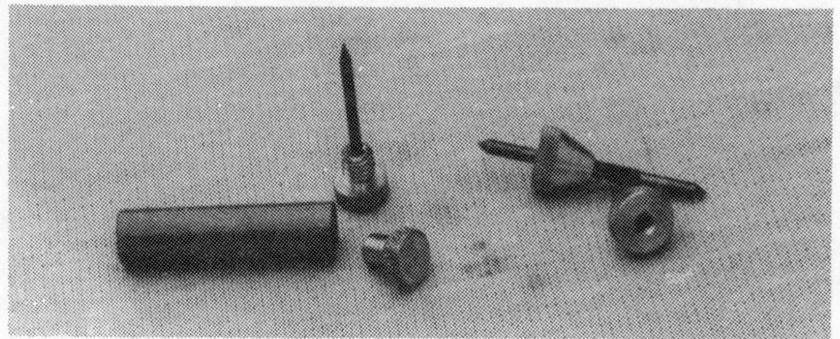

Fig. 4-12. A Du Bro prop balancer on the left and a Prather blancer on the right.

then sitting the prop on the vertical needle as shown in Fig. 4-13. The heavy blade will drop lower than the lighter blade. You then sand the front, or curved part of the heavy blade, and try the balancer again. *Never sand the back side of the prop*. It will change the pitch if you do. The DuBro balancer is extremely accurate, but the knob is sized only for a one-fourth of an inch hole in the prop. This means it can't be used for balancing the smaller props.

The Prather balancer, with the two cones that screw down into the prop mounting hole, works for any size prop. You hold it lightly between your thumb and forefinger as shown in Fig. 4-14. A light hold is essential so that you don't create friction and stop the heavy blade from dropping. This balancer might not be quite as accurate as the DuBro, but it is much handier to use at the field. Either one will do the job for you.

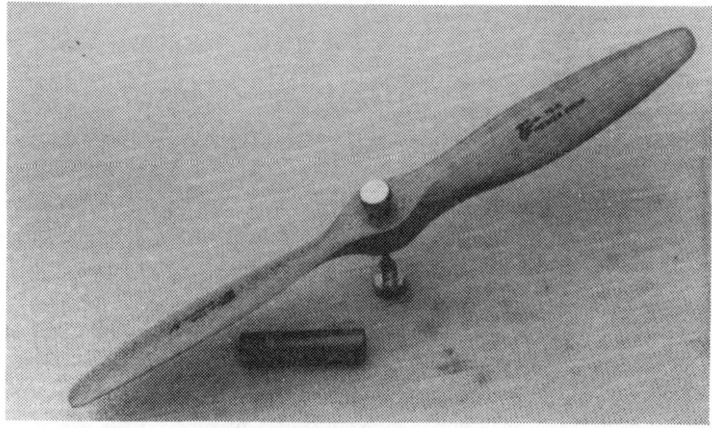

Fig. 4-13. The Du Bro prop balancer in use.

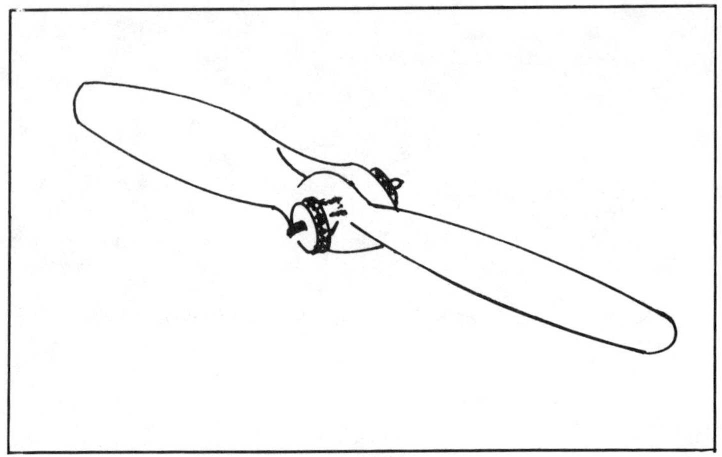

Fig. 4-14. The convenient Prather prop balancer.

Safety

I have already mentioned that some large, powerful engines have been known to sling the blades off nylon props. Actually, this is a possibility with any prop and any engine. With the smaller engines, it becomes a remote chance, but still worthy of mention. An unseen flaw in the prop, a casting flaw in the nylon or a hidden bad spot in the wood, can make any prop a potential hazard. Even closer to home, suppose that you tick the prop on landing and just grind off a little of the tips. It's not enough to warrant a replacement, so you continue to fly it. It looks good, but is it? Maybe the hub area was overstressed and is ready to let go.

No, I'm not recommending that you change your prop every time it gets a tiny nick, although many fliers do and it's wise from a prop-balancing standpoint. What I *am* recommending is that in addition to the safety rule about keeping fingers out of the way of the prop make it a strong rule that you stay out of the line of the prop. If it does break, that way you won't get hit. An 11-inch propeller on a .60 engine turning in the 13,000 to 14,000 rpm range has a tip speed of about 500 mph. If a blade breaks off, you have the equivalent of a 500-mph throwing knife coming at you.

Use caution. *Do not get in line with the prop*. It is common for a flier to lean over the engine (Fig. 4-15) to adjust the needle valve. If the engine is running, the pilot's head will be in the danger zone—in line with the prop. Lean back from the engine, or better yet, get behind the prop (Fig. 4-16). It could save you an injury.

Fig. 4-15. The wrong way to adjust the needle valve (leaning over the propeller). A prop blade failure in this case could result in serious injury.

FUEL AND FUEL TANKS

The life blood of your engine is the fuel. When the fuel is flowing properly, the engine usually runs fine. When it's not flowing properly, more problems seem to be traced to fuel and fuel tanks than you'd think.

Fuel

Most model airplane engines operate on a mixture of methanol and nitromethane. Because they are two-cycle engines, a lubricating oil is mixed with the fuel. This fuel, without the oil, is the same type used by Indianapolis race cars and fuel dragsters. And in any event, whether it's model airplanes or Indy, increasing the nitro increases the speed. It also increases the wear on your engine. For

Fig. 4-16. The correct way to adjust the needle valve (from behind the prop).

this reason, plus the added fact that nitormethane is very expensive, most sport fliers stick to regular sport fuel.

The usual fuel mixture is 10 percent nitromethane, 65-70 percent methanol and 20-25 percent oil. Some fliers like a fuel with 15 percent nitro and other fliers, for economy, choose 5 percent. It varies according to cost and need, but standard sport fuel is usually 10 percent. Fuel for other uses varies a great deal from the 50-65 percent nitro used in racers to the 2½ percent used by some competitors who use a certain type of foreign engine.

Model airplane fuel always comes with the oil premixed. Other two-stroke engines might require you to mix oil with gasoline before you use it. The oils used are not petroleum based. They are either castor oil or one of several synthetics.

At one time, the oil used in model engine fuels was exclusively castor oil. However, the rising cost of castor oil compared to the newer synthetics has made the synthetics very popular. Most fuel used today is either all or part synthetic oil lubricated. There are advantages of each type oil and there will probably be proponents of each type at your flying field. My own recommendation is to use a fuel with both castor and synthetic oils in order to get the advantages of both.

The best thing going for castor oil is the way it handles heat. Castor oil will work to a higher temperature than the synthetics, a definite plus, and it also has an affinity for heat. This means that if your engine starts running lean and hot, the castor oil will flow *toward* the hot spot. Synthetics won't do this. A bad lean run on an all synthetic oil fuel can mean a burned or melted piston—a ruined engine.

On the other hand, castor is more expensive than the synthetics, so let's look at the synthetics and their advantages. There are three main synthetics used in fuel today: Klotz, one of the Union Carbide Ucon oils and a Monsanto synthetic. Of the three, Klotz is very recognizable by its pinkish-red color. A pink fuel, one that looks like cherry fruit-flavored drink, is bound to have Klotz in it. The price of any of these is lower per gallon than castor oil.

The synthetics burn very cleanly and leave little or no residue in your engine. Castor oil, on the other hand, leaves a varnish on your piston and cylinder and carbon on the cylinder and head fins where it has baked on. Synthetic oil fuel exhaust residue is also easier to clean off your plane. This is especially true in cool weather when the castor turns very thick.

One final note on castor oil. It provides protection against rust. You might not think that an engine that is run regularly on a fuel that has oil blended in could have a problem with rust, but it can. The parts most easily ruined by rust are the ball bearings. Synthetic oils give virtually no rust protection. Couple that with a methanol (or alcohol) fuel that draws water out of the air and you can have a rust problem. Castor gives you a measure of protection. Not the protection you'll get if you pull the fuel tubing off and run the engine dry to shut it down after your last flight and then fill it with a light machine oil like 3 In 1, but more than the synthetics offer.

I recommend a fuel with both types of oil. A typical fuel using both castor and synthetic oils will have about 5 percent castor and 17 to 20 percent synthetic. This combination keeps the price down, gives you the heat protection of castor and some rust protection. It burns fairly clean and the residue isn't too hard to clean off your plane.

Your main problem with fuel might come from a local fuel blender who uses only synthetic oil. This fuel works absolutely fine and it's inexpensive. But if, and it's a big if for a beginner, you get a lean run on your engine, you won't have that castor oil there to help protect your engine. The best bet is to use fuel with some castor in it. The major fuel manufacturers wouldn't add the more expensive oil if they didn't feel that it is necessary.

Fuel Tanks

R/C fuel tanks are usually white, translucent polyethlene plastic with flexible pick-ups so that fuel can be picked up when the

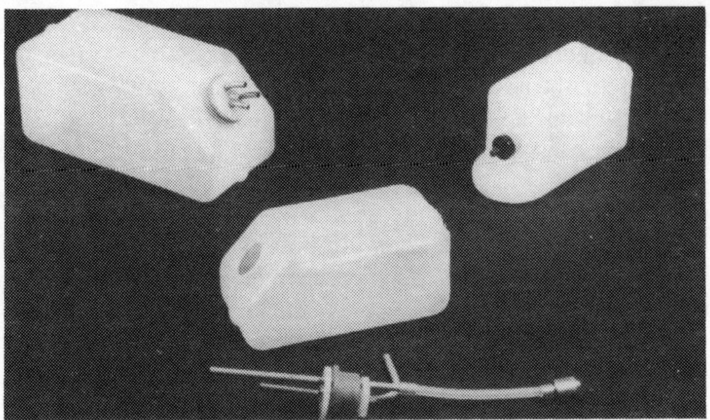

Fig. 4-17. Sullivan and Kraft fuel tanks. The tank in the foreground has the plumbing removed showing the flexible fuel pickup tube.

Fig. 4-18. Muffler pressure hook up. The white pressure line runs from the fitting on the muffler to the fuel tank inside the fuselage.

plane is in any attitude. They come in various sizes and shapes to fit any type of plane. The major manufacturers in the United States are Sullivan and Kraft. Figure 4-17 shows examples of each type. Take a look at the tank in the foreground with the inside plumbing removed. The long fuel pick-up line is made from flexible silicone rubber tubing with a weighted pick-up on the end so that it will stay with the fuel no matter what attitude the plane is in. The other two lines are the vent and filler lines. The vent line curls upward to the top of the tank and the filler merely goes into the tank anywhere. This tank system, using separate fuel pick-up, vent and filler tubes, is called the three-line system. It is preferred by many fliers because each line has its own function with none doing double duty.

The other fuel tank hook-up method is the two-line system. In this system, the filler line is omitted and the tank is filled through the fuel pick-up line. This requires you to remove the fuel line from the engine every time you fill the tank.

Most fliers will use muffler pressure to aid fuel flow. Because the pressure inside the muffler is slightly higher than atmospheric pressure, it is put to work helping to move the fuel to the engine. A line is connected from a fitting on the muffler (Fig. 4-18) to the tank. When the engine runs, some of the higher pressure exhaust flows through the line. This helps to force the fuel to the engine. This pressure is not great enough to require any regulation or special carburetors like the fuel pumps described earlier. It just keeps a slight pressure on the fuel so that the engine doesn't have to work as hard to draw fuel.

Muffler pressure is connected to the vent line. This means that the filler line on a three-line set-up must be capped off or pressure will be lost. This is easily done by putting a plastic fitting or a spare bolt in the soft fuel line. With a two-line system you don't have to worry about this.

There are some other advantages of the three-line set-up. For example, in a tightly cowled engine, the fuel line connector on the engine might be hard to reach. In that case, the three-line set-up with its separate filler would be mandatory. An example of this is shown in Fig. 4-19, on a scale Steen Skybolt. The engine fuel line is back under the cowling, but filling is easy because the filler and vent/muffler pressure lines are routed out a convenient spot on the bottom of the cowling.

Filters

Another reason I like the three-line system is because of my use of fuel filters. Many fliers use a filter in the fuel line that runs from a fuel can to the engine. I go a step farther. I use an in-line filter between the tank in the plane and the engine. Examples of fuel filters are shown in Fig. 4-20.

They might be made from plastic or aluminum, but they all use a fine wire mesh to trap lint and grit before it gets to your carburetor. Foreign material in your fuel line and carb can turn a sweet running engine into a beast. This single problem, a clogged car-

Fig. 4-19. Three-line fuel system. One fuel line, hidden under the cowling, supplies fuel to the engine. The second runs from the pressure tap on the muffler to the tank. A third line, which is capped during engine operation, is used to refuel the tank.

Fig. 4-20. Examples of in-line fuel filters. Using one of these on your engine can prevent many carburetor problems.

buretor, seems to be the major engine problem I run into. Most, if not all, of the trouble could be avoided by the use of a filter. I use one on every engine and I recommend that you do, too.

The use of a filter in the fuel line makes a three-line fuel set-up more desirable. With a filter, you never want to take the fuel line off at the engine to fill it. Sending fuel back through the filter to the tank would be flushing any foreign matter caught in the filter back into the tank. At the same time, you would be trapping grit and dirt from your fuel can on the *engine* side of the filter. Not a good idea. If you use a filter, you must take the line off at the tank side of the filter in a two-line system in order to fill. Since this part of the line is usually very short and hard to handle, you can see the advantage of having the separate filler line.

Fuel Pumps

The former control line or free flight flier will question my recommendation that you use a fuel pump to fill your tank. In their cases a 4- to 6-ounce squeeze bulb is sufficient (Fig. 4-21). Free flight and control line planes usually only carry a maximum of 4 ounces of fuel. Therefore, the squeeze bulb works fine. However, a large R/C plane with a 16-ounce tank takes a lot of squeezes to fill it. Also, you do not run the tank dry as often in R/C as you will in control line, so the capability to defuel through the pump is a big help.

There are two types of fuel pumps: mechanical and electric. With the mechanical ones you turn a crank and the fuel is pumped into or out of your tank. Mechanical pumps are a little slower, but they are self-contained and require no power other than for you to turn the crank.

Electrical fuel pumps use either a 6- or 12-volt battery for power. They work fast and do not require any effort. Many fliers

Fig. 4-21. Squeeze bulb used for filling small fuel tanks and priming the engine.

have a 12-volt motorcycle battery in their flight box to power their fuel pump, engine starter and other accessories. Figures 4-22 and 4-23 show examples of mechanical and electric fuel pumps. As for choice, there is no real advantage to either type unless you're worried that your battery might go out and leave you without power.

STARTING AND ADJUSTING

After you know all the theory and all the extra items that go with or on your engine, it comes down to getting it started and adjusting the carburetor. It is best to get some experienced help at

Fig. 4-22. The Du Bro handcrank fuel pump.

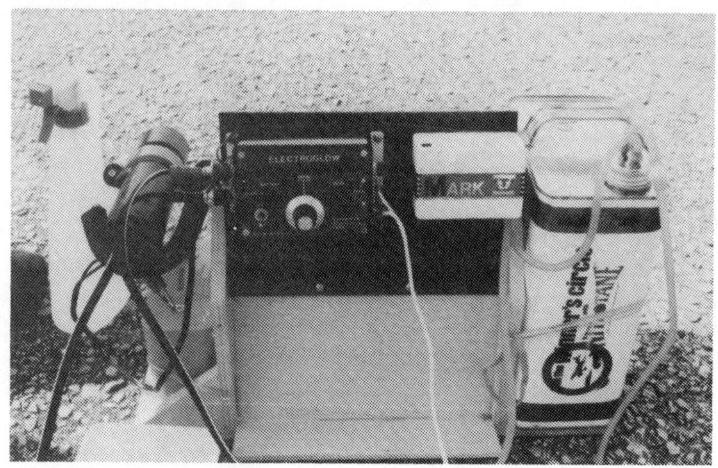

Fig. 4-23. A Mark V electric pump.

this point. A demonstration and first adjustment of your engine is worth a thousand words. Because you will be adjusting your own engine sooner or later, I'll go into the details of the process.

Starting Battery

You will need a 1½-volt electrical source for the glow plug. This can be from a battery or a power panel. The battery can be the old standby that's been around model airplanes for years, the dry cell, or one of the newer rechargeable NiCads. Both work equally well. You will also need a hook-up lead to connect the battery to your engine and glow plug. There are several available and none is really any better than the others. It's a matter of choice.

Power Panels

Another starting power source is the power panel. It takes a 12-volt source (sometimes a 6-volt source) like your car battery or a motorcycle battery and gives you a connecting point for several different items—with the correct voltage supplied for each one. Usually (see Fig. 4-24) there are connections for the fuel pump, the glow plug lead and an electric starter. The more expensive panels have ammeters so that you can check the current through the glow plug lead to tell if it is still good. Others have an LED that glows when the glow plug circuit is good.

Starters

In the previous paragraph I mentioned an engine starter. Former control liners and free flighters are probably not very

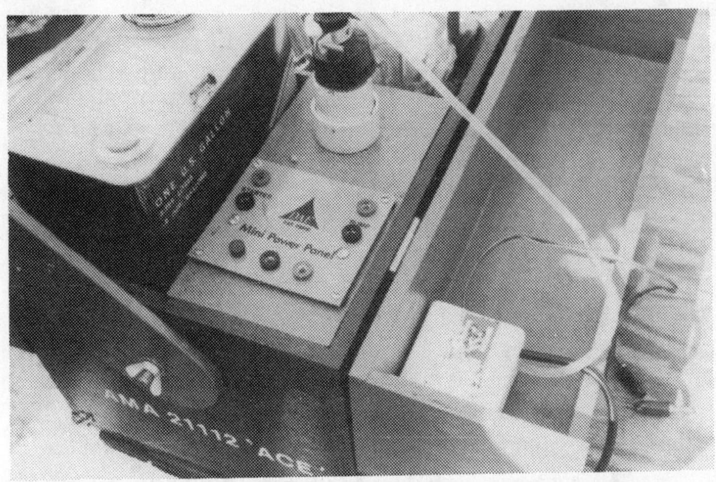

Fig. 4-24. The DAE Mini Power Panel, used in conjunction with a car or motorcycle battery, supplies power for an electric engine starter, the fuel pump and glow plug hook up. The round object on the left, below the word "Mini," is a light emitting diode. It indicates electrical continuity with the glow plug.

familiar with electric starters. These are small, hand-held 12-volt electric motors that, when pressed up against the spinner or prop hub, turn the engine over at a fast rate. This is in lieu of flipping the prop by hand. About the time the .60-sized engines became popular, so did starters. Flipping a .35 is one thing, but getting your finger bitten by a prop swung by a 1.5 horsepower .60 can really hurt. This is not to say that a starter (Fig. 4-25) is necessary. Many fliers still handstart their engines. A starter is nice in the event that you have a balky or flooded engine.

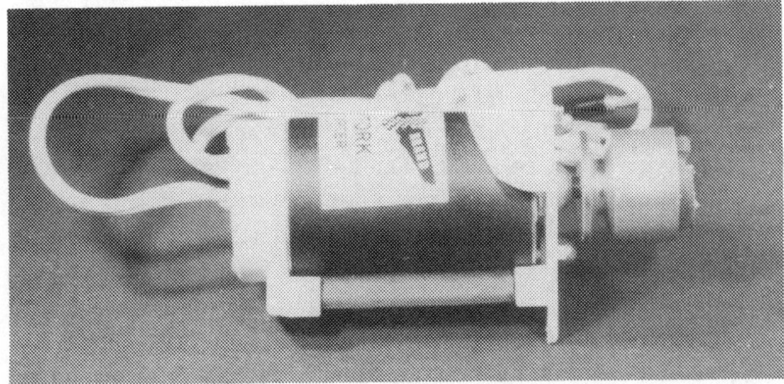

Fig. 4-25. The Sullivan Hi-Torque electric starter saves both effort and bruised fingers.

Starting the Engine

Follow the manufacturer's instructions for your engine. Be sure that the battery is hooked to the glow plug securely and with a starter or by hand-flipping, you should get it running. Your instructor will give you a hand here, but if you are doing it on your own for a ground test, I recommend that you start the engine at a fast idle. That is somewhere between idle (carburetor closed) and one-quarter throttle. Many former control line fliers will want to start at full throttle because control line engines are started that way. Look at it this way. You start your car at a fast idle and warm it up a bit before you drive off at high throttle, don't you? Try your R/C engine the same way. It'll start easier and last longer.

Adjusting the High Speed Needle

On most engines you adjust the main needle valve for high speed running first. The exception to this is that Fox engines require the idle jet to be adjusted first. After the engine is running, slowly advance the throttle to full open carburetor. If the engine coughs and quits, it's too lean. Open the needle valve a turn and restart. What you want is the engine running rich. You can tell that the engine is running rich by its lower pitched sound and by the exhaust. The exhaust will be smoky and the engine will seem like it is slobbering. Once the engine is running rich, slowly turn the needle valve in until you hear it start to change from the low pitch sound to a higher pitched one. At this point it is breaking into the lean running area. If the engine is new, you will want to stop here and run it slightly rich for a few flights to give it a break in.

To further adjust the engine for maximum power, turn the needle valve in further until you hear the power peak. This is the maximum power setting *on the ground*. Upstairs with 50 to 60 mph air blowing into the carburetor, the engine will lean out farther and possibly go over-lean and run hot. What you need to do is to open the needle valve a quarter-turn to a half-turn until the engine slows down slightly. This position should give you maximum power in the air. Bear in mind that you are guessing at the correct setting and you can't actually tell if it is right until you fly it and listen to the engine.

Now give your plane the *nose up test*. With it running at full throttle, pick the plane up and hold it so that the nose is up—in a steep climb attitude. The engine should lean out more and go to maximum power. What happens in this test is that the nose-high attitude places the tank, which was level with the engine, several

Fig. 4-26. The Nose-up test. Holding the nose of the plane up at a steep angle with the engine running at full power to check for proper high-speed adjustment of the carb.

inches lower. This makes it slightly harder for the engine to draw fuel from the tank—causing it to run leaner. If the engine coughs and slows down, it is too lean and you should open the needle valve a little until the engine can pass the test. The nose up test is shown in Fig. 4-26.

Some final recommendations on needle valve adjustment. First, it's better to have your engine running a little bit rich than for it to be on the lean side. A lean running engine is hot and has higher wear. Conversely, a rich running engine stays cool and has minimal wear. In addition, the engine will always run leaner toward the end of the tank than it does with a full or nearly full tank. If you are set for maximum rpm with a full tank, you are going to be over lean at the end of the flight. When you get a good needle valve setting, leave it alone.

If you use a filter, your needle valve setting will not change very much unless the weather changes drastically. I continually see fliers who change their needle valve settings every flight. Invariably they have poor running engines. From a hot, humid day to a cool drier one you might need a small (one-quarter turn) needle valve change. If you find that you need a big adjustment, something else is wrong. Your filter might be clogged or you might have a pinhole in the fuel line that is letting air in and causing the engine to run lean.

Fig. 4-27. The pinch test. Squeezing or pinching off the fuel line with the engine running at idle to check for proper low-speed adjustment of the carburetor.

Adjusting the Idle

Most R/C beginners get the hang of adjusting the top end quickly. Either because it's easy or because it's the same as on a control line engine, they seem to learn it much quicker than they learn how to adjust the idle. There is no magic formula for adjusting the idle mixture. You must, however, follow the procedures and learn to recognize the symptoms of a lean and rich run just like you did at the top end. It's a little more difficult because it's not as graphic a change as you'll hear when you set the top end.

First, get the engine running with the top end adjusted. (Except in the case of Fox engines, which require that you set the idle first.) It is also best to adjust the idle when the tank is between one-half and one-fourth full. This will give you a slightly rich setting for taxi out and takeoff. On the other hand, it will give you the correct setting for your traffic pattern and landing when a good engine run is more critical.

Now that the engine is running, leave the glow plug wire connected and throttle back to near idle. Maintain an rpm at which the engine will run. Next, pinch the fuel line to shut off the fuel flow and listen to the engine. If it quits almost immediately or just "winds down" to a stop, the setting is too lean. Figure 4-27 shows the *pinch test*. If your engine quit too lean, follow your engine instruction sheet to richen the mixture. Be careful! Some carbs have very sensitive idle mix adjustments. Perry carburetors in particular need only a barely perceptible movement to change the mixture.

Restart the engine and perform the pinch test again. If the mixture is too rich, the engine will speed up noticeably after a few seconds and then wind down to a stop. Release the tubing before the engine quits and adjust the mixture to a leaner setting. The correct setting you are looking for is one where the engine speeds up just slightly before it tries to quit.

Once the idle mixture is adjusted, you need to make a throttle acceleration check to get a final adjustment and setting. With the engine at idle, move the throttle quickly to full power. The engine should accelerate smoothly to full power with only a slight hesitation in the mid-range. Fuel metering carbs will have less or no hesitation compared to air bleed carbs. If the engine coughs and tries to quit, it is slightly lean. You probably misjudged the setting during the pinch test. Richen it up and try again.

If the engine has a very slow, blubbery acceleration, it is too rich. Lean the mixture slightly and try again. With an air bleed carb as found on smaller and on older engines, you might never get rid of the slow rich acceleration through the mid-range. You must make a distinction between a normally slow acceleration and a rich, very slow acceleration. Ask your instructor to give you a hand the first time and to demonstrate the correct setting.

Now that your idle mixture is set, leave it alone. It might change slightly as your engine is broken in. New engines will not idle as slowly as well broken-in ones. It might have to be adjusted slightly between winter and summer, but normally it should stay the same. You might notice that it seems a little rich when you first start up and taxi out. Remember, you adjusted it for best idle under landing conditions, so you might have to accept a slightly faster idle at first. When you first start up, your engine has not yet warmed up to operating temperature and, just like your car, it might not have its best idle until it does.

ENGINE RECOMMENDATIONS

Not knowing every beginner's needs, it is difficult to make a blanket recommendation for what size engine to buy. The best recommendation is for the beginner to buy an engine for his *second* plane, then buy a trainer to fit that engine. Let me explain. There are quality trainers available for any size engine made. If you have an engine, there will be no difficulty in finding a good plane for you to learn to fly on. The concern is that you do not make your engine obsolete after you do learn to fly. As you get out of the trainer class, there is less of a variety of planes for each size engine, except in the .60 size. There are fewer kits available in the .40 size than in the .60 size, for example.

You will also probably want to specialize more on your second plane. You'll want a scale plane or an acrobatic one or some other. Get a general idea of the type of kit you'll want as your second plane, or at least what size engine you'll need, and buy this size. Then pick out a trainer kit to go with it. When you learn to fly and move up to that plane you've always wanted, you won't have to buy a new engine. Just take the one out of the trainer you've retired.

What if you have no idea what you want next? What's a good engine size to start with? I recommend a .40. A .40 is a mid-sized engine. It is about half way between the very small engine and the .60s in size and also mid-range in price. The most outstanding trainers, or at least the ones most fliers have learned on, are in the .40 class. After you learn to fly, there are many kits of all types: scale, acrobatic, biplane, etc. that are sized for .40 engines. You can't go wrong with a .40.

I'd also like to make one more recommendation in the engine area: buy American. With the lowering value of the dollar, foreign engines are becoming more and more expensive. If you already have one, you'll notice that the spare parts are also becoming more expensive. Compare the parts lists and you'll see. You might also find that you are waiting a long time for parts after a crash. It is not unusual to wait 6 months for parts for a Japanese or European made engine. It is very unusual to wait more than two weeks for parts from an American manufacturer. Cox, Fox, K&B and Kraft are American made engines. In a rush, a long distance call to one of these companies on a Monday will usually get you the parts in time to fly the next weekend.

5 The Airplane

There are many different types of R/C planes. There is one suited to every type person and all of them are fun. If you haven't decided on what type you'll want to fly after you pass the trainer stage, you'll want to look at all of them and get some ideas. I won't say that there are advantages or disadvantages for any one type. However, some types may have a particular difficulty or consideration that you might want to know about beforehand.

TYPES OF PLANES

It's hard to put many of the R/C planes on the market into a neat category. Just about every one overlaps into two or three categories. Much depends on how the flier uses it. For example, a biplane might not fit simply in the *biplane* category. It might also fit into the *scale* and *giant* categories. It's a point to keep in mind. You can use a *competition plane* for sport or turn a racer into a docile Sunday flier if you want to.

Sport Planes

This is a big category of planes. You'll see some that are called *sport planes* on the kit, but these aren't the only ones by a long shot. Just about any type of plane that you want to fly, not for competition, but not for sport, is a sport plane. You'll see high or shoulder wing planes, the advanced trainer types. Usually these are overpowered compared to regular trainers. Two of the most popular that you'll see at just about any flying field are the Jensen Ugly Stick (a .60 engine) and the Midwest Sweet Stick (a .40). There are also low-winged sport planes. These are a bit more acrobatic than the shoulder wing planes. They look more like a real plane and they are very popular. Two outstanding planes of this type are the Alley Kat (Fig. 5-1 and the Kougar (Fig. 5-2).

Fig. 5-1. The Alley Kat.

You can find sport fliers with competition-type acrobatic planes. As a matter of fact, these planes, perhaps without the more exotic accessories (retracting landing gear, engine fuel pump, tuned exhaust pipe) makes flying, excellent sport planes. They are, of course, more acrobatic than the "sport" planes and you have the added prestige of flying one like the champions fly. Another type of plane you see many sport fliers with is the scale plane. There is a competition class called *sport scale* that caters to planes that are a little less scale and a little better in the flying category. Most of these sport scale planes never see a contest. They are flown by fliers who want to be the pilot of a Mustang or some other scale plane. Whether it's WWI, WWII, classic, 30s racers or some other type, flying scale planes is very popular.

You will find sport fliers with everything from sailplanes to helicopters. You'll also see unusual and original designs in the sport catagory (Figs. 5-3 and 5-4). There is everything from futuristic X-wing fighters to my own Maltese Falcon (Fig. 5-5) which was featured in *Model Airplane News* magazine in 1977.

Fig. 5-2. The Kougar.

Fig. 5-3. An acrobatic plane.

Fig. 5-4. An amphibian.

Fig. 5-5. The author's original sport/acrobatic plane,—the Maltese Falcon.

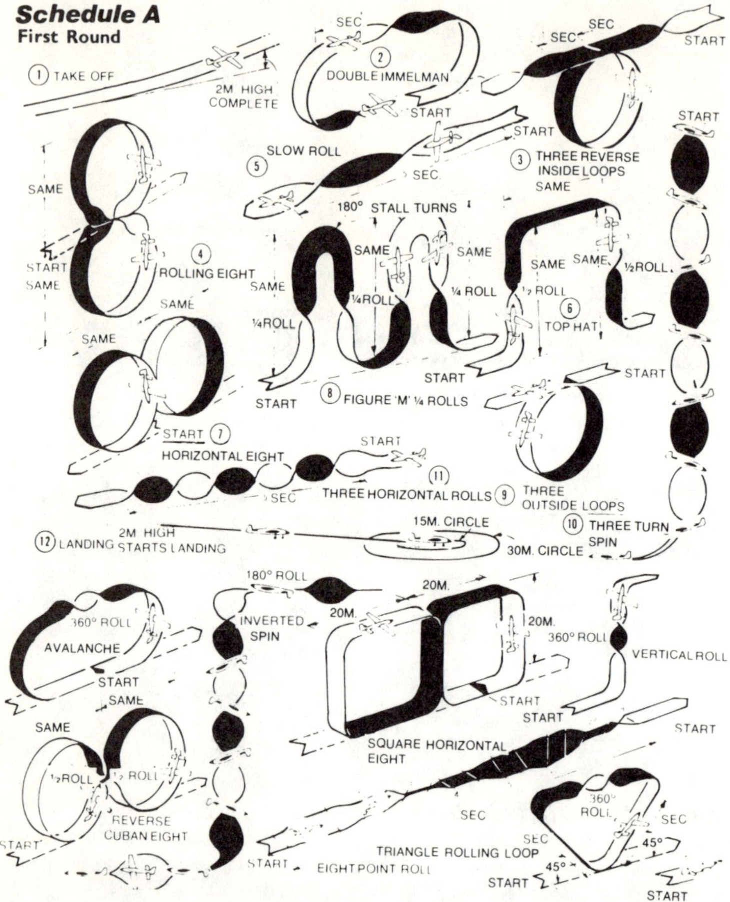

Fig. 5-6A. The master class acrobatic pattern.

Acrobatic Pattern Planes

When an acrobatic plane is mentioned to a non-flier, he usually thinks of a biplane. In R/C this in not necessarily the case. In acrobatic competition the planes fly a certain pattern of maneuvers. This gets them the nickname *pattern planes*. These planes are specifically designed for, and optimized to perform, the current international (FAI) acrobatic pattern. When the pattern changes, the plane designs will change to one that performs the newer maneuvers better. Generally speaking, pattern planes are .60-powered, sleek, high-speed planes. Most competitors use retracting landing gear, tuned exhaust pipes, engine fuel pumps and very powerful engines. The pattern requires many large and vertical maneuvers. Figure 5-6 shows the pattern.

Many of the planes designed for earlier patterns are sometimes still available at lower prices than the latest up-to-date version. In particular, the Kaos and Super Kaos by Bridi were supplanted by the Dirty Birdy and then the UFO. These earlier two are super flying planes at a much lower price than the newer two. Examples of pattern planes are shown in Figs. 5-7 and 5-8.

Biplanes

Many R/C biplanes are scale models, but because they are so popular, they deserve coverage in a class of their own. Biplanes are

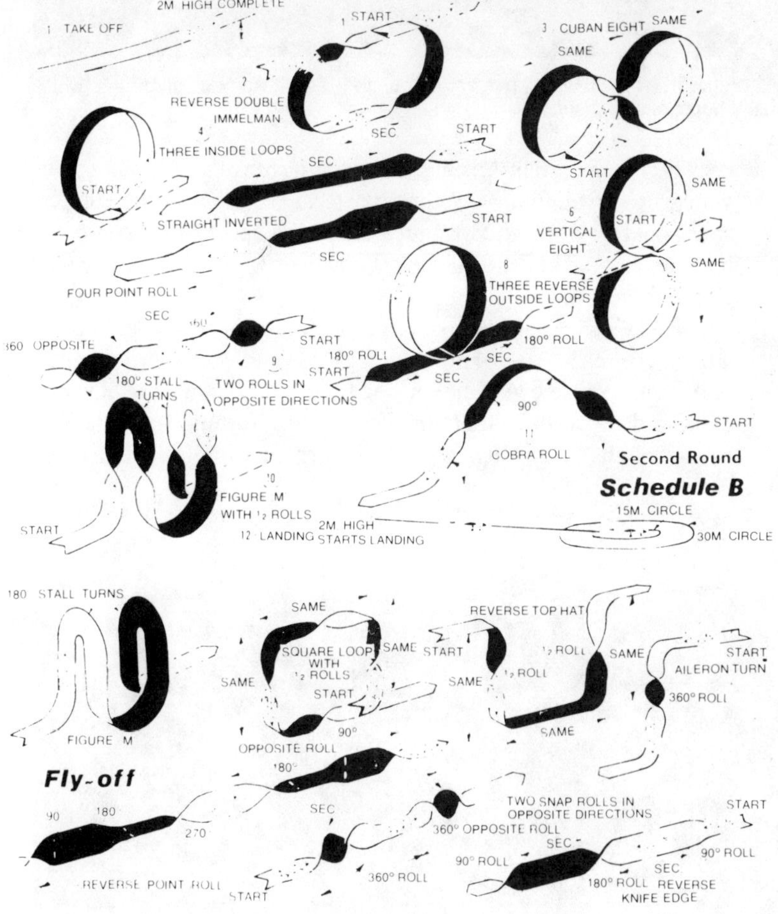

Fig. 5-6B. The master class acrobatic pattern.

Fig. 5-7. A .60-sized pattern plane, the Atlas, from a kit of the world championship plane.

crowd-pleasing, tight-turning, snap-rolling fun planes. Someone in your club can be flying a 100-mph pattern plane doing the complicated contest acrobatic maneuvers and if a sport flier taxis out a biplane, any old biplane, and takes off, every spectator will turn to watch the bipe.

Biplanes bring back memories of barnstorming and air shows. They are able to turn very tightly and perform maneuvers down where everyone can see them. For example, a bipe can usually do a nice 50-foot diameter loop. Nothing special. You recognize that it's a loop. Now if a pattern plane pulls up for a loop,

Fig. 5-8. The Desperado is a .40-sized original design pattern plane.

Fig. 5-9. The Aeromaster is one of the most popular biplanes for a .60-size engine.

it usually pulls up and up until the top of the loop is often at 400 feet! Pattern requires three consecutive loops. A pattern plane will do then very precisely, but they are so big that although they might score well with the judges, they lose their identity. The biplane, on the other hand, does its maneuvers right down where you can see them. Not as good for the judges, but a sure hit with the spectators.

If you like the biplanes, you will find a myriad of kits, that range from the .09 engine size to monsters powered by converted industrial and chain saw engines that are one-third the size of the real plane. One of the most popular biplanes, and not a scale model, is the Aeromaster by Andrews (Fig. 5-9). This one is finished in the color scheme of a WWI Fokker D-VII. Another popular biplane is

Fig. 5-10. The author's .60-sized scale model of the homebuilt Skybolt biplane from a Sig kit.

Fig. 5-11. The Smith Miniplane, a .40-sized biplane, from a Sig kit.

the scale model of the Steen Skybolt by Sig. An example of this kit is my plane shown in Fig. 5-10. Both of these planes require a .60-sized engine. In the .40 engine size, a good flying kit is the Sig scale kit of the Smith Miniplane (Fig. 5-11).

Earlier I mentioned that some types of planes might have a particular difficulty. Well, biplanes have one: they are invariably conventional gear planes. They do not have tricycle landing gear. You'll hear them called *tail draggers* because they have a tail-wheel. Airplanes with conventional gear do not have the inherent ground handling stability that a trycycle gear plane has. This does not mean, however, that they are difficult to takeoff and land—only different. Any well-designed popular kit will be easy to fly. The three shown in this section will pose no problem to a flier past the trainer stage.

Scale Planes

While not usually the best flying planes around, these are some of the most popular. Notice that three of the categories in this chapter deal principally with scale planes; this catagory, biplanes and the giant planes. You might also include the ducted fan planes, helicopters, and racers, because these are also mostly scale planes. I'll cover these separately. This scale section will be limited to prop-driven, normal size, monoplanes. In this area are the planes of the 30s, WWII planes, post-war prop planes and civil prop planes—quite a large selection. The "war birds" planes of the WWII era are especially popular. You'll find many kits of these in the .60 size. Recently, several .049 powered scale plane kits have been introduced. These are becoming very popular because they can be flown from a small flying area.

Fig. 5-12. A .60-sized scale model of a P-51 Mustang from a Top Flite kit.

The flier without too much experience should look for a kit that specifies *stand off* or *sport* scale. These kits have been modified to make them much better R/C planes. If you are concerned about how these planes look, don't be. The modifications made are so subtle that only an expert can tell that the tail of your Mustang is slightly enlarged so that it will be easier to control at the slower speed of an R/C plane.

Take a look at the planes in Figs. 5-12, 5-13 and 5-14. Are they true scale or stand off scale? These are actually stand off scale planes that are excellent fliers. As you can see, much of the scale look comes from the detail the builder puts into it. This takes extra time and effort, but except for a slight weight penalty, it doesn't

Fig. 5-13. The hero of the Battle of Britain, the Spitfire, from a Dave Platt kit.

Fig. 5-14. A Blacksheep Squadron F4U Corsair waits to have its wings unfolded before flight.

detract from the plane's flying ability and it adds a lot to the appearance.

Just like biplanes, most scale planes are tail draggers. Again, don't let this deter you from trying one. Any well-known kit will have manageable ground handling. Relocating the landing gear slightly for good R/C performance is one of those "usual" modifications the manufacturer makes from true scale.

Helicopters

Helicopters are in a class by themselves. As I mentioned, many of them are scale. All of them require special training to fly. Just like the big ones, you use some of the controls differently and even some different controls when you are flying. The newer models have copied technological advances made on the full-scale ones. Some of them are fully acrobatic like the one shown in Fig. 5-15. You'll see them do loops, rolls and other acrobatics that were previously unheard of in a helicopter.

One thing that keeps the R/C helicopter from perhaps gaining the popularity it deserves is cost. Like the full-scale ones, helicopters are expensive. Expect to pay well over $200 for one. This does not include the cost of the radio or engine, so your total investment in a helicopter outfit can easily top $500.

Race Planes

There are several classes of R/C racing for engines from .049 to .40 cubic inch displacement. All of the classes are fast and competitive, but none tops Formula I. These are scale models of the full-size racers called *midget* or sometimes *Goodyear racers* that were popular just after WWII and have enjoyed a revival in the past few years. These .40 powered R/C Formula I planes are the fastest R/C planes in the sky except for a special record speed plane or two. They sometimes reach speeds of 175 mph as they race, four at a time, around a three-pylon race course. Figure 5-16 shows a Formula I racer owned by Bob Violett. He is the national champ and owner of Bob Violett Models.

As you might have guessed, Formula I is for very experienced pilots only. The next lower engine size in racing, for planes in the .15 size engine range, is also for racing. These racers are called Quarter Midgets. They are fast, but they are not as fast as the Formula I birds.

Half-A racers for the .049 engines are quite popular. This is a good and inexpensive place to start in racing. Another race for the less experienced pilot is the Quickie 500 race or club race. Quickie 500 racers are light and easy-to-build planes of 500-square inches wing area. Generally speaking, the power is a .40 engine with the type or even the manufacturer restricted by the club or locality. This is to keep costs down and insure competitive races. Other club races might specify the exact plane and engine. These are usually easy-to-handle planes that most novices can fly.

Giant Scale Planes

The most recent boom in popularity has been in the area of giant R/C scale planes. These planes, with wing spans of 7 to 9 feet are powered by modified industrial or chain saw engines or by .60-size engines with a gear or belt reduction drive unit. In the last

Fig. 5-15. A .40-sized American Revolution helicopter.

Fig. 5-16. The Polecat is a .40 size pylong racer by Bob Violett.

few years, their popularity, and the number of kits and accessories available, has increased by leaps and bounds. They far outstrip the former new plane on the block—the helicopter.

You might hear these planes referred to as *quarter scale planes* because many of them are one-fourth the size of the real thing. Others are one-third scale or just large models. These planes generally fly very slowly and stable and they are nearly trainer-like. The only thing detracting from their value as a trainer is expense. All that wood and covering just adds up to more cost than an identical, but smaller plane.

The popular scale models you'll see in giant scale are mostly those of light planes and biplanes. The full-sized planes they were taken from tend to fly slowly and the models do a great job of realistic, scale-like flight. In many cases, they are hard to tell from the real thing at any distance. If you plan to give a giant scale plane a try, get with an experienced flier who flies them. There are several areas he will want to explain to you before you buy one. In particular, the choice of heavy duty hardware and radio are important. Some of the new radios come with small servos that do not have the strength to safely handle the big planes.

Ducted Fan Planes

Another specialized area of scale planes is the *ducted fan plane*. This concept uses a conventional glow-plug engine turning a small, multi-bladed prop in a close fitting duct to simulate jet thrust. With the invention of the ducted fan, the modeler could add the military and civilian jets to the planes he had to choose from to model. Generally speaking, only single engine planes are seen due to the complications of using two engines. The fan has to turn at a

Fig. 5-17. A scale ducted fan A-4 Skyhawk from Bob Violett Models.

very high speed. Usually a racing .40 or .45 is used, along with high nitro racing fuel. The planes normally have long takeoff rolls, but when they are airborne they gain speed rapidly. Due to their scale jet look, which is different from any other model, ducted fan planes are usually show stoppers when they appear. They do, however, need careful tuning of the engine and careful flying. At slow speeds, their controls are not as precise due to the lack of prop blast flowing over the tail surface. Figure 5-17 shows a scale ducted fan model. It is the Bob Violett Models A-4 Skyhawk II.

Sailplanes

These are the silent R/C planes: the gliders. Their long, skinny wings are ultra-efficient for catching a rising thermal of air and staying aloft for extended periods of time without power. Sailplanes are towed up to about 400 feet by a winch (Fig. 5-18) or by a long length of surgical tubing. They are released and then go hunting thermals. They use as little as two channels for control of

Fig. 5-18. Electric winch with a spool of nylon line used to tow R/C sailplanes to a height of 300 to 500 feet.

Fig. 5-19. Two R/C sailplanes. These have wing spans in the 100-inch plus range. Some are as large as 12 feet.

pitch and roll or might have more channels in use for other features like spoilers and a special tow hook release.

Sailplanes might seem like an easy-flying, low-pressure catagory, but don't be fooled by your first impression. Like most aspects of model flying, it's as easy or as challenging as you choose to make it. Sailplane competition is some of the most hotly contested there is. Planes like the ones shown in Fig. 5-19 compete in national and international competition. If you decide to try a sailplane, it will be hard not to compete. You'll probably get caught up in the spirit and the events appear easy at first glance. Sailplanes are smooth, easy-to-fly planes. After you've mastered them, the sky's the limit.

Old Timers

Old Timers are replicas of free flight planes that were designed before 1942. A wave of nostalgia hit the R/C modeling world a few years ago and the result was the Old Timer. Full size replicas, beefed up in a few places, with R/C steering began showing up at fields. Planes like the Buzzard Bombshell (Fig. 5-20), designed by the Buzzard's club of Chicago and said to have hit the 1940 Nationals "like a bombshell" setting a new record on its first flight, are now seen at nearly every flying field.

Old Timer afficianadoes are organized into the Society of Antique Modelers. There are competitions similar to sailplane events. These planes often make excellent trainers because they are self-stabilizing and will get the novice pilot out of most trouble. He can release the controls and let the model fly itself. In fact, they are so easy to fly that they do not train you to fly anything else. This can cause a problem if you should want to transition to another type of model. However, if you remember one of these old plane designs

Fig. 5-20. A replica of the 1940 Nationals winning free flight plane converted to R/C.

or heard about one from your father or grandfather and want to give one a try, the plans or a kit is probably available.

Combat Planes

Another relatively new category of R/C planes is the R/C combat plane. Most of these are takeoff-on-control-line planes and the event is flown much the same way. Each plane tries to cut a crepe paper streamer attached to the other plane. These planes are light, easy to build, and very maneuverable. Figure 5-21 shows two combat planes. The power is usually a .19 or .25 sized engine. While a mid air collision is a possibility, it rarely happens. When it does, little damage is done because of the light weight of the

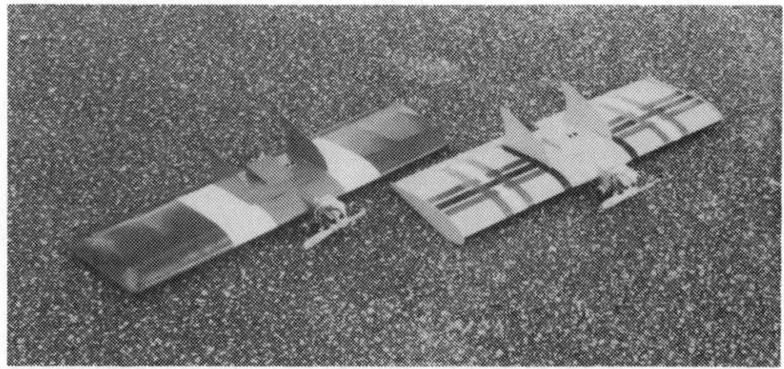

Fig. 5-21. Two King Kombat flying wing combat planes. Long crepe paper streamers are attached to these planes and they take to the air trying to get a cut on each other.

Fig. 5-22. The Colt, an excellent three-channel trainer featuring a cast foam wing. The kit is by Sig.

planes. The event is fun, inexpensive and can add some spice to your R/C life when you become tired of "just plain" acrobatics.

Trainer Planes

There are quality trainers of every size and price range. Any of them will do a more than adequate job of taking you through the fledging stage of your R/C flying. The whole group of trainers can be split into two classes, aileron trainers and trainers without ailerons, or three-channel planes. There are pros and cons of each type and when it gets down to the bottom line, personal preference really makes the difference. Aileron trainers on the whole require closer monitoring by an instructor at first, while the three-channel trainers are more self-stabilizing.

On the other hand, three channel planes are very limited in what they can do. Once you learn how to actually land, you will probably want a more maneuverable plane to start learning some acrobatics with. In this case, the aileron trainer can also be your advanced trainer. The choice might also be based on abilities. If

Fig. 5-23. The Falcon 56. It is claimed that more people have learned to fly R/C on this plane than any other.

Table 5-1. Aileron Trainers.

PLANE	MANUFACTURER	ENGINE SIZE
Falcon 56	Goldberg	.30-.40
Kadet	Sig	.30-.40
Fledgling	Sterling	.30-.40
Sweet Stick	Midwest	.40
Trainer .40	Bridi	.40
Kavalier	Sig	.40
Ugly Stick	Jensen	.60
Sr. Falcon	Goldberg	.60
Gazariator	Sterling	.60
Trainer .60	Bridi	.60
Trainer .20	Bridi	.19-.25
Little Stick	Midwest	.19-.25
Freshman	TopFlight	.30-.40
A-Ray	Andrews	.30-.40
E-Z Flier	Southern R/C Products	.30-.40

your reflexes are slower or you are the type of person who could be called "all thumbs", then you might want to start with a three-channel plane. Many of the kits available can be built as a three-channel or an aileron trainer. One of the best of this type is the Sig Colt (Fig. 5-22).

Those of you with full-scale flying experience will probably want to start with an aileron trainer. The controls will be familiar to you. After all, a plane is a plane. There are several trainers in this category. One, shown in Fig. 5-23, is the Falcon 56 (by Goldberg). The Falcon can probably be said to have trained more R/C pilots than any other trainer. It was developed years ago as a three-channel trainer (it can still be built that way) and evolved into the aileron trainer it is today. You will recall that in an earlier section I recommended a .40-sized engine if you had no other specific choice. Let me now list some trainers and their engine size specifications (Table 5-1). You'll see plenty of .40-sized ones and other sizes. These are shown in Table 5-2.

Table 5-2. Three-Channel Trainers.

PLANE	MANUFACTURER	ENGINE SIZE
Kadet	Sig	.25-.35
Colt	Sig	.19-.25
Klipper	Sig	.19-.25
Q-Tee	Airtronics	.049
Alpha	Ace	.15-.25
H-Ray	Andrews	.25-.35
M.E.N. Trainer	M.E.N.	.15-.25

Fig. 5-24. A disassembled R/C plane showing the fuselage and removable wing.

THE PARTS OF A PLANE

I'll cover each part of a plane and a helicopter by name and explain its function. As you go through this section you will probably recognize many of the names. Generally speaking, they are the same as for full-size planes. Some, like the name *firewall*, are the same for planes and cars.

Fuselage

Essentially, the *fuselage* is the body of the plane. Everything else attaches to it. This is especially true for R/C planes, because the wings are usually removable to make the plane easier to transport. See Fig. 5-24. The nose of the fuselage is where, in most cases, the engine mounts. The motor mount usually bolts to a piece of heavy plywood called the firewall. On the back side of the firewall is where the nose gear mount will attach. You can see that the firewall is the attachment point for a lot of equipment. It must be very strong and securely glued to the fuselage sides.

The compartment behind the firewall is the tank compartment (Fig. 5-25). Sometimes the battery is placed in this compartment if nose weight is needed to get the plane's balance point correct. The tank compartment must be fuel proofed, of course, either by painting it or coating it with resin or epoxy.

The area behind the tank compartment and over (or under) the wing is where the radio is installed. It is called the *radio compartment*. The edge of the fuselage where the wing sits is called the *wing saddle*. Behind the radio compartment is the *aft fuselage*.

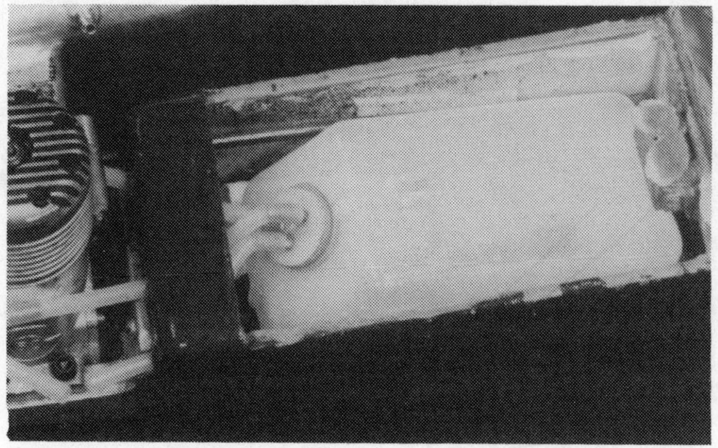

Fig. 5-25. The tank compartment behind the engine in the fuselage.

Figure 5-26 shows the radio compartment, wing saddle and pushrods extending into the aft fuselage.

The Tail

There are several parts of the tail, or *empennage*, as it is called. The *vertical tail* controls the yaw of the plane. As you will learn later on, this does not turn the plane. The fixed part of the vertical tail is the *vertical fin* (or just *fin*). The moveable part is the *rudder*. See Fig. 5-27. Some planes, mostly competition acrobatic planes, have an additional fixed vertical tail on the underside of the fuselage. This is the *sub fin* and is shown in Fig. 5-28.

Fig. 5-26. The radio compartment in the fuselage. Servos with pushrods are hooked up and the receiver and battery are wrapped in foam.

Fig. 5-27. The fixed vertical fin and moveable rudder.

The *horizontal tail* controls the pitch (the up and down movement) of the plane. The fixed part is the *horizontal stabilizer* (or just *stab*). The moveable part is the *elevator*. The horizontal tail is shown in Fig. 5-29. A very few planes have a horizontal tail similar to modern jets. The whole unit moves. You'll hear these called a *flying tail* or *stabilizer* (a coined word that is a combination of stabilizer and elevator). If the horizontal tail happens to be in the front (Fig. 5-30), this is called a *canard configuration* and the horizontal tail is the *cancard.*

The Wing

The wing is the most important part of the airplane. Wings come in various shapes and sizes. They can be *straight* (Fig. 5-31),

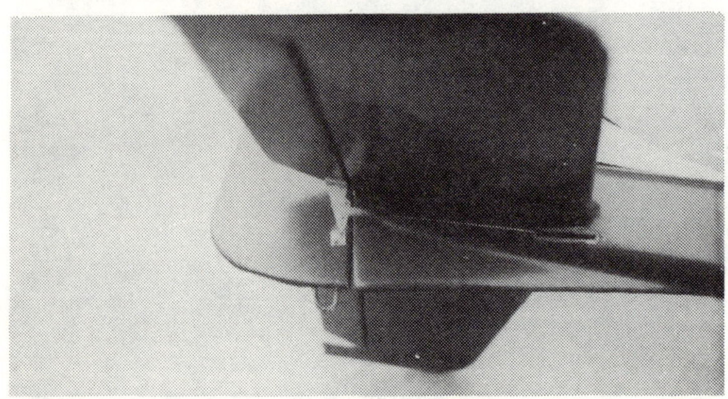

Fig. 5-28. The fixed subfin underneath the fuselage.

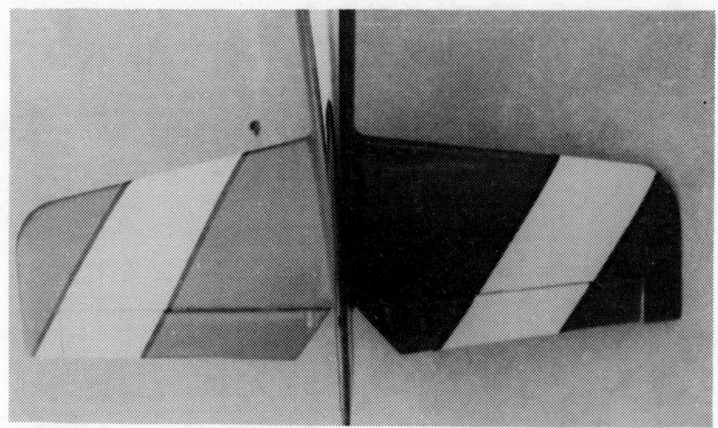

Fig. 5-29. The horizontal tail. The fixed portion is the stabilizer. The moveable parts are the elevators.

swept (Figs. 5-32 and 5-33) or *tapered* (Fig. 5-34). In addition to the various shapes, there is considerable nomenclature that goes with the parts of a wing. Refer to Figure 5-35 as you read through the new terms.

The length of the wing is its *span* and the width is the *chord*. The chord of the wing where the fuselage is is the *root chord*. The end of the wing furthest from the fuselage is the *wing tip*. Its chord is the *tip chord*. The thickness of the wing has no special

Fig. 5-30. A canard is a horizontal tail located in the front of a plane. This plane, the Zonker, has the wing and engine in the rear.

Fig. 5-31. An example of a straight wing. This one is on a Falcon 56.

name, just thickness, but a cross section of the wing is its *airfoil*. The front of the wing is the *leading edge* and the rear edge of the wing is the *trailing edge*.

The measure of the slimness of the wing is the *aspect ratio*. It is the number found by dividing the wing area by the square of the chord. As an example, sailplanes, with long, slim wings have a high aspect ratio. Acrobatic planes with shorter wings have a low aspect ratio. You might also hear the term *wing loading*. This is the weight of the plane divided by the wing area. A sailplane that is very light has a low wing loading, in the area of 6 to 8 ounces per

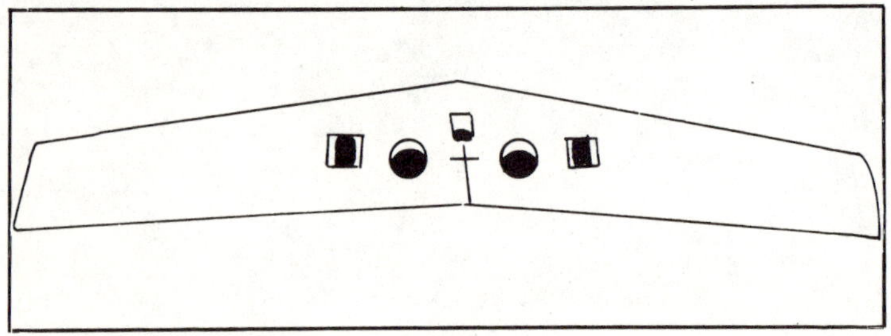

Fig. 5-32. The uncovered foam cores for a swept wing model.

Fig. 5-33. The Upper wing of this biplene is a swept wing.

square foot, while a pattern type plane has a higher wing loading, in the area of 25 ounces per square foot.

The moving controls on the wing are the ailerons and sometimes spoilers and flaps. *Ailerons* move in opposite directions, one up, one down, to make the plane bank or roll. Aileronscan be long and slim like those shown on the wing in Fig. 5-31. These are called *strip ailerons*. Those that are more rectangular and similar to

Fig. 5-34. This acrobatic pattern plane features a tapered wing.

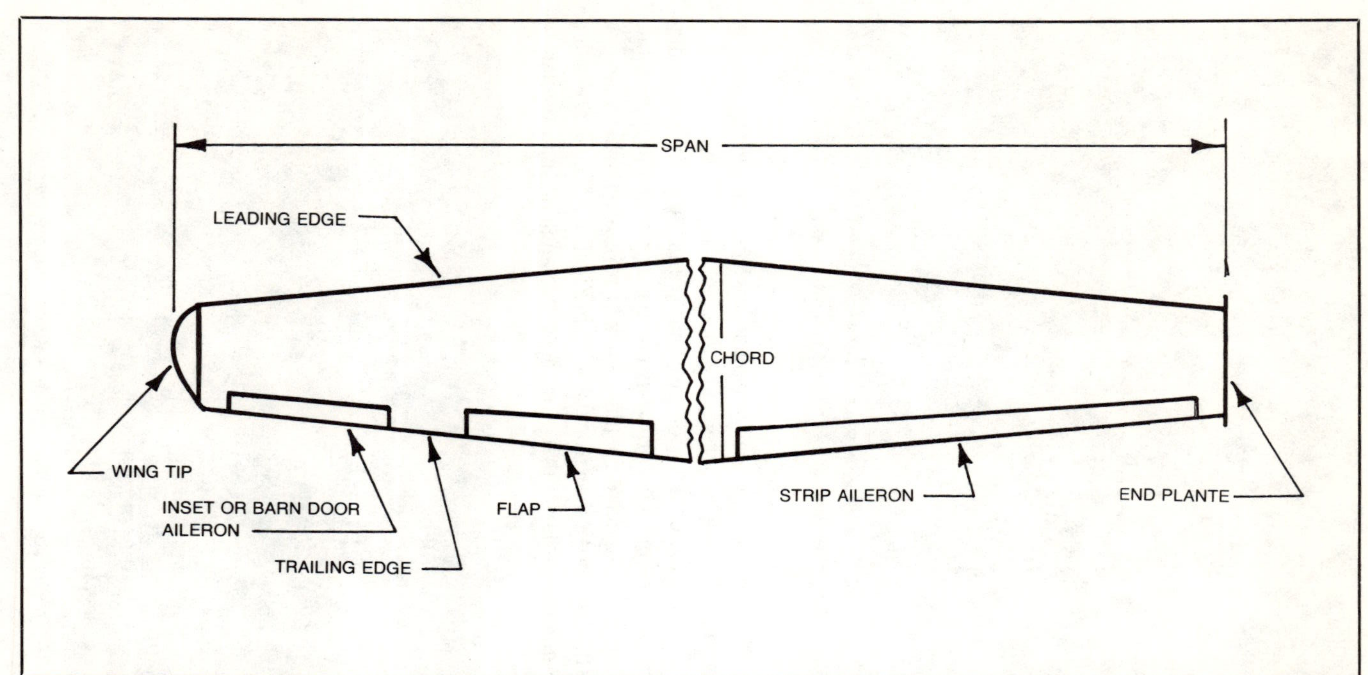

Fig. 5-35. The parts of the wing.

Fig. 5-36. Inset or barndoor ailerons.

ailerons on full-scale planes are called *inset* or sometimes *barndoor ailerons* (Fig. 5-36).

On sailplanes, you sometimes see a control called a *spoiler*. These are on top of the wing (see Fig. 5-37) and usually located at the high point. When raised, the spoilers "spoil" some of the tremendous lift the efficient sailplane wing has. Spoilers are often used as an aid to spot landing in a contest.

Many scale planes and some other types have *flaps*. Flaps go down only and are used to increase the lift of the wing for takeoff and landing. Figure 5-38 shows a plane with the flaps down.

Most low-wing planes have the main landing gear located on the underside of the wing. These are generally a torque rod assembly supported inside the wing (in the case of fixed-gear planes).

Fig. 5-37. The spoilers on the top of this sailplane's wing are used to kill lift and cause the plane to descend.

Fig. 5-38. This scale B-25 has its flaps (on the inboard sections of the wing) down.

There are several arrangements possible for retractable landing gear systems (Fig. 5-39).

THE PARTS OF THE HELICOPTER

The helicopter has many parts that are different from those of an airplane. There are many mechanical parts on a helicopter that have no counterparts on an R/C plane. The centrifugal clutch is one. Let's take a look at the two parts that are most obvious at first glance: the rotors.

Rotor Blades

The large horizontal propeller or rotary wing is called the helicopter's *rotor blades* or *main rotor* (Fig. 5-40). This is what

Fig. 5-39. An underside view of a scale P-51 showing the landing gear retracted.

Fig. 5-40. The large propeller on the top of the helicopter is the main rotor.

generates lift like the wings do on a conventional plane. The main rotor also gives the helicopter its forward thrust and turn capacity.

Tail Rotor

The small propeller at the rear of the helicopter is the *tail rotor* (Fig. 5-41). The tail rotor functions about the same as the vertical fin and rudder on a conventional plane. It provides yaw stability.

TYPES OF CONSTRUCTION

In addition to the different types of planes, there are many different ways to build a plane and a huge variety of different materials to choose from. There are so many, in fact, that the beginner is often confused and ends up making a poor or wasteful choice of materials, adhesives or finishes.

Fig. 5-41. A close up of the tail rotor (the small propeller on the rear end of the helicopter).

Fig. 5-42. An example of a balsa wood built-up fuselage and wing. This one is of a scale Corsair.

Fuselage Construction

Former control line and free flight modelers will invariably think of fuselage construction in terms of balsa wood. This is still one of the favorite construction materials. Balsa is light, very strong for its weight and, even with recent price increases, still relatively inexpensive. Balsa is also easy to carve, shape, and sand. Those are additional reasons why it's still a big favorite. Figure 5-42 shows a good looking Corsair fuselage and wing built of balsa.

A second type of fuselage material is fiberglass that is made either with polyesther or epoxy resin. Figure 5-43 shows a fiberglass fuse. Most of the kits of .60-size acrobatic planes have fiberglass fuselages. A kit with a fiberglass fuselage is easy to build. The fuselage itself is practically finished and requires only installation of motor mounts (and sometimes these are already installed), wing hold-downs, servo rails, sanding and painting.

With fiberglass, a complicated design is easy to build because all the compound curves which normally would require so much carving and sanding are molded in by the manufacturer. Fiberglass fuselages have another advantage. They are totally impervious to fuel. Fuel and oil soaking in over a period of time causes the demise of many planes of wood. Not so with fiberglass. If fuel spills inside the plane, you just wipe it up and forget it. Naturally there is a price

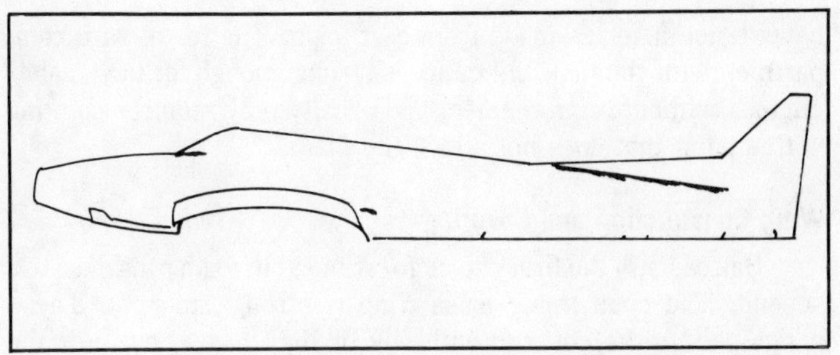

Fig. 5-43. An example of a molded fiberglass fuselage. This one is of a Phoenix V and needs very little work to complete it.

to pay for all this convenience and that price is in weight and cost. A fiberglass fuselage is naturally a bit heavier than one built from balsa. However, the little additional weight gain isn't too detrimental in the big pattern planes. A well-made uniform, strong, fiberglass fuselage is hand-made. Expect to pay for it than you would for a balsa and glue fuselage that you put one together yourself.

Another fuselage material is ABS plastic. This is a common material for ready-to-fly or almost-ready-to-fly (ARF) type kits. The fuselage is formed with a vacuum machine and then assembled. It has many of the advantages of fiberglass for fuselages, but it is not as resistant to vibration. It might develop cracks. This is especially true in the larger models. For small models, such as the Pilot Skywagon shown in Fig. 5-44, it is ideal. A lot of detail and complicated curves can easily be put in a small, light model made from vacuum formed plastic.

Another fuselage construction material is foam. That's correct: foam like styrofoam. Very small planes (.049) to (.15) can

Fig. 5-44. The Pilot Skywagon features a formed plastic fuselage and a plastic covered foam wing.

have a nice fuselage made from cast foam. The foam, with compartments for the tank and radio, is strong enough for the smaller engines without reinforcement and usually only requires painting with a paint that does not attack the foam.

Wing Construction and Covering

Balsa is still the first choice for wings, but foam runs it a close second. The open frame balsa wing is strong and light. These wings used to be covered with silk or light paper, but now the covering is usually a heat-shrinkable colored mylar. It is sold under several brand names, but the most popular are Monokote and Solarfilm. Monokote by Top Flite is the strongest, but also the heaviest. It is preferred by fliers of large planes. Solarfilm (by Pactra), as well as most of the other films, is not as strong or puncture resistant as Monokote, but it is very light. Fliers of sailplanes and the very small planes like the light weight of these. Solarfilm also requires less heat to make it adhere. It can be used directly on foam without danger of melting it.

Another wing covering for a balsa framework wing is a heat shrinkable polyesther cloth called Coverite. It also comes in various colors and some of it comes with a thick coat of paint already on the cloth. Although the advertisements for these products claim advantages for one or the other of these good products, I've found it's usually a matter of personal choice. Some folks like the way Monokote goes on, others prefer the handling of another. Each of them does a good job.

Foam runs a close second to balsa in popularity for wing construction. The foam construction I am refering to is a foam wing core covered with balsa or some other sheeting for strength. The foam core is cut from a sheet of 1-pound per cubic foot styrofoam with templates and a foam cutter made from nichrome wire. This very light core, as shown in Fig. 5-32, is sheeted with a skin of balsa, very thin (six-sixty-fourth inch) plywood or posterboard. The wing tips are added, the wing is joined in the center and then painted. You can see that this makes for a quick wing. This method is just about always used with fiberglass fuselages. In fact, it is so common that you will often hear kits called fiberglass and foam kits. At first, taking a foam core and a stack of balsa and turning it into a finished wing seems like a formidable task. You'll find, however, that once you've done one you'll be telling yourself "this is the easiest wing I've ever done." Don't hesitate to try a foam wing.

A third type of wing, and one that is found only on small planes, is the all foam wing. This is a cast foam wing made the same way as the cast foam fuselage mentioned earlier. The wing is used either as is or it can be painted or covered with the low-heat film. Both Sig and Midwest make excellent .15-sized planes with cast foam wings. The Colt mentioned in the section on trainers is one of them. See Fig. 5-22 for another look at the Colt. Another company that makes a wing of this type is Ace. Their wing comes straight or tapered and is sold separately as well as being standard on many of their kits.

ADHESIVES

In the past, modelers knew only one adhesive: model airplane cement. Cement is still available, but it is rarely used in R/C construction. Modern adhesive technology has produced quicker setting, stronger and more fuel resistant adhesives. You'll find that most modelers use a variety of adhesives and they pick the best one for each specific job.

Epoxy

Epoxy glue combines strength and fuel resistance to be the R/C flier's number one choice for an adhesive on high stress areas like firewalls and wing hold-downs. It is a two-part adhesive with a resin and a hardener that must be mixed just prior to use. This can be an inconvenience because you always have to find something to mix it on. You cannot save the mixture so you must estimate fairly accurately or some is wasted. Epoxy glue is also heavy compared to other adhesives and should be used sparingly on smaller planes where weight is a factor. These disadvantages, when compared to the strength and quick set-up time, are inconsequential.

Generally speaking, two types of epoxy are sold: a 30-minute working time variety and a 5-minute working time type. The 5-minute epoxy is extremely popular for at-the-field repairs or for the got-to-get-it-finished-before-the-weekend flurry of building. My wife likes it so much that she builds whole planes with it. Once you've used it, the 5-minute working time and the quick 20-minute cure time become very attractive. Several manufacturers offer both 30-minute and 5-minute epoxies.

Aliphatic Resins

The cream or light tan colored aliphatic resins are another type of glue that is very popular. There are many good brands, but

Titebond and Wilhold are the ones you'll usually find in hobby shops. These water-based glues are strong, light and easy to use. Their plastic containers with the applicator tips make for a no-mess, no-waste application. For building balsa wings and fuselages, this is a good glue to choose. Like the old model airplane cement, however, it shrinks as it dries. Care must be taken to insure that parts are held straight while the glue sets. This is particularly true for wings and tails where a warp can result from the shrinking action.

Super Glues

The super glues, or alpha-cyanoacrylates, are also extremely popular with modelers. Several are sold by model accessory manufacturers with catchy names like *Hot Stuff*, *Zap*, and *Jet*. You'll even hear remarks at the flying field, after a plane has picked up some minor damage, like "Just Hot Stuff it," or "Give it a Zap." The super glues set nearly instantly—5 seconds for most of them—on porous materials like balsa and hardwood. This makes them ideal for repairs and also for quick building if the parts to be joined fit very tightly. A tight fit is absolutely necessary. These adhesives work by causing a molecular combination between the two pieces. As such, they will not bridge a gap like a real "glue." Small gaps can be filled very readily with, of all things, baking soda. When touched by a super glue, it turns to a rock-hard substance.

Contact Cement

Contact cement is used sparingly in the construction of R/C planes and usually only to attach the skin to the core of a foam wing. Where it is used on styrofoam, a special type of contact cement is necessary. The average contact cement you would buy in a hardware store has a solvent base that literally melts foam. Use of it in an attempt to cover a foam wing will give predictably disastrous results. What you need is a water-based contact cement. These are available in some hardware stores, or more safely, at your local hobby dealer's.

The cements made specifically for model use are packaged in small amounts and sold under such names as *Blue Goo*, *Sorghum*, and *Core Bond*. Contact cements are easy to use. Just brush a light coat on the foam core and the balsa or plywood wing skin, let it dry for about 45 minutes and then press the skin onto the core. Be careful that it is aligned straight because you don't get a second chance with contact cement. As I mentioned in the wing construction section, it looks different at first. But when you've done one you'll be amazed at how easy it is.

PAINTS AND FINISHES

Like many of the other construction materials, there are several finishes available. I'll first cover how to finish, then lightly touch on the types of base coats and paints on the market.

Preparing The Wood

By preparing the wood, I mean sanding it very smooth. You might think that a lot of wood filler and paint will take care of the rough spots. It won't. The better you have the wood sanded, the easier your finishing job will be and the better it will look.

If you have done a lot of carving, start sanding with coarse sandpaper. This will help to get rid of the biggest rough spots. Then change to a black "wet or dry" type paper of about 150 grit. When smooth, go to a paper in the 220-240 range and then to 320. Many people take it down to 400 for this initial sanding. The idea is to get the wood very smooth because, in most cases, any bad spot or blemish will show through.

Blow the dust off the plane. A vacuum cleaner hooked up backwards works very well for this. Look the plane over for any nicks and gouges that the sanding didn't take care of. You can fill these with spackling paste. That's the same stuff you use to fill nail holes in your wall. DAP and several other manufacturers make it and it's sold in any hardware or dime store. Fill the dings with the spackling paste and, when dry, sand it off with 220 paper. This is the beauty of spackling paste—it is lightweight, it doesn't crack with time and it sands very easily. It is great for filling in any cracks you might have between two pieces of wood you joined. Now that the primary sanding is done and the major dings are filled, we can look at hardening the wood.

Hardening The Wood

Although not absolutely essential, especially on a trainer, hardening the wood can be the next step to a good finish. The process actually does two things: It hardens the soft balsa so that the paint does not soak in or crack after it's dry and it also begins to fill the wood grain.

There are several ways to harden the wood. One favorite way is the use of a polyesther finishing resin. Finishing resin is a special, easy-to-sand formula of the resin that is used to make most fiberglass fuselages. The best way to apply the resin is to mix up a batch with its catalyst and paint it on. Then take a paper towel or two and wipe most of the resin off. This cuts your sanding time and also forces some of the resin into the wood. When dry you sand lightly with medium grade sandpaper, apply a second coat, sand again and then go on to the next step.

Polyesther resin sands relatively easily and has been the base to many a glass-like finish. There is one disadvantage, however, in addition to the fact that the application can be a rather messy affair. Resin does not cure well over epoxy glues. If you use epoxy to glue the tail on, you cannot put resin over that glue joint. It's something to keep in mind when you're selecting the materials.

An alternative to the polyesther resin is epoxy glue itself. The slow-cure type is the kind you'll use for this application. Mix up a large batch in a mixing cup, then sit it in a pan of hot water. The heat will cause the epoxy to become very liquid (almost like water). You can now brush the epoxy on with a stiff brush and wait for it to cure. After curing, the high rough spots are sanded or scrapped off. The scrape method is quick and easy. Use a single-edge razor blade held perpendicular to the wood. Just run it along the surface and scrape the high spots off. Apply a second coat if you think it is necessary, scrape and sand again, and then proceed to the next step.

A third way of hardening the wood, and my personal preference, is with lightweight fiberglass cloth. Both K&B and Sig market a very light fiberglass cloth that weighs in the area of three-fourths ounce per square foot. It is a very light material, but it is also very strong. The fiberglass cloth is adhered to the wood with epoxy paint. However, thinned epoxy glue will work just as well. You merely lay the cloth across the balsa area you want to cover, the tail for example, and then paint clear or colored epoxy paint through it onto the wood. The fiberglass cloth sticks firmly, needs little filling and adds tremendous strength to the wood.

Some of you might remember a fourth way to prepare the wood for filling: silkspan or silk and dope. If you can find nitrate dope, this is still a good method to use. It's very light and also very strong if you use silk instead of the silkspan paper. It is alright to use the butyrate or fuel proof dopes if you are going to use a dope finish (rare for R/C planes). If you use butyrate dope and then put epoxy paint over it before the dope has had time for all the solvents to evaporate out of it, (about two weeks), you can get blistering. In the long run, it is usually better to use a complete base/primer/

paint system from the same manufacturer or at least of the same type, like epoxy, to insure that the solvents in each are compatible. This way you can put the final coat of paint on your beauty without worrying about it blistering.

Filling And Priming

There are several products on the market for filling the wood grain on a balsa plane and providing a base coat for the paint to adhere to. These products are called *fillers* or *primers*. They are marketed through hobby dealers and are packaged especially for model use.

For a dope finish, balsa fillercoat or clear with talcum powder is used. You don't see dope much any more, but some of you might still want to use it. The key to filling with dope and talcum, or for that matter with any filler, is a lot of sanding. Paint on or spray on your first coat or coats of filler, let it dry, then sand it down nearly to the hardened wood surface. Do this a second time and then check for grain. Usually twice gets everything filled if you sanded enough. Also check for any nicks or gouges that need filling with spackling paste. Remember that because spackling paste is so porous, anyplace you fill with spackling paste must be reprimed for a good, uniform paint finish. When the grain is filled and sanded, you are ready for paint.

One excellent primer is K&B Super Poxy Primer. It is a two-part epoxy primer that fills well and, when dry, sands like dope and talcum. It is white and shows up any blemishes so that you can spot them and fix them. Another filler I use a lot is Hobbypoxy *stuff* by the Pettit Paint Company. It is a brown, one-part primer. It also fills well and sands easily. Pettit also makes a Filler that is thicker than Stuff and can be used to fill nicks and gouges. If you intend to use acrylic enamel or lacquer automobile paint, then you might want to use auto primer on your plane. It works very well, but it tends to be very heavy unless you really pay attention to your sanding.

Paints

If your base and primer are done correctly, the paint should go on smoothly for a perfect finish. There are any number of different types and brands of paint. All of them will work well.

Epoxy Paints. These are two-part paints. Measure amounts of the color and the hardener must be mixed before use. These paints cover very well and only require two coats at most for a contest finish. They are also very hard, scratch resistant and completely impervious to fuel and oil. The hardener for epoxy paints is available in a slow cure type for brushing and a quick cure for spray applicaton. Naturally it is necessary to use a matched system. That is, a hardener from one brand will not give good results when added to a color of a different brand. Keep your paint and hardener matched. Also, although they are epoxies, and as such will harden after mixing if left to stand, you can prolong the useable life of mixed epoxy paints by placing it in the refrigerator. It will usually remain liquid for a couple of days. K&B, Prettit and Pactra all market epoxy paints in many colors (including some metallics.)

Polyurethane Paint. This is a one part paint that is a bit softer than epoxy. It does have the advantage of needing no measuring or mixing of parts. Simply open the can, stir and paint. Polyurethane paints are not as fuel resistant as epoxy, but for normal usage with the lower nitromethane content fuels, they work just fine. Pactra's Formula U and R&S Perfect Paint are examples of polyurethane paints. The colors available are in about the same range as the epoxies. In addition, there are flat camouflage colors.

Acrylic Paint. Acrylics, or automobile paints, are not available from hobby shops. But the wide range of colors, especially in the metallics, that are used on cars makes them so attractive that some modelers buy the paint from auto parts or paint stores. Either acrylic enamel or acrylic lacquer can be used. Lacquer should be sprayed in several coats, then buffed or hand rubbed just as on a car. Acrylic enamel must be used a catalyst added to really be fuel proof. It covers more like other two hobby paints—epoxy and polyurethane. Unlike lacquer, enamel should not be buffed.

Model Airplane Dope. The old standby for control line and free flight is not seen very often in R/C. Dope, marketed by Sig, Pactra, and Testors requires many coats and therefore large quantities. It is just easier to put on two coats of epoxy than it is to apply six to 10 coats of dope and also more fuel proof. Dope is light, however, so it can be a good finish for a small plane where you're trying to keep weight down. There is also a very good selection of colors to choose from with dope.

Applying the Paint

Any of the paints mentioned can be applied either by brush or spray. In either case, you should thin the paint before you apply it.

For brushing, thin slightly. For spraying, you will have to practice with your airbrush or spray gun until you get the kind of paint flow you need. But generally, thinning about 30 to 50 percent will be in the ball park. Naturally, this figure will vary according to the temperature and humidity (among other factors).

Before you actually paint, go over the plane with alcohol to remove all traces of oil from where you touched it. You should also wipe the plane down with a tack rag, available at any hardware store, to remove dust. Now you are ready to put on the paint and get a great finish on your trainer.

THE FINAL SET UP

Many kits come with complete, easy-to-follow building instructions written on a level that beginners can follow. Too many do not. Often a kit will come with a plan and only the barest skeleton of directions and the manufacturer assumes that the buyer has had enough previous building experience to make do. This can make it very puzzling to a rank newcomer who never built control line or free flight kits and has difficulty following the procedures. There are always people in your local club who will be glad to lend you a hand and I urge that you seek them out.

A little experience is truely worth 1000 pages of instructions. Either way, by muddling through on their own or with the help of an experienced builder, beginners generally get their plane and wing built. The problems come when they try to deal with the final set-up of the plane, wing attachment methods, getting the landing gear right for the best performance, setting the proper control throws and balancing the plane. These are four areas that are all-too-often ignored or dismissed lightly in kit plans and instructions. Let's look at each one.

Wing Attachment Methods

There are two methods of wing attachment: rubber bands and bolts. Rubber bands are usually used on trainers, small planes and some biplanes. Bolts are used on just about everything else. There is a lot more to holding a wing on with rubber bands than meets the eye at first. You need to get the wing on straight and centered, put the rubber bands on correctly and in the right number, and you need to care for the rubber bands after you take them off.

When I say the wing must be straight, I mean when that you look down on the top of the plane, the wing should be square with the fuselage. And it is centered with the center of the wing directly over the center point of the fuselage? To insure that you get the wing on correctly, you need marks on both the wing and the fuselage. Put them at the exact center of the wing on the leading and trailing edges. A narrow piece of colored trim tape works nicely. Just measure the wing to find the exact center and stick the tape in place. Do the same with the fuselage right next to where the leading and trailing edges of the wing will be. Put a narrow strip of tape or a thin paint stripe in these two places. Figure 5-45 shows how one flier has marked his wing for centering. When you put the wing on, all you have to do is align the marks, check to see if the wing is square to the fuselage, hold it in place and put on the rubber bands.

It is important to put the rubber bands on *correctly* and in the proper number. For medium and large planes, use no. 64 size rubber bands. For smaller planes, check your local hobby shop for the size that will fit. As for actually putting them on, there is a correct way and a way that might or might not work. It will probably be fine for your flying, but there's a chance of trouble. The *safe* way is to hook the rubber bands on the front dowel, then stretch them over the wing and hook them over the back dowel.

Notice that I specified the front dowel first. There is a reason for this. Suppose you did the natural thing and started the rubber band on the rear dowel. You would then stretch it forward, hook it over the front dowel and release it. When you release the rubber band, it is not stretched as tightly in the front as it is near the rear dowel. If there were no friction, the tension would even out. But with the rubber band rubbing against the wing and the other rubber bands, it stays under the uneven tension—with the rear part of the rubber band tighter.

Most of the time this doesn't make any difference, but in a hard pull-out, the slack in the front might allow the leading edge of the wing to lift. This causes all sorts of funny movements from your plane. It can lead to breaking the rubber bands and disastrous results. For safety's sake, start at the front with your rubber bands and go to the rear so that the tightest part will be at the leading edge. Figure 5-45 shows rubber bands being put on in this way.

When it comes to specifying how many rubber bands to use, the rule is: don't skimp on rubber bands; they are all that hold your plane together. When you make a hard pull-out from a dive you want the wing to stay on firmly. You can be assured that if the wing comes off there won't be enough left to repair. Generally, for a .30-size or larger trainer, you'll need at least 5 rubber bands on

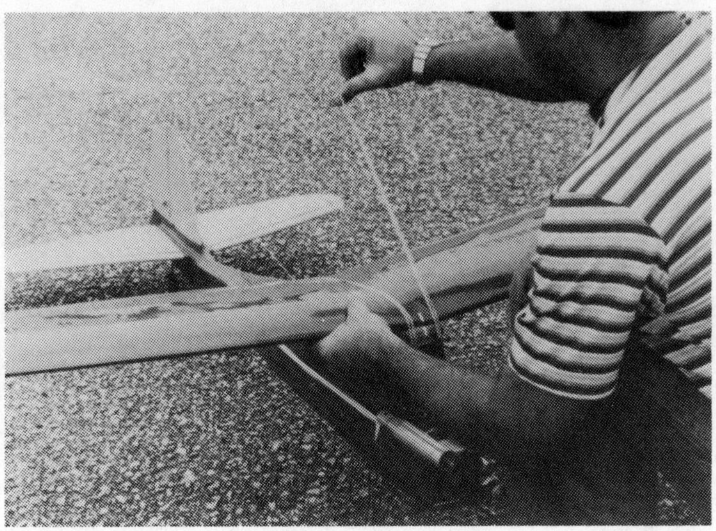

Fig. 5-45. How to properly place a rubber band on the front first and then stretching it back to the rear. The two white marks are tape alignment marks on the fuselage and wing.

each side (for a total of 10). This assumes that the rubber bands are in good condition.

Several things will destroy rubber. Among these are oil and sunlight. Both are abundant at the flying field. It's hard to keep your plane out of the sun all the time, but it's a good idea to try. Sitting it in the shade or covering it with a white cloth or rag while you aren't flying will not only serve to protect your rubber bands, it will also keep the temperature inside the fuselage down and protect your radio components. When you remove the rubber bands you need to get all the oil off them that you can.

Some fliers spray them with the same detergent they use to clean the oil off their planes. Whether you do this or not, a good way to help absorb any extra oil is to store them in something that soaks it up. The best thing I've found is kitty litter. I use an old jar with a cap and a couple of inches of the stuff. When I remove the rubber bands I just toss them in the jar, cap it and shake it up. The next time I fly, the oil has been soaked up and all that is necessary is to take them out, stretch and snap them a few times to get the dust off and they're ready to use. Every time you stretch them, look for cuts, cracks or signs of old age. If you find any, throw the rubber band away and get a new one. They only cost about a penny apiece and they keep you flying so keep only the good ones.

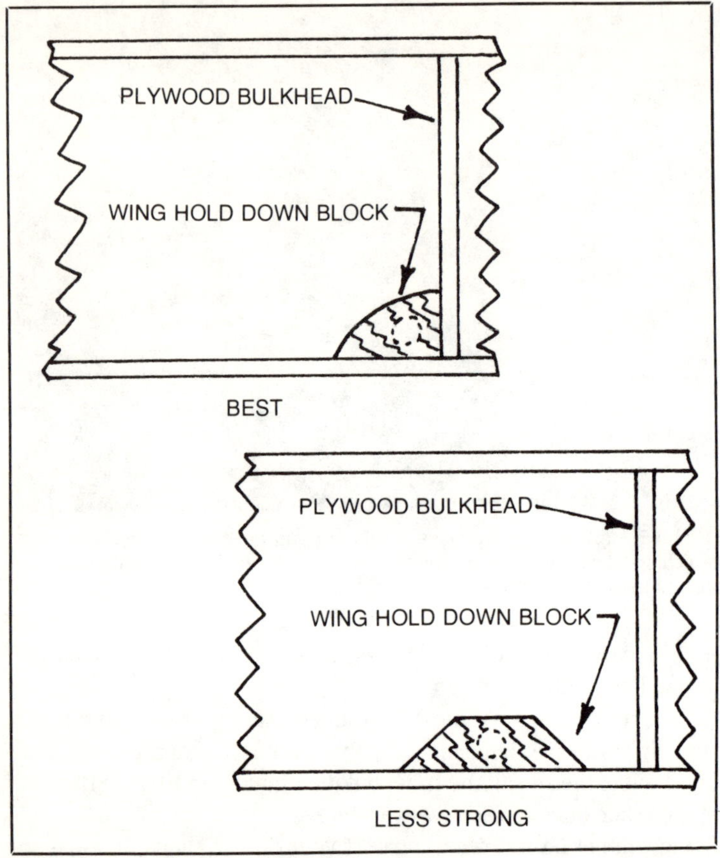

Fig. 5-46. The top view of a wing block installation.

If you bolt your wing on, there is a whole different set of things to watch for. The alignment problem goes away, because if you aligned the wing correctly when you drilled the bolt holes, the wing will be straight every time. The problem can come in the strength of the blocks that the bolts go into. These blocks are made of hardwood or one-fourth inch plywood. They are glued into the fuselage, then drilled and tapped for the one-fourth × 28 nylon wing bolts. When they fail, it is nearly always the block-fuselage joint that gives way.

Here is how to correctly install wing bolt blocks. First, glue them in the corner between the fuselage side and the bulkhead that is even with the trailing edge of the wing. Having the block glued on two sides makes it much more resistant to being twisted out. See

Figs. 5-46 and 5-47 for a look at a wing block installed in this manner. Next, glue the block in the fuselage so that it is flush with the wing saddle. When it is flush with the wing saddle and touching the wing when it is bolted down, it will not be under a twisting force as it would be if it were not flush. If it is not flush, you can actually tear the block out just by tightening down too much on the bolt. Even if it holds in this case, it pre-stresses the fuselage block joint. This makes it easier to break it loose later. If the block is installed correctly, then all you can do by tightening the bolt too much is crush the wing.

Glue triangle balsa stock on the underside of the wing mount block to give it some extra reinforcement. Always use epoxy glues

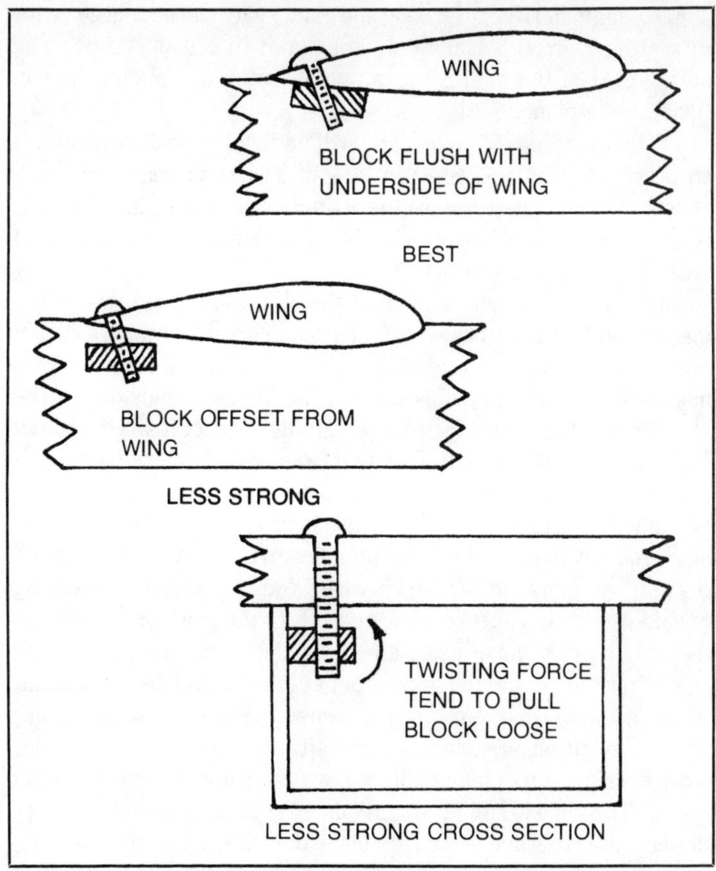

Fig. 5-47. The side view of a wing block installation.

in this high-stress area. An additional reinforcing trick I use is to drill through the fuselage side into the wing hold-down block with one-sixteenth or three-sixty-fourth inch drill. Then I coat a toothpick with glue and shove it in the hole. When the glue is dry, I cut the toothpick off and sand it flush. I now have a dowel-pegged wing block. Like rubber bands, wing bolts are all that holds your plane together. Make sure the entire assembly is strong.

Landing Gear

The landing gear is a part of the plane that is usually taken for granted by the novice flier. That is, if it is strong enough and is set so that the plane rolls reasonably straight on the ground. There is, however, a good bit more to it than that. Your landing gear can have a big effect on your takeoff and landing performance. The relationship in length between the nose and main gears can be a large factor in getting a smooth landing as compared to a bouncy one. The springiness of the main gear can also change the landing characteristic of a plane.

The main gear of your plane will be fixed in position, and, for all practical purposes, fixed in length. The nose gear can be adjusted. Its length determines the attitude your plane sits in when it is on the ground. This attitude is what causes the difference in takeoff and landing characteristics.

The next time you are out at the R/C flying field, watch the takeoffs and landings of several planes—especially trainers. You'll probably see at least one that screams down the runway, gets nearly to the end and jumps into the air. After it lands, check the attitude that the plane sits in on the ground. I'll bet it sits nose low. Now look around for a trainer that bounces on every landing. It could be that the pilot is not a very good one yet, but check the attitude of the plane on the ground. It probably sits nose high. It also probably has a landing gear attached to the fuselage bottom and made from unbraced 5/32-inch wire. You're probably wondering how I know this. Take a closer look at how the gear, or specifically the length of the nose gear, affects landing and taking off.

First, you'll find that just about every plane is designed to sit level on the ground. That makes sense, but it is actually a compromise position. Visualize a plane sitting in a nose low attitude. Now visualize this plane rolling down the runway at near takeoff speed. The wing is angled slightly down so that the air hits the top, deflects upwards and forces the plane down firmly on the runway.

Now take your plane and push the tail down and turn loose. The plane rotates on the main gear while on the ground. You can see that the center of gravity or weight concentration of the plane is forward of the main gear. The center of pressure of the wing is forward of the main gear, too, and it acts just like the weight when the plane is rolling along the ground at high speed. The pressure on the wing pushes the nose down.

For you to make a takeoff in this situation, you need to put in enough up control to lift the weight of the plane and also to overcome the downward force on the top of the wing. Once you get this amount of control in, the plane will rotate on its main gear and is ready to lift off. However, because the nose low attitude of the plane caused you to require a lot of up control, as soon as the plane gets to the level attitude and the downward force on the wing disappears, you instantly have too much up control in and the plane zooms upward—appearing to jump into the air.

Before you thing that a short nose gear is all bad, take a look at its effect on landing. Suppose you come in level or slightly nose high (which is correct) and then mix up your timing and make a firm landing that would give you a small bounce. The main gear touches first. Because the weight of the plane is forward of the main gear, the nose drops down. Because the plane sits slightly nose low, when the nose gear touches the wing will be at that same negative angle. Air will hit the top of the wing, just like it did on takeoff, and hold the plane on the ground—negating the bounce. Not bad for a beginner. This is why you might see trainers set up with a slightly short nose gear. The pilots like the landing characteristics, the way the plane stays down once it is down, and they are willing to accept the poorer take-offs. You might want to try this if you are having trouble with bouncy landings.

What about the reverse; a slightly long nose gear? If you guessed that because a short nose gear gives you a poor takeoff and a good landing, a long nose gear gives you the opposite—you're right. With a long nose gear, the plane will sit nose high on the ground. On takeoff roll, the wing is automatically at an angle near to the correct one for takeoff and the plane flies itself off pretty as you please.

But watch out for landings. If you get the nose up so that the main gear touches first, you might get a good landing. I say might because the wing will still be at a positive angle and might tend to lift the plane off if your landing was not just right. More than likely, you'll touch the nose fear first since it's on the long side and thus guarantees a bounce. The long nose gear set up is not a very good one for beginners. I do, however, see a lot of beginners' planes set up this way.

A beginner can easily get his plane into a nose-up condition on the ground simply by being a beginner and landing a little harder than perfect. You'll probably notice that many trainers have landing gear made from 5/32-inch wire attached to the bottom of the fuselage. This type of gear is too springy to start with and after several firm, beginner-type landings, it gets flattened out. This makes the main gear shorter than it was to start with, shorter now than the nose gear, and your plane—which originally sat level on the ground—now sits nose high. This happens little by little and the bouncy landings sort of sneak up on you. Sometimes it will happen after you have already soloed. You'll start thinking you've lost the touch for making a good landing, when all it is is a squashed main landing gear. I have all my students add a spreader bar made out of one-sixteenth inch wire wrapped and soldered between the two legs of the main landing gear. This will keep the landing gear from spreading and make the landings much nicer.

I'd like to make one more recommendation with regard to the plane and landing gear. Have as much prop clearance as possible. I recommend 2 inches. Set your plane and landing gear up so that when the plane is on the ground there is as much prop clearance as you can get between the prop tip and the ground when the prop is vertical. This much, and it might seem like a lot, will give a beginner enough clearance so that he is not always nicking the prop.

Use larger wheels or lengthen the gear. Do whatever you can to get the clearance you need. You'd be surprised at how much that seemingly firm nose gear bends on a hard landing. With props over a dollar apiece, breaking them gets expensive. You'll probably still break your fair share of props, even with the full 2 inches of clearance, but you'll sure break a lot more with one-half inch.

Control Throws

This is a frequently overlooked item on nearly every kit plan. Your instructor should check the amount of control movement you have, but it is best to have it in the ball park to start with. You might also find yourself in a club with no formal instructor program and end up asking just any competent flier to test your plane. He might not make a control check as he should. Therefore, you should have your plane set up as best you can before you bring it to the field.

If you are a former control line flier, you are probably accustomed to control movements of up to 45 degrees. This is much too much throw for an R/C plane. The control movements of an R/C

Table 5-3. Recommended Control Movements.

	AILERON	RUDDER	ELEVATOR
Aileron Trainer	3/16"-¼"	1"	¼"-⅜"
3-Channel Trainer		½"	¼"-⅜"

Measurements are from center to full deflection.

plane are very small and it's easiest to measure the amount of movement in fractions of an inch at the edge of the control surface. Table 5-3 shows the approximate control movements needed for trainer planes. Your plans or instructions might also give you specific amounts of movements. If they don't, these will work until after a test flight. The test flight will let your instructor determine the plane's sensitivity and he will recommend adjustments to the control movements accordingly.

Balancing Your Plane

The balance point, or center of gravity (CG) of your plane can have a great effect on its performance. The difference between the location of the CG of a trainer compared to a fully acrobatic plane can be considerable. You should have your balance point in the correct, recommended position for a trainer. This should be in the range of 20 percent ot 25 percent of the distance back from the leading edge of the wing. Check your plans to be certain.

A different CG from the one the plans specify can make a marked change in the performance of your airplane. The most dangerous location is having the CG too far back. An aft CG will make your plane much too sensitive. It will react to the slightest control input. That is not the thing you need when you are learning to fly. In pronounced cases where the CG is too far back, the plane will try to snap roll at an up-elevator input.

On the other hand, when the CG is too far forward, the plane will be very sluggish. You might think that this is a great way to set it up, but there are drawbacks. As the plane's speed decreases, like when you are going to land, the nose tends to drop. As the speed gets even slower, you might run out of up-elevator. Even with full up control, the nose will still drop. The result is, at best, a hard landing and probably a broken prop. The best place for the CG is where the plan says.

Now that you know the problems of having a mislocated CG, the question becomes, "how do I get it in the correct spot?" You can do two things to get the proper CG: move the radio components or add weight. If you plan ahead while you are building, you can locate the heavy parts of the radio, the servos and the battery, so that the CG will be in the right spot.

Here's how to do that planning. After the plane is finished, but before the servos are installed, lay them in place along with the battery and receiver and check the balance. If it's not on the money, shift them around to try to move the CG to the correct location. On most planes, there is a tendency to come out tail heavy (CG too far back). If this is true, try placing the battery further forward—perhaps up under the fuel tank. Now you have the room to move the servos forward in the radio compartment if necessary.

If shifting the radio components won't correct the CG for you, you'll have to add weight. Don't be upset; this is common—especially on scale planes. Add stick-on weight to the motor mount or lead next to the firewall in the tank compartment if you need weight up forward. Lead fishing weights work very well.

Once I get the balance correct, I epoxy the weight in place so that it can't be dislodged and shift around during maneuvers. If you do epoxy weights up front like I described, be careful not to get epoxy in the nose gear steering mechanism. For adding weight to the tail, the long, thin stick-on weights available at hobby shops are great. You cut the weight to the length (and weight) you need, pull off the backing and press it in place—usually on the fuselage under the stab.

Remember, it is very important to have the CG in the correct location. Relocate the radio or add weight, but get the CG correct.

Radio Controlled Flight

A radio controlled airplane *is* an airplane. All airplanes, from the smallest model to a 747, fly basically the same. Each one follows the exact same laws of aerodynamics. People tend to forget that R/C planes are really airplanes. They tend to classify them as "models" and think that they fly differently. Certainly there are differences. These come from the fact that models are on one end of the scale of aerodynamics and the 747 (indeed most full-size planes) is on the other end. R/C planes just happen to operate in the low speeds. Even the ones that appear to be fast are actually slow compared to most full-size planes. Also, an R/C plane's wing is so small that it tends to be very inefficient.

As an example, a full-scale light plane like a Cessna or a Beechcraft has a wing loading (weight divided by wing area) in the range of 10 to 16 pounds per square foot of wing area. A heavy model is in the neighborhood of only 2 pounds per square foot. This inefficiency of R/C plane wings is common to all designs and is one reason why an exact scale R/C plane is often difficult to fly. To give you a better idea of the ins and outs of R/C flight, I'll first discuss aerodynamics and then I'll go through the differences that are peculiar to R/C. Included will be wind effects, hand-eye coordination versus the feel of being in the plane, perception and orientation.

AERODYNAMICS

I won't go into a very detailed discussion of aerodynamics, only enough so that flight won't be a total mystery. I'll cover the practical aspects that will help you understand your plane and the reasons for some of the things we do in R/C.

Lift

The *lift* of a plane comes from the wing. Nearly everyone has seen a drawing of an airfoil (Fig. 6-1). The air traveling over the top

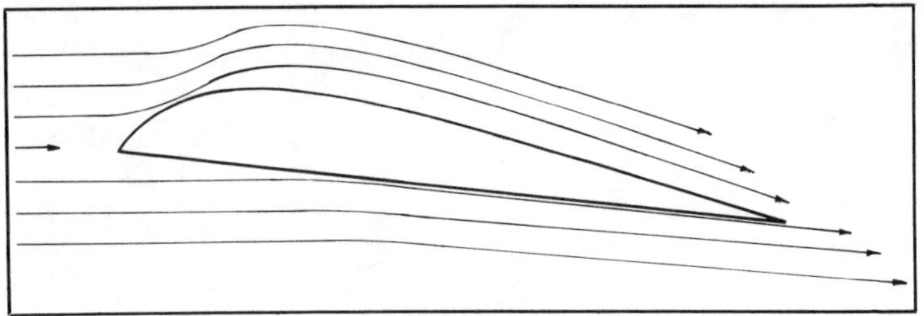

Fig. 6-1. Air flowing over an airfoil to produce lift.

goes at a faster rate. This reduces the pressure and produces lift. Some air hits the bottom of the wing, too, and produces reaction lift like a kite.

You can see that if the wing is tilted at a greater angle to the airflow (Fig. 6-2) it might produce more lift. Actually it does, up to a certain point. The angle that the wing makes with the airflow is called *angle of attack*. You might hear someone say at one time or another that a plane is flying at a high angle of attack. This will be with the nose high and the wing at a large angle to the airflow. This is usualy at low speed and the pilot has the nose up to produce more lift at this speed. At cruise speed, the plane is about level and the wing is at a low angle of attack.

Stall

When the wing gets to a critical angle of attack it is said to stall. This is when the wing cannot produce enough lift to hold the plane up. The wing is stalled and the plane drops. Do not confuse stalling in a plane with stalling a car. When you stall a car, the engine quits. Stalling a plane has nothing at all to do with the engine.

If you want to make a comparison, it's when the wing quits flying. You'll notice a stall by the after effect it has on the plane. The nose doops. What has happened is that the wing has stalled, but the tail, which also produces lift, hasn't. Therefore, the wing drops and the tail still holds its end of the plane up (and the nose points down). This works great since the altitude with the nose down causes the airspeed to build back up to above stalling speed again rapidly and your wing will begin to fly again. This works out well, of course, *if* you have enough altitude for recovery after the nose drops. You certainly don't want a stall near the ground.

Airspeed

I mentioned stalling speed. This is the airspeed at which the wing stalls. Note that I said *air*speed. R/C pilots cannot actually tell what the airspeed is like full-size plane pilots can. What we see is the *ground speed*. The speed of the plane in relation to the ground. This does not take into account wind. Consider what happens with a 10 mph wind. Suppose our plane is goint 30 mph. If we head directly into the wind, the speed we see (ground speed) is 20 mph. Don't be fooled. The airspeed is still 30 mph. An airspeed indicator in the R/C plane would read 30 mph. Now take the plane and turn it around so that it is going with the wind. The ground speed you see will be 40 mph—really moving along. However, the airspeed is only 30 mph.

Keeping this difference between airspeed and ground speed in mind, suppose that the stalling speed of your plane is 20 mph. Now, still going downwind, we slow down to a ground speed of 30 mph. This *looks* fast enough to fly, but we have forgotten the wind pushing on the plane. The airspeed is now the ground speed (30 mph) minus the wind speed (10 mph) or 20 mph—right on stall speed!

You must keep this in mind when you are learning to land. If you practice low approaches and landings during a time when the wind stays about the same, you will learn the speed the plane needs to be at for a good final approach and landing. Then, if you come out to fly a week or so later and the wind has changed, you'll be in for a surprise. The speed you learned to be comfortable with will be different. With the change in wind, the plane will have a very different airspeed and will therefore fly differently. If the wind has changed appreciably, have your instructor give you a hand until you have adapted to the new situation.

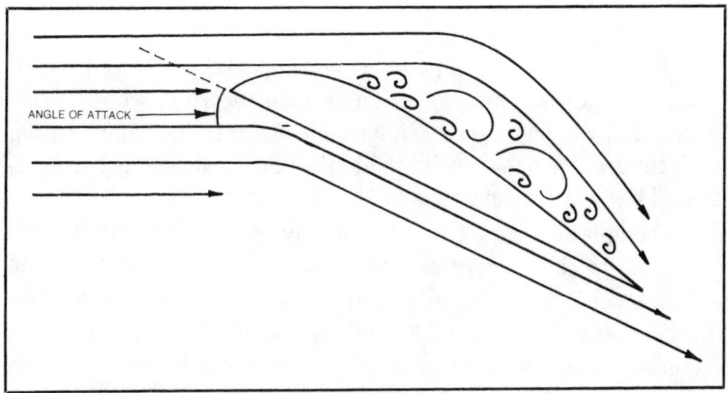

Fig. 6-2. Air flowing over an airfoil at a greater angle of attack.

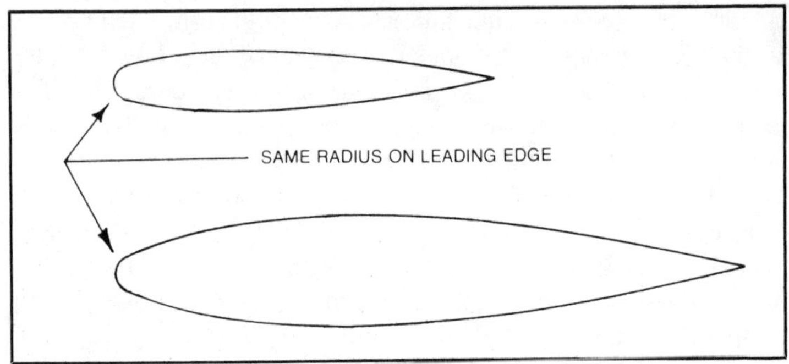

Fig. 6-3. Two airfoils with the same radius leading edge. To the larger airfoil the leading edge is relatively sharp, but to the smaller airfoil it is quite blunt.

Tip Stall

One of the design differences in R/C models as compared to full-scale planes has to do with tip stall. When a plane has the wing tip area stall before the root area close to the fuselage, it will tend to roll over rather than having the nose drop straight ahead. If the plane is high enough, it will enter a spin. Down near the runway, a tip stall can be down right disastrous. A straight ahead stall might cause a hard landing, a broken prop or maybe a bent nose gear, but a tip stall will usually result in a cartwheel and a broken wing, nose or tail (perhaps all three). The problem with an R/C model is that you have no way of knowing about the stall—unlike the burble or shudder you feel in a full-size plane. For this reason, R/C models are normally designed to be very, very resistant to tip stall. This is done by using washout in the wing, thicker wing tips, a constant radius leading edge on tapered wings or by using, as nearly all trainers do, a constant chord wing.

Washout is a built-in twist in the wing. The wing tips are built such that they are at a lower angle than the root section. This means that when you are at a high angle of attack, the root section, with its greater angle, will stall before the lower-angled tip section. This will prevent a tip stall.

On tapered wings, two common ways of designing out tip stall are using thicker wing tips and using a constant radius leading edge. A very thin airfoil will stall quicker than a thick one. The thickness of the airfoil is measured in percent with the figure being attained by dividing the thickness by the chord. A common thickness is 15 percent. This could be one, for example, that has a thickness of 1½ inches and a chord of 10 inches. On a tapered wing, you would normally use the same airfoil for the whole wing and just scale it down as you get closer to the tip. This will, of course, give you a nice taper. But to design in tip stall prevention, you would use a thicker (perhaps 17 percent) tip section. If the tip chord is 8 inches, then the thickness will be about 1⅜ inches at 17 percent as opposed to about 1 3/16 inches for the 15 percent tip. You'll probably never notice this if you build kits, but it is nice to know how it's done.

The other method, the use of a constant radius leading edge, is easier to see. Take a look at the two airfoils in Fig. 6-3. Both have the same radius leading edge. This leading edge curve appears, when compared to the rest of the airfoil, to be a relatively sharp one on the large airfoil and a relatively blunt one on the small airfoil. This is exactly what we are looking for. A sharp leading edge stalls faster than a blunt one. If you use the large airfoil for the root of the wing and the small airfoil for the tip section, you will have designed in tip stall prevention. The constant radius leading edge is easily done on a balsa covered foam wing. A block is used for the leading edge and it is carved the same for its whole length. The result is a constant radius leading edge.

Rectangular wing plan forms have nicer stall characteristics than sharply tapered ones. This is why most trainers use this type of straight, rectangular wing. They are also easier to build.

Dihedral and Stability

You will notice that, when viewed from the front, the wings of most planes (real or R/C) are angled upward at the tips. This is called *dihedral*. A head-on view of a plane (Fig. 6-4) shows the dihedral of the wing. The opoosite of dihedral is called *anhedral* and is seen on the stabilizers on some acrobatic planes (Fig. 6-5).

Dihedral gives your airplane inherent roll stability. It will tend to make your plane keep its wings level. Consider the two halves of

Fig. 6-4. Dihedral (the upward angling of the wings) as shown on this scale P-51 Mustang.

Fig. 6-5. Anhedral is the downward angling of the wings or tail. In this case a tail is shown.

the wing. Each one has the same amount of lift and this lift acts *perpendicular* to the wing (Fig. 6-6). Each wing panel has an upward component and a sideward component. The upward component holds the plane up and the sideward component opposes the sideward component of the other wing. Put the plane in a bank (Fig. 6-7) and the lower wing panel has a larger vertical component than the upper one. The difference in lift tends to roll the plane back to level. The greater the dihedral, the greater this leveling tendency will be.

Turns

Before I can discuss the remaining effects of dihedral, I'll have to go into how a plane makes a turn. Everyone knows that a car turns by turning its front wheel and a boat turns with its rudder. These are vertical controls that do the turning. We are able to do this because of the friction between the vehicle and the road or the water and the fact that the altitude can't change. You are, for all practical purposes, stuck to the surface of the road or water. A plane has none of these. There is not enough friction to keep you from skidding and your altitude certainly can change. A plane does not turn with its rudder, it turns with its wing. This might be a little hard to understand at first, but the lift of the wing actually pulls the plane around the turn.

First, however, you must get the plane in a bank (Fig. 6-8) so that there will be a horizontal component to the lift of the plane. You get the plane into the bank with the ailerons, for a plane that has them, and the rudder for a two- or 3-channel plane. For an aileron plane, you move the stick. The ailerons move, one up, one

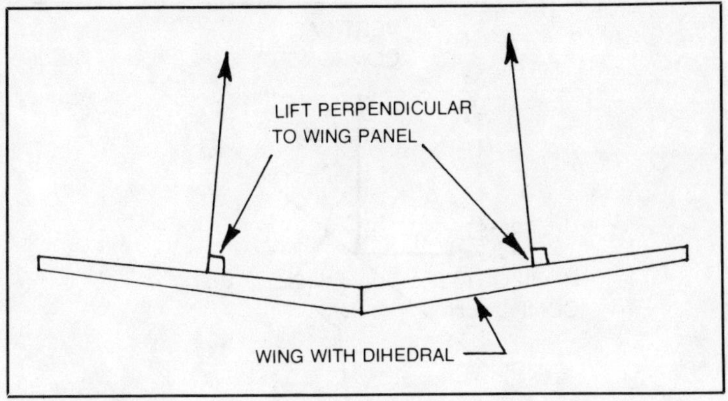

Fig. 6-6. The different directions of lift due to the dihedral in the wing.

down, causing the plane to begin rolling. The plane will continue to roll as long as you keep the ailerons deflected. When you get to the bank you want, you release the aileron stick.

Look again at Fig. 6-8. As your horizontal lift component increases, the vertical lift component *decreases*. This means that in a bank, the plane will tend to descend unless you add some up elevator to increase the overall lift. This will be discussed in more detail in the flight instruction section of the book. Right now you need to understand what makes the plane turn.

For a three-channel plane the turn is the same, but how the plane enters the turn is different. The roll control is the rudder. It causes a phenomenon called *roll due to yaw.* The rudder, when it is

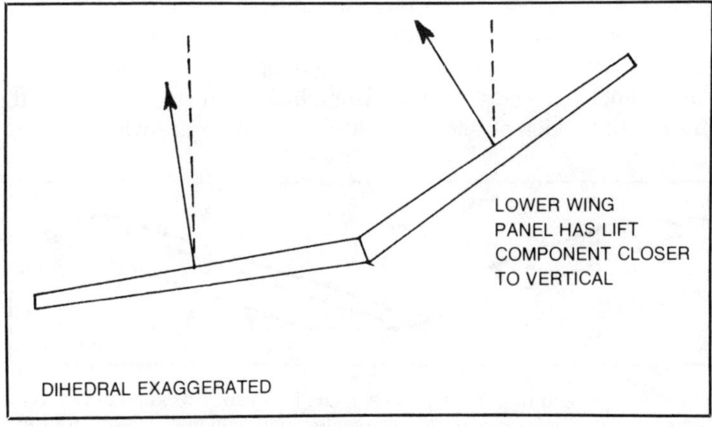

Fig. 6-7. Lift components of a wing with dihedral in a bank.

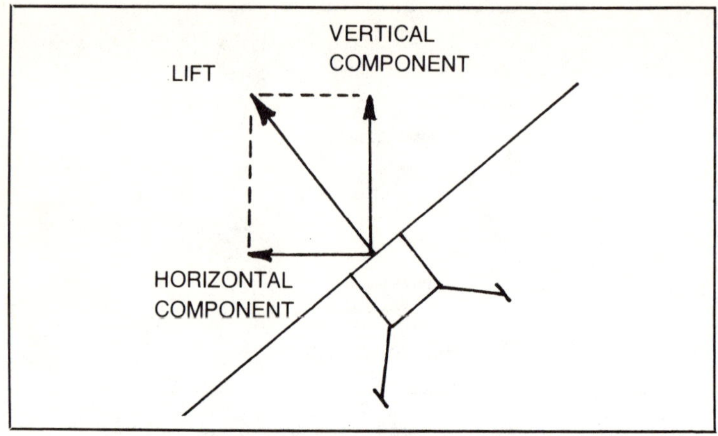

Fig. 6-8. The horizontal lift component of a wing in a bank.

deflected, actually yaws the plane sideways. When this happens, the underside of the forward wing panel faces the airflow very slightly and the top side of the rearward wing panel faces it more directly. See Fig. 6-9. You can also look at the trainer with dihedral from a front quarter view. If the airflow is blowing from you to the plane, some air will get under the forward wing and lift it. Some air will also be forced down on top of the rearward wing. This causes the plane to roll. Just like a bank in a plane with ailerons, when you get to the bank angle you desire, neutralize the rudder control stick and add some up elevator to compensate for the lost lift.

Other Dihedral Effects

Because dihedral causes stability and also roll, you might guess that it would be undesirable in a competition acrobatic plane. This is not true. There are needs for dihedral effect in just about all planes. Let's look at some of these effects and see why.

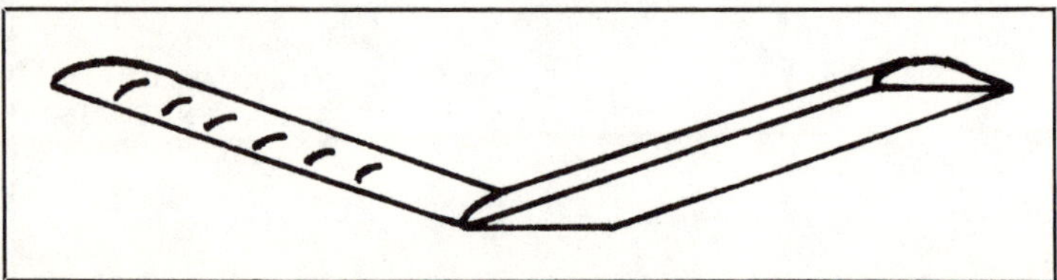

Fig. 6-9. The wing of a three-channel plane in a yaw. Roll is produced from the yaw by the air flow hitting the underside of the wing that is yawed forward and the upper side of the wing that is yawed rearward.

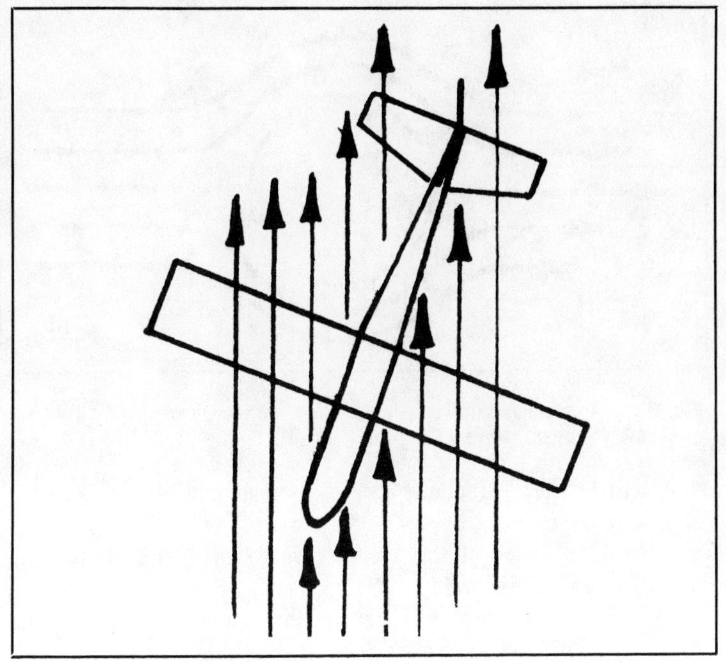

Fig. 6-10. Right rudder put in and held yaws the plane's nose to the right.

In an acrobatic plane that is required to use rudder in point rolls to hold knife edge flight (with the wings in a 90 degree vertical bank), roll-with-rudder is undesirable. The solution, however, is not to design out all of the dihedral. It is sometimes better to *add* dihedral. Wing location on the fuselage can cause dihedral type actions, Consider your plane when you put in right rudder. The plane yaws to one side, as in Fig. 6-10, and air flows over the fuselage. It hits on the left side first. Now look at a cylinder shown in Fig. 6-11 with air flowing over it. This is a simulation of a fuselage. Notice how the airflow splits. Half goes over the top and half over the bottom. Now let's attach a high wing to the cylinder/ fuselage. We have a drawing, as in Fig. 6-12, of a plane coming out of the page. See how the airflow lines strike the underside of the wing, tending to raise it, and then later it strikes the upper surface of the wing, tending to force it down. This will cause a roll to the right. Remember that the plane had a right rudder input, so that right rudder gives us a right roll. This means that a plane with a high wing location will have dihedral effect and steer with rudder application the same as a plane with dihedral. It will, however,

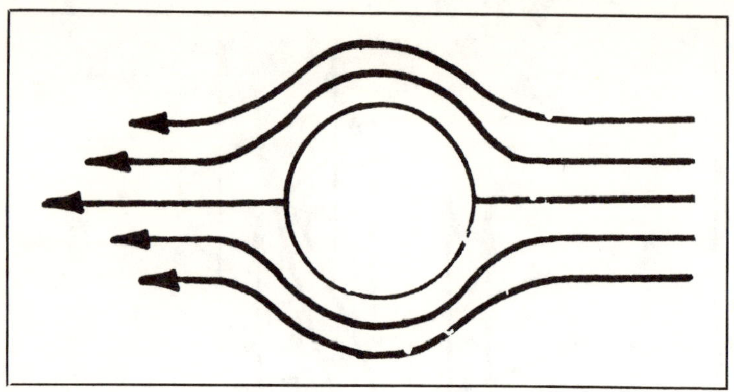

Fig. 6-11. A cylinder, simulating a fuselage, with air flowing ove: it as in a right yaw. (Nose on view.)

steer a little more sluggishly for the same amount of control input. That is undesirable.

Now let's look at the cylinder again, with the air flowing around it. This time, we'll put on a low wing. See Fig. 6-13. Again we are in a right yaw with right rudder input. Notice how the airflow this time tends to force the wings in the opposite direction from when we had a high wing. In the case of a low wing plane with no dihedral, a rudder input will cause a roll in the *opposite* direction. That is, right rudder, left roll. I should also point out that this is known to every aeronautical engineer, but it is not well known or understood by modelers. Many modelers seriously damage their low wing acrobatic planes' performance by taking the dihedral out "to make it fly better."

The mid-wing location, of course, gives not roll with rudder input. Why, then, don't acrobatic planes use a mid-wing location? Generally, it is for practical reasons. If you raise the wing to the exact middle of the fuselage, while keeping the size of the fuselage the same, the room for the radio equipment is greatly reduced. Due to streamlining, modelers are not inclined to enlarge the cross section of the fuselage unless it is absolutely necessary. Because the wings of acrobatic planes, or for that matter nearly all R/C planes, are removable, putting the wing on the centerline of the fuselage weakens the structure and also makes it harder to build and remove. These are some of the reasons you usually see R/C acrobatic planes with low or semilow wing locations.

The obvious question is, "How do we get rid of the opposite direction roll with rudder application in a low wing plane?" The

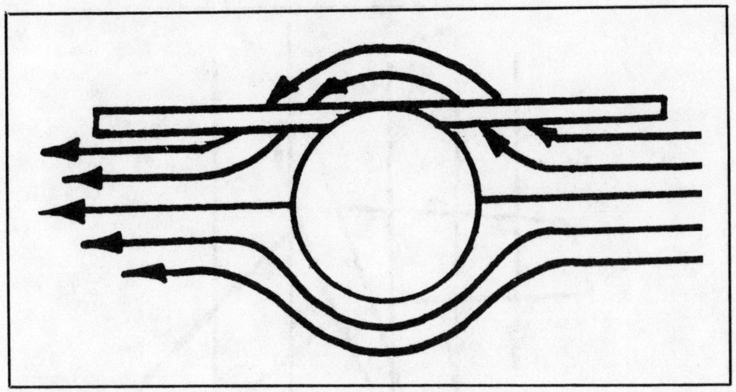

Fig. 6-12. Nose on view of a cylinder/fuselage in a right yaw with a high wing attached. Notice that the force of the air causes a roll to the right (the same direction as the applied rudder).

answer is, "put in some dihedral." This sounds simple, but lets look at how it works. Dihedral makes the plane roll in the direction of the rudder, while a low wing location makes the plane roll in the opposite direction. If the plane is designed with just enough dihedral to exactly compensate for the rolling tendency due to the low wing location, you will have an acrobatic plane which will hold knife edge flight with rudder only.

There is no way to calculate this amount of dihedral. The R/C plane designer uses experience and a cut-and-try method. If his experience causes him to make a wrong guess on the proper amount of dihedral required, he cuts the wing in two, changes the

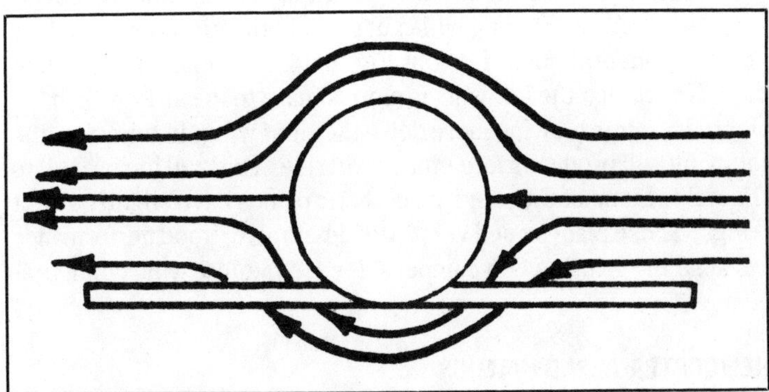

Fig. 6-13. Nose on view of a cylinder/fuselage in a right yaw with a low wing attached. Notice that the force of the airflow causes a roll to the left (the direction **opposite** to the applied rudder).

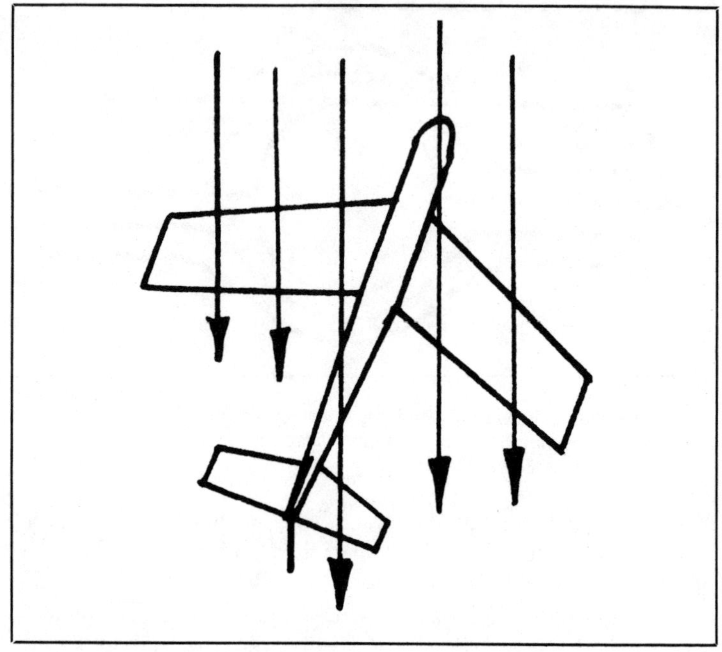

Fig. 6-14. Swept wing plane in a right yaw. Note how the left wing is more perpendicular to the airflow than the right. This caused more lift and a roll in the same direction as the applied rudder.

dihedral angle, then fiberglasses the wing back together and gives it a try. Often two or more trials are needed before the plane's performance suits him.

Let me touch on another configuration that has dihedral effect: *wing sweep*. A swept wing will cause roll in the direction of rudder just like dihedral does. Look at Fig. 6-14. The plane is in a right yaw. Notice that the left wing is more square to the airflow than the right. The air is blowing more down the right wing. In this case, the left wing will produce more lift and will rise. This will mean a roll to the right. Some of the present acrobatic planes have slightly swept wings. These planes need very little dihedral for good performance because the wing sweep compensates for the low wing configuration.

HELICOPTER AERODYNAMICS

Helicopter aerodynamics is quite different from that of fixed wing aircraft. The reason is immediately obvious when you look at a helicopter. It has a rotary wing. This large lifting propeller is called the *main rotor* and is shown in Fig. 5-38. Helicopters with only one main rotor, and I will restrict the discussion to that type because R/C model helicopters are single main rotor types, also have a small propeller on the tail called the *tail rotor* (Fig. 5-41).

Main Rotor

The main rotor supplies the lift for the helicopter to fly. Like the wings of a fixed wing plane, it also causes the helicopter to bank. In addition, and unlike the wing of a fixed wing aircraft, the main rotor causes pitch changes. These changes in the attitude of a helicopter are caused by changes in the pitch of the main rotor. This main rotor pitch, or angle of the rotor blade, can vary two ways: collectively and cyclically.

Collective pitch is easy to understand. Both rotor blades change their pitch angle at the same time. The increased angle causes the blade to get a bigger bite of the air, creating a lifting force, and the helicopter rises. Lower the collective pitch and it descends.

Cyclical pitch is a little more difficult to comprehend, but it is the key to helicopter flight. It works in two ways. First, it is used for control and is changed by the pilot—either full scale of R/C. Second, it is used during forward flight and is changed automatically. A complex pushrod—swashplate arrangement in the rotor head, the area around the shaft to which the main rotors are attached, makes the cyclical pitch changes. See Fig. 6-15.

Fig. 6-15. The light colored, ring shaped object in the center of the picture is the swashplate.

Suppose that you want to bank the helicopter left. Put in the left control. It tilts the swashplate. Pushrods that control the rotor pitch ride on the swashplate and cause the rotor blade pitch to be increased at a point that will cause the right side to lift and decreased at a point that will cause the left side to drop. The result is a left bank. Because the rotor blades are constantly moving, the pitch has to change, or cycle, from high on one side to low on the other side. This is where the name cyclical pitch comes from.

You would normally think that these points of increased or decreased pitch would be exactly on the right and left sides of the helicopter much like ailerons on a fixed wing plane. This would be true except for a phenomenon called *gyroscopic precession*.

If you have ever seen a toy gyroscope, you know what I mean. When a gyroscope is spinning and stabilized, you can push on it and it moves as if you pushed on it from another point 90 degrees away from where you actually pushed on it. This is gyroscopic precession. A force on a gyroscope acts at a point 90 degrees away.

Everything that spins has some gyroscopic action. The larger and heavier the object, the greater the action. The propeller on a conventional R/C plane has gyroscopic precession, but because the prop is small and light, we can disregard the effects. The main rotor of a helicopter, on the other hand, is much larger and heavier. It displays a considerable amount of gyroscopic action, enough so that it must be taken into account by the cyclic pitch control.

In addition to gyroscopic action, there is another consideration in cyclic pitch. You must consider the effect of forward speed on the lift of the rotor blades. This is important because one blade is traveling in the direction of flight and the other one is traveling opposite to the direction of flight. You need to think of each of the rotor blades as a small wing to see how this happens.

Picture a helicopter in forward flight at 25 mph. Now let's say that each rotor blade tip is going 100 mph. We will wait until the rotor blades are exactly 90 degrees to the fuselage, like the wings of a fixed wing plane, and then take a picture. See Fig. 6-16. Because the rotor turns clockwise, the rotor blade on the right side of the helicopter is traveling toward the rear of the copter. The air actually flowing over it is traveling at the speed of the blade *plus or minus the speed of the helicopter*. The blade is going 100 mph, but at this point, the helicopter is actually carrying it backwards 25 mph. The net speed of the air over the blade is only 75 mph.

On the other side, the reverse happens. Here the speed of the air over the blade is 100 mph plus the speed of the helicopter (125

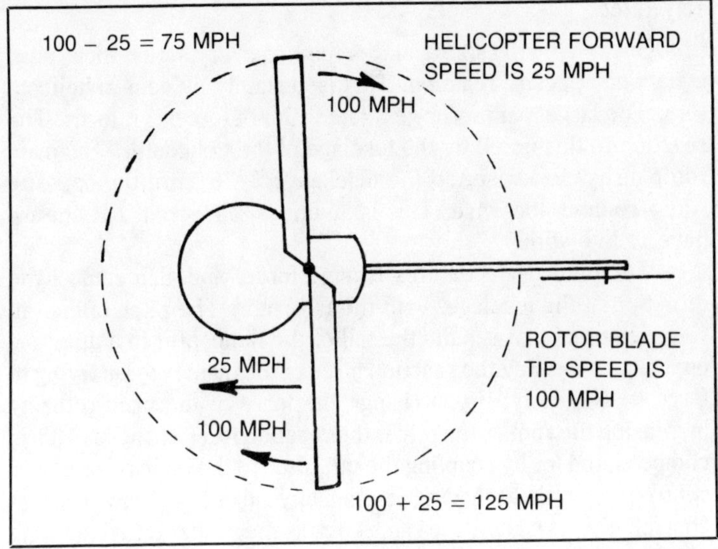

Fig. 6-16. The speed of the rotor blades due to rotational speed and the forward speed of the helicopter.

mph). This means that at the same pitch, the blade going forward (the one on the left) generates more lift than the blade going in the direction opposite to which the copter is flying. This phenomenon will cause the helicopter to tend to bank more and more to the right as speed increases. To correct for this rolling tendency, the swashplate is tilted a certain amount so that in normal level flight the rotor blade going forward has a slightly lower pitch than the other one.

Now let's look back over cyclic pitch and put it all together. To make a bank and turn, you need a cyclical pitch change to tilt the rotor—causing a bank. You must also cycle the pitch to compensate for different rotor blade tip speeds during forward flight. Along with this, you must also consider gyroscopic precession. This turns out to be a very complicated set of calculations, but it is all done for you by helicopter designers in their design of the main rotor swashplate and controls. The main rotor is set to cycle in varying amounts depending on the situation. You should not attempt any adjustments other than those in the manual that comes with the kit unless you have expert help. In any event, you should have a helicopter expert help you set up your chopper and teach you to fly it.

Tail Rotor

One of Newton's laws states that for every action there is an equal and opposite reaction. This is certainly evident in helicopters. The large main rotor generates a lot of force as it turns. The reaction to this is felt by the fuselage of the helicopter. The main rotor turns clockwise, so the fuselage tries to turn the opposite way—counterclockwise. This is an undesirable trait, but one we have to live with.

We compensate for this turning force, and also control the direction of the fuselage, with the tail rotor. The pitch of the tail rotor is set so that it pulls the tail of the helicopter in a direction opposite to the way the reaction force of the main rotor is trying to force it. Naturally, if you change the force of the main rotor by increasing the rpm or the pitch, the reaction force changes. This is compensated for by coupling the tail rotor to the main rotor power controls as well as having it manually adjustable with another control. This is usually the same stick as the rudder on a fixed wing plane.

As you can see, helicopter aerodynamics are quite different from fixed wing aerodynamics. If you are a fledgling chopper pilot, be sure to get with one of your club's helicopter experts. The helicopter, even a training type helicopter, is not as stable and docile as a corresponding fixed wing plane.

R/C AND FULL-SCALE FLIGHT COMPARED

The aerodynamics of airplanes, large and small, is the same. There are, however, some differences in actually flying R/C and full-scale planes. Predominate among these are wind effects and the fact that R/C flight entails hand-eye coordination while full-scale flying has "feel."

Wind

I have already explained the difference between airspeed and ground speed, but let me review them. Air speed is the speed the plane is traveling through the air mass. (Wind is actually a moving air mass.) Ground speed is the speed of the plane relative to the ground. Wind has an effect on ground speed.

How does wind affect a plane? First consider its speed. To be more specific, consider the wind's speed in relation to the plane's speed—in particular the plane's landing speed. An R/C plane lands at approximately 15 to 25 mph. This depends on the size and type of plane. A full-size light plane like a Cessna lands at around 75 mph.

A wind of 10 mph is negligible to the Cessna, but it can be *one-half* of the R/C plane's landing speed. Talk to a real pilot about landing with a wind in the 30 to 35 mph range and he'll tell you about taking special precautions and really being cautious—maybe even struggling with the plane. This relative wind velocity is commonplace with R/C planes, so if you have a "light" wind and bounce around and struggle with your model, it shouldn't surprise you.

The same thing can be said for cross winds, the second thing you should consider about the wind. A 10 mph cross wind is really nothing to the Cessna, but it can cause all sorts of problems for the novice R/C flier. The same problems would be encountered if the Cessna were to attempt a landing in a 30-mph cross wind. More than likely he would not even make the attempt, but would land on another runway more nearly aligned with the wind.

The third factor to consider about the wind is gusts. These affect both full scale and model planes, but R/C planes, of course, are affected more severely. A wind gusting 5 to 10 mph is changing about 25 percent of the plane's landing speed—a significant amount. This requires careful planning and judicial handling of the plane to prevent a hard landing. The full-scale Cessna, on the other hand, sees a wind of 5 mph gusting to 10 mph as a very minor problem only requiring a slight increase in landing speed.

As you can see, even in the slightest breezes, an R/C plane is getting close to a severe environment. Your instructor will brief you on how to handle the various winds, but until you get a lot of experience you can expect to encounter some difficulties unless the wind is down the runway and very light.

Hand-Eye Coordination Versus Feel

The next area of difference between full-scale aircraft and R/C planes is in how and when you know to make a control input. The pilot of a full-scale plane relies on a visual appearance of the horizon and on sensing of movement and g-forces. This "seat of the pants" feel is what you do not have in an R/C plane. You also do not have a horizon to judge references.

With an R/C plane you must first see the plane, then determine its attitude, decide on the correct control input and then make the input. The lack of feel and the inability to use the plane itself for the references needed causes a good deal of concern to many people. This is especially true for pilots of full-scale light planes. In a sense, you have a variable reference. At varying altitudes, level flight will look different and turns will look different. As a matter of fact, everything you do will appear different as you do the same maneuver at a different altitude or from a different position. Theoretically this makes flying an R/C plane a more difficult task than flying a full-scale plane. See what you think after you learn how to fly.

PERCEPTION

Because flying an R/C plane is a hand-eye coordination function, the key to good control is an accurate perception of the plane's attitude. When an R/C flier gets his plane too far away, he'll probably say, "I can't see it." He actually can "see" the plane, but what he means is that he can't perceive its attitude to tell which way to move the controls to bring the plane back. What then, do you need to "see" in order to get a good perception of the plane's attitude?

Perceiving the Attitude

Perceiving the plane's attitude is being able to tell the angle and location of the wings, fuselage and tail in relation to yourself. For example, if the tail (vertical fin) is on the bottom, then the plane is upside down. However, if the plane is so far away that you can't determine where the tail is, it becomes difficult to tell if you are upright or inverted. The best attitude indicator at a distance is the wing. If you can't see the wing or if you see just an end or front view of it, the plane is level or nearly level. In a bank, the wings clearly show up.

You can see that distance has a lot to do with perception. The closer the plane is, the easier it is to perceive. You might feel that as a beginner you will keep the plane in close. Nothing could be farther from the truth. A beginner will invariably be behind the plane and let it get too far away before he turns. This tendency to get too far away causes most of the perception problems I see in beginners. Remember that in a full-scale plane the student can fly straight ahead, collect his thoughts and then decide what to do next. The R/C student who pauses very long lets his plane get farther away and harder to see and perceive.

Some people have more difficulty with perception than others. This is natural, just like some people having more athletic ability than others. Those with extremely poor attitudinal perception, of course, make poor R/C pilots. You might find that you have trouble at first and then improve as you gain experience. This, too, is natural and part of the learning process. You will begin to remember subconsciously the last attitude of the plane and instinctively know what position it should be in if you've lost it briefly. This knowledge of the plane's position will aid your perception even more at long distances.

You should also notice that there are times when your perception is not as good as others. If you wear glasses and you do not have them on, you will not see the plane as well and this will reduce your perceptual abilities. Early in the morning and late in the evening can also be difficult times. With diminished light, you will have less perception. Too much light can also hurt. If you fly your plane in line with the sun, it will be just plain hard to see. For a beginner, this is not difficult to do so be careful. Try to fly in an area on the other side of the field from the sun if possible. This can be extremely important to people who get mild sun blindness or lose their sight for several seconds after they look at the sun.

This concern about the sun might lead you to believe that a nice, gray, high-overcast day is a great one for flying. Unfortunately this is not true. An overcast day is the worst time for perceiving your plane. Without any sun shining on the plane, the parts tend to blend together in your vision and you end up seeing a shapeless blob. These are days to really concentrate on staying in close. If you had perception problems before, then have a friend or your instructor stand with you in case you lose perception of the plane and can't tell which way it is going. You will find many R/C pilots who simply will not fly on an overcast day.

Aids to Perception

Even though perception is a physical ability that some people are better equipped with than others, there are ways to enhance your perception. The suggestions I list here might already have been mentioned, but I want to put them all together in one spot for easy reference if you have a perception problem.

- Have an experienced flier or your instructor stand with you if you notice any perceptual trouble. This is even after you solo. Some days you will feel good and fly well. Other days you won't feel so hot and your perception will be affected. If this is one of your off days, have an experienced flier stand with you. Think of it as insurance against losing perception of your plane's attitude, getting disoriented and dinging it.
- Be extremely careful if you are taking any type of medication. Real pilots are grounded when they take medication. R/C

pilots, while there is no restriction, should observe this rule if the drug is one that slows you down or makes you drowsy. Not only will your perception be affected, but your timing, reflexes and judgement will be also. If a cold has you down, stay on the ground.

- If you have perception problems, avoid flying on an overcast day. I have already discussed how this is the worst time for perceiving your plane's attitude. You should avoid flying on these days. If you must fly, have another flier stand with you. Two sets of eyes are better than one.
- Fly as close to yourself as you can. The closer the plane is the easier it will be to see and also to perceive. Unfortunately, you can't fly very close in until you gain some experience. With more experience you might not need to fly close for good perception. At any rate, try to keep the plane in as close as you can.
- By all means, wear your glasses if you need them. It is much harder to determine the attitude of a plane that is an out-of-focus blur than it is for one that is sharp and well defined. On bright sunny days, wear sun glasses or clip-ons over your prescription glasses. I have also found that a baseball cap with a long bill helps a lot on sunny days. The shade from the cap will keep you from squinting and allow you to see better.
- Paint your plane to enhance your ability to perceive it. My paint and color scheme recommendations might seem to limit your choice of finish—but they work. Tests run on Air Force RPV's and several years of modeling have gone into the suggestions.

Perception of a plane is the ability to distinguish the fuselage and tail from the wing and the top of the plane from the bottom. This is what clues you in to which way the plane is going and whether it is climbing or diving. With this in mind, you need to paint the plane to help you see these clues more easily. I recommend that the bottom of the wing be finished a dark color. It will be in the shadow most of the time anyway, so you might as well finish it in a dark color.

It is important that the bottom of the wing be easily distinguishable from the top. For the top of the wing, I recommend a large pattern of light and dark colors. A large black and white checkboard has been shown to give the best visibility in tests. But for our purposes, any light and dark pattern will work. The pattern can be a checkerboard, a sunburst or just wide bands or stripes. It must be large and bold and have strong contrast.

Avoid small patterns and complimentary colors that will blend together at a distance. You might also want to repeat the pattern on the top of the horizontal tail. Paint the fuselage a brighter color than the bottom of the wing. This will make it easy to tell them apart in the air.

Colors I have tried are: dark blue wing bottom, dark blue and light yellow checkerboard wing top and stab, and orange fuse; blue wing bottom, orange fuse, and white, orange and blue wing top; and a dark green wing bottom, light yellow, orange, and green fuselage, and green and yellow checkerboard wing top. There are dozens of others, of course, and you will be surprised how some color schemes will make it easy to perceive your plane. Figure 5-10 shows one of my planes with a green, light yellow and orange color scheme. When this plane is in a bank it is instantly visible and always easy to keep in sight.

ORIENTATION

Another difference between full-scale and R/C planes is in how you orient yourself. In the full-scale plane, you are actually in the plane and going the same way it is—all the controls are directional. If you want to go left, you put in left control. This is so natural you don't even think about it. An R/C plane, however, is a different ballgame. You are not going the same direction the plane is; you are fixed. Making the plane go to the left, for example, might be a left turn or it might not be a turn at all. This is what is initially confusing about R/C flying, but it is easily explained and learned.

Flying Away From Yourself

When you first start flying R/C, you'll find that the easiest thing to do is to fly away from yourself. This is because you are looking in the same direction that the plane is going and the controls are directional. When your plane is flying this direction, left control makes the plane go right. Unfortunately for R/C'ers, you can't keep the plane headed away from you all the time. You must turn the plane around and come back.

Flying Toward Yourself

Flying toward yourself is the hard part of flying R/C. Were it not for this, you would probably learn to fly in a couple of flights and there would be no challenge to it. Don't think it is hard to learn. It's like learning to ride a bicycle or like learning to back a trailer. The trailer is a good analogy since you steer it backwards and that's just what you do when you fly an R/C plane toward yourself.

To understand this steering technique, take your plane or any model, even a small plastic one, and put it on the floor. Stand behind it facing the same direction it is pointed. Now, think about putting in some controls. If you put in right control stick, the plane will bank and turn right. Remember which direction in the room the plane will be going in the right turn. Now walk around in front of the plane and face it as though it were flying toward you.

Visualize putting in the same right stick control. Recall which direction in the room the plane is going to turn toward. It will still turn to its right, but this will be to your *left*. When the plane is coming toward you and you put in right control, it will go to *your* left. Walk around the plane and think about the controls again until you get this apparent control reversal fully understood.

Notice that everything associated with the roll control is apparently backwards when the plane is coming toward you. This will be confusing at first. But like riding a bicycle, it will come to you and you'll suddenly wonder what all the fuss was about. It will definitely come a lot faster if you have an instructor and follow a regular program of instruction.

SCHOOL'S OUT

Now that I have covered radio controlled flight, your ground school is finished. You whould have a working knowledge of rules and regulations governing R/C flight. You should also have an understanding of the radio, its parts and how to choose one, the engine, how it operates and the accessories available, and the plane, how it is constructed and how it flies. By this time, you probably have your plane ready to go. Or at least you have it started. It's time to get out of the classroom and get down to the fun—learning to fly your own plane.

R/C Flight Instruction

While the first half of this book was written as a textbook to explain radio controlled flying to the student, this half is intended as an instructional guide for the instructor. The student is also encouraged to study this part in order to learn in advance what he will be doing. However, the actual learning must take place at the flying field with an airplane.

THE PROGRAM

The R/C flight instruction program is structured to help the instructor teach students the most about R/C flying in the least amount of time. It is a complete program that produces students who are competent pilots able to handle their planes well in nearly any situation. It is designed in four sections: familiarization, figure 8s, low approaches, and landing. The student will progress through each phase at his own speed and stay in one until he is ready for the next, more advanced one.

The chapter on each phase is detailed with learning outcomes for the student, what you should demonstrate and how to demonstrate it, how the student should practice, common errors he is likely to make (and how to correct them), and instructional techniques that will help you get R/C flying across to the student. By the time you get to the later chapters, some of the techniques might seem repetitious, but each chapter was written as an independent entity so that it can be used for instructing a student at that phase without refering to previous chapters. But before I get into the details of the flight instruction program, there are several general areas you should be made aware of.

BUDDY BOX VERSUS SINGLE TRANSMITTER

When the idea of electrically connecting two transmitters in a master-slave arrangement first came out, it was thought that this innovation (shown in Fig. 7-1) would revolutionize R/C flight instruction. It did not. In a buddy box set up, the instructor has a master transmitter with override capability over the student's slave transmitter. The problems with this quickly became evident. In the first place, the master transmitter actually flies the plane. The student has to own two transmitters or at least have another one available for use. In most cases, it is the instructor's transmitter that is used. The very least among the problems is that after each instructional flight the instructor's transmitter trims are out of the positions they need to be in to fly his plane. And of course, many student's transmitters, especially the less expensive ones, do not come equipped for buddy box use.

By far the biggest factor against the buddy box system is that it tends to become a crutch. Having the instructor hooked in and ready to immediately assume control of the plane, tends to make students overconfident, but also afraid to go it alone. I know students who have flown for three years and never given up their buddy box. This dependence really slows down the progress of learning.

As you probably have guessed, I do not favor the use of buddy-box instruction. It can, however, be used with the R/C flight instruction program. It is particularly useful in special cases such as teaching a student with a physical handicap or other problem that requires extra close monitering. It is also helpful if your student insists on learning on a plane that is well beyond his capabilities. An example would be a low-winged, high-performance plane. If you decide to use the buddy box, you must follow these rules or your student might become "addicted" to it.

- Make sure your student always knows who has control. State clearly "I have it" when you take control. This lets him know if he did not make a certain input or correction. Failing to let the student know precisely when he is actually flying the plane can be the biggest failure of most buddy box instructors. If the student does not know that you had control of the plane when a correction or input is made, there is a good chance he will think he did it. Then, if he was actually using the wrong input at the time, his mistake will be reinforced. Even though the wrong input was sent, the plane performed the proper maneuver. It is absolutely critical for the student to know when he is and when he is not flying the plane.

Fig. 7-1. Two transmitters connected with a "Buddy Box" cable.

- Use the buddy box sparingly. The longer you use it the harder if will be to get him flying solo. It is better to let him gain confidence in his own abilities than to let the buddy box become a crutch that he will have a hard time turning loose. Once you pass the familiarization phase you should not need it.
- Don't rush him into landing just because you can save him with the override function. The student should only go as fast as he can assimilate all the necessary information to perform a task. Going faster will confuse him, scare him and make him more dependent on you and the buddy box.

WHERE THE INSTRUCTOR SHOULD STAND

If you use a buddy box, it doesn't really matter where you stand in relation to your student. If you don't use a buddy box, as most instructors won't, it is very important to place yourself so that you can both instruct the student and also be able to rapidly take control of the airplane. Your position is on the student's left side. When the student first starts flying, you should hold on to the transmitter while he flies. You do this by reaching across your body with your left arm and holding the transmitter with your left hand (Fig. 7-2).

This might seem awkward at first, but there is a reason for holding on with your left hand. It allows you to take over quicker than any other method of holding the transmitter. As the student gets better, you will stop holding on to the transmitter except in a critical situation. As he progresses farther, just standing next

Fig. 7-2. The instructor lets the student fly while holding on to the transmitter with his left hand ready to take over if necessary.

to him and giving verbal instruction will usually suffice. With some students, especially those who are extremely nervous or frightened, you might want to place a hand on their left shoulder just to let them know that you are nearby and can take over if necessary. Always keep your left hand free to take the transmitter if the situation dictates.

HOW TO TAKE CONTROL

Taking control from a student, or actually taking the transmitter from the student, should be smooth and quick. It can be very haphazard and result in the loss of a plane if you don't specifically teach him how you are going to take the transmitter and how he should give up control. You should be standing on his left side and holding on to the transmitter lightly with your left hand.

When you need to take control of the plane, you should give him a verbal command. At that time, he should release the transmitter and you can pull it over in front of you and begin to fly. I recommend the words, "I have it." They are short, quick and to the point. They are also the natural thing to say in a tight situation. When you say, "I have it," he should immediately stop flying the plane and release the transmitter (Fig. 7-3). You can now, in one motion, pull the transmitter towards yourself with your left hand and reach for the aileron/elevator stick. You can try transferring control while standing on the other side, but you'll have to change hands and lose time. Practice this way a few times if you have been using some other method and see if it doesn't seem faster.

One thing that you must stress to the student is that he must turn loose of the transmitter on command. He might think that he has the situation well in hand, but his judgement is not as good as yours. If your student is one of those who tends to freeze and really hang onto the transmitter when he gets into trouble, practice taking it from him a lot. I've seen too many planes crash while a scared student was frozen on the sticks and the instructor was frantically grabbing for the box. There is no time for wrestling the student for the transmitter.

INSTRUCTING TECHNIQUES

There are several instructor techniques or procedures that you can use to enhance your instruction. Many of them are just

Fig. 7-3. At the command, "I've got it," the student releases the transmitter and the instructor's right hand reaches for the control stick.

good common sense. Make it fun. Don't growl or yell at your student. He is learning R/C because it is a fun and relaxing hobby. Just because he is a slow learner or makes the same mistake repeatedly is no reason for you to lose your cool or shout. Other techniques come from learning theory. These are the ones that the student might not notice, but will help immensely in his learning.

Feedback

Feedback is telling the student how he is doing. You would think that feedback is one technique that every instructor uses with every flight, but it isn't. Many instructors just let the student practice and say very little to him unless he really gets into trouble. This is just about the slowest way a student can learn. Give your student feedback often and immediately and give him feedback for both good and bad performance.

The immediacy of feedback is very important. A student must know before he goes to the next part of his practice whether or not he has done the previous part properly. Most times just a word like "good" or "not bad" will suffice. It is extremely important that you do this to reinforce good performance. This quick method of letting him know that he has done the maneuver correctly will speed his learning process. You also need to give him feedback for everything he does—every turn, level off, altitude correction, line up; everything. This can be just a word or a phase. "Good bank angle," "nice turn" or "you overshot, roll out" is a sequence that could cover making a turn and rolling out in line with the runway. You can see that you don't have to say very much, but you are telling your student a lot. He can get an immediate picture of a correct bank, a correct turn, and realize if he went too far in the turn and overshot the runway. This type of feedback, immediate and frequent, makes every minute of his practice meaningful and will speed his learning.

The student needs immediate correction when he does something wrong. A small correction like the overshot turn in the previous example can be handled like the feedback on good progress. A quick word like, "You overshot a bit," works fine. The handling of a long correction requires a different approach. If your student has missed a concept or you need to explain something to him, you need to take control of the plane while you do it. This is extremely important. Your student, at his stage of learning, is struggling to just concentrate on keeping the plane from crashing. He will not be able to listen to a long, detailed set of instructions and also fly well. If you need to explain something, it is important enough for him to give you his undivided attention. Take control, let him relax for a moment and then give him your explanation.

Saturation

Another factor the instructor should be aware of is what is called saturation. As the student first starts learning to fly, he will be able to control the plane fairly well for a short period of time and then he will begin to overcontrol and make large errors. What happens is that the student is able to keep the plane within reasonable limits for a short period of time. Then at some point, he starts to get behind in control input, tries too hard to correct and overcontrols. This causes large errors. The time that this starts is called the *student's saturation point*. It is the point where the intense concentration needed by the student in these early flights shows up as strain. At first, this might be after only a minute or so of flying. Later it will become less and less of a problem until the student is able to fly out the whole tank.

The instructor needs to look for the student's saturation point and learn to recognize it. He will learn very little by continuing to fly after this point. He will tend to scare himself by making the mistakes, compounding the problem, and he'll end up putting the plane in danger of crashing and forcing you to take control. When you recognize the symptoms of excessive over-controlling, it's time to take the plane and let the student relax for a moment. You can kep the plane in the air and use this time to demonstrate, explain his errors and talk to him about what he is going to practice next.

Learning Rates

Another thing to consider in your student is changes in his learning rate. These are natural as he moves from learning an easy task to a more difficult one. As an example, learning a simple turn is an easier task than learning how to land. The point you must make to him is that each task has a different learning rate (as does each student). He might become concerned and not think he is making any real progress when he starts figure 8s and low approaches. Tell him beforehand that this is a difficult and more lengthy phase than familiarization and learning a turn. Remind him while he is on these harder phases that learning is slower here. It is also important to remember that feedback, immediate and frequent feedback, really works wonders. A "pat on the head" during this time keeps him trying hard.

Even though some phases naturally take a little longer to learn, you should be on the lookout for plateaus and regression. The rate of learning in any endeavor can be represented by a graph that shows the amount learned compared to time. Figure 7-4 shows a typical learning graph. Initially, learning is very rapid. Then the rate drops off as the amount of knowledge to be assimilated becomes greater and the tasks harder.

At times, the student will hit a plateau or flat spot in the curve where he seems to be making no progress. Of course he *is* making progress during this time, but it is hard to see. These plateaus can be difficult for the anxious R/C student. He might come to you and say, "I just don't seem to be learning anything. Maybe I should: "get a new plane," " get a new engine," "get a new instructor," "try a new method," "fly on Wednesdays instead," or just about anything else.

Students tend to look for a magic cure to a perfectly natural learning plateau. Some have long plateaus, others, especially the more gifted, have short ones—but they all have them. If the quote is, "maybe I should get out and get more practice," he would have had the proper answer. All he needs is more experience.

This is not to say that a student can not outgrow a plane. A trainer is a limited performance airplane and nearly every student, with rare exceptions, will eventually reach a point where he needs a higher performance plane to progress any farther. That point, however, is beyond this book. Any trainer can take any student through the basic four R/C flight training phases. Most trainers can also perform the acrobatics described in a later chapter. No student should have to change trainers to learn how to fly.

The other thing to watch for is regression. The downward dip in the curve in Fig. 7-4 shows that the student has forgotten some of the knowledge or skill that he had learned or had something happen, like a crash, that set him back. This is perfectly natural if the student is flying only on weekends. He just can't be expected to fly as well on Saturday after a five-day layoff.

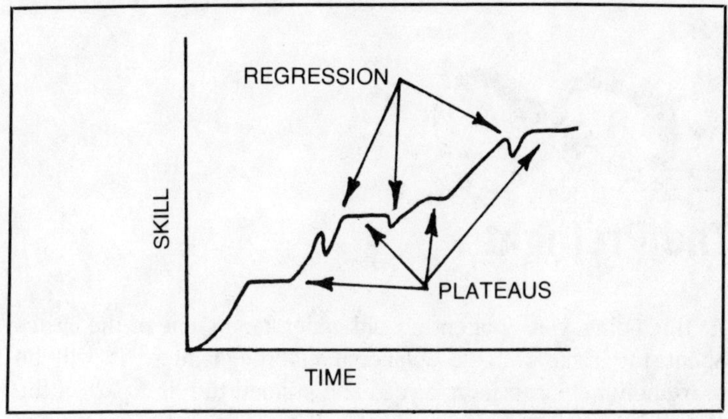

Fig. 7-4. Typical learning graph showing regressions and learning plateaus.

When you explain this to your student, make an analogy with learning to drive a car. Ask him to think about how long it would take to learn to drive a car if he only got to practice on weekends. Be sure you point out that he can expect to regress after missing a week or more and especially if he misses longer. Of course, the ideal situation would be to fly every day *and* on the weekends. However, for most of us that's not possible.

The other reason I mentioned for regression can be plain old fear or lack of confidence. If your student makes a serious error, particularly one that damaged his plane, he is going to be frightened and very cautious the next few flights. I've had some students come back after a crash so nervous they felt too weak and shaky to control the plane. As with regression from any other reason the cure for this lack of confidence is experience—lots of experience.

As I describe each of the four phases of the R/C Flight Instruction course (familiarization, figure 8s, low approaches, and landing) I will discuss each of these techniques and learning fundamentals again. During that discussion, however, I will concentrate on more specific cases and cover more specific techniques that you can use to help your students.

The Preflight

At this point, your student should understand some of the basics about the radio, engine, plane and aerodynamics. It will be extremely helpful if he had read and studied the first part of the R/C flight instruction course where these basics were explained in detail. If he has not, then you should give him a briefing on these items. You can do this at the field when you are checking over his plane and engine or before he is ready to fly. Don't take him up if he has no knowledge of flying.

PREFLIGHT CHECK

After the student has a knowledge of the basics, you must conduct a preflight. For the first flight, it should be extensive and cover the plane, engine and radio for proper construction, installation and operation. A sample preflight checklist is given in Table 8-1. It looks quite long (20 steps), but after you read through it, you'll see that it really isn't long. Most of the items can be covered with a quick look at the plane, you would the ones covering the engine and radio even without a checklist.

Don't forget that your student might not be familiar with modern adhesives and might not realize the importance of solid and strong engine and wing mounts. Your student might be a former control line modeler and have the elevator adjusted for 45 degrees of up and down travel. That might be just right for a CL stunt plane, but it would be an extremely large amount for an R/C trainer.

I was once presented with a plane to test which, I luckily discovered before the flight, had unbraced one-thirty-second wire for the pushrods. The controls would move, due to very free hinges, but they were springy and floppy. In the air, I would have had no control at all.

You will see that the latter items on the checklist include a test run of the engine and a taxi test. You'll need to do this

Table 8-1. Instructor's Preflight Checklist.

1. Check for frequency flag on radio and proper use of frequency control method.
2. Range check radio.
3. Take wing off, check servo operation, wiring, switch, and antenna.
4. Check control linkages, pushrods, and clevices for clearance and strength.
5. Check structural integrity around wing hold-downs.
6. Check tank installation and fuel lines.
7. Check wing integrity and replace the wing.
8. Check the CG of the plane.
9. Check the wing and tail for alignment and warps.
10. Check control hinges and horns.
11. Check landing gear: wheel collars tight, wheels roll free, nose gear strong and with right amount of throw.
12. Check engine mount for strength and engine for proper incidence.
13. Turn on radio and set trims to neutral. Recheck control surface alignment. Check for proper throw and for binding.
14. Check controls for proper direction.
15. Check engine and prop for proper size and for strength.
16. Start engine and check idle and full power.
17. Check for excessive vibration at full power.
18. Hold nose up at full power and check for signs of leaning out.
19. Make a check of all controls at full power.
20. Check that the plane will taxi straight.

anyway, but it is a god time to start teaching the student about the practical aspects of getting his plane airworthy. Explain to him how to listen for the sound of the engine to change as you adjust if from rich to lean. Show him where to be when he adjusts the needle valve and how to do the nose-up test. Likewise, show him how to adjust the idle and explain to him how you determine when it is set properly. Setting the idle seems to be difficult for most beginners. Make the instruction detailed.

Taxi the plane and show him how to check the steering. The most common problem is having the nose wheel steering set too sensitive. Help him get it set correctly and show him about how much steering he'll need for your field.

TEST FLIGHT

This flight should be just what it is called, a test flight, not an instructional flight. First, you need to get familiar with his plane. It's not so much that any instructor can't handle any trainer, but it might very likely need the control throws adjusted for more or less movement. Because it was probably built by an inexperienced person, it might have a strange quirk or two. This flight is the place to find out and also to decide how you are going to teach the student if the plane does respond differently from what you expected.

The second reason you want to keep the first flight as a test flight only is that your student will probably not be ready to fly. He'll be watching his "baby" and waiting for your judgment. That's only natural when you consider all the time and work he's put into it. Many students will even be surprised that it flies. It is the first hurdle in their learning to fly, building an airworthy plane, so let him relax and enjoy watching it.

After you take off, climb up to a safe altitude and level off. Throttle back to instructional speed, two-thirds to one-half throttle, and check the trim and control response. If the trim is way out so that you can't get it to where you can let it fly hands off, you'll have to land and reset the controls. This might mean a warp in the wing if the ailerons are way out or incorrect incidence if the elevator is off. An improper engine thrust line can also cause the elevator to be way off.

Assuming that you can get the plane to fly straight and level within the limits of the trim switches, the next thing to check is the control response. Both the pitch and roll sensitivity should be set for a beginner. Don't overdo it thinking that your student can handle it.

Let's face it, if the ailerons are set so that the plane can do three rolls, pattern style, they are very much too sensitive for a rank beginner. Just because he has an aileron trainer doesn't mean that it has to be set up sensitive.

The ailerons should be set slow enough so the student can make an incorrect input to roll out from a medium bank (30 degrees) turn, notice that he has moved the stick the wrong way, and reverse it before the plane gets over on its back. Anything else is too fast and he will, at first, get inverted and in a panic situation. This scares him and retards his learning. It also scares instructors who have to recover the plane.

During the test and trim flight, don't do any acrobatics or

hard maneuvers. Even though the plane might look strong, it might not be. There might be a weak spot that was painted or covered over. He also might have used a glue that is not too resistant to vibration. There are many other little things that might be wrong with a beginner's plane, but they all point to the same conclusion: don't overstress it on the first flight. You'll more than likely need to land and reset the trims. After this is done, take a look at the plane again. In particular, you should check the engine mount area, wing mount area, the tail and the radio mounting. If these areas fail, the plane is gone. You can, and should, give the plane a good post-test flight check.

FIRST FLIGHT BRIEFING

Now that the plane has been rechecked and the trims adjusted, it is ready for the first instructional flight. But wait, don't go leaping off into the blue and shoving the transmitter into the student's hands. First you need to give him a preflight briefing. He needs a briefing before his first flight and then a short briefing before every flight. More on this later. For now we'll start with what he should be briefed on before that all-important first flight.

The Controls

Before his first flight, you need to give the student some hands-on work with the transmitter so he will at least have an idea of which way to move the sticks. Get the frequency pin, turn on the transmitter and receiver and let him see for himself how the controls work. Sure, he has played around with them while he was installing the radio, but he probably won't be as familiar with the controls as you think.

Have the student move the controls while you explain what they do. Be sure that you are very careful in explaining the direction to move the stick for up elevator. Some people want to hold the transmitter in a vertical position. To them, if they have had no previous experience with airplanes, "up" should be an upward movement of the stick. This, of course, is down control and can cause no end of excitement in the air. Explain that the transmitter was designed to be held horizontally and the stick movement follows the full-scale aircraft practice of having a pull toward yourself give "up" control. The student can and should hold the transmitter in a way that is comfortable to him. Just make sure he understands which direction is up control.

Let the student try the other controls: the rudder, nose wheel steering, aileron, and throttle and explain each of these in detail as he moves them.

Trim

After he has practiced with the main controls, teach him how to use the trim. It will take a while for him to learn to trim, but it will go quicker if he understands it in advance. The major difference between the main controls and trim controls is that the control sticks are spring loaded to the center and the trims stay where they are set. This fact is much more significant than it sounds at first. The trims are used to readjust a neutral position, while the main controls are used to move the plane *about* the neutral position. Let me explain more fully.

Suppose the plane is in level flight and you release the controls. If it is not trimmed properly it will move from level flight attitude. Let's say, for this example, that the plane enters a slight dive. We say that it is trimmed for a dive or has too much nose down trim. This diving, or elevator down attitude, is the plane's neutral position. That means that when you release all the sticks and the controls go to neutral, the plane dives. You need to change the trim so that when you release the sticks the plane stays level. You do this with the trim levers.

But before you actually do this, look at the main control sticks (in this case, the elevator stick). Suppose that you pull back on it and cause the plane to level off or even climb. You have moved the plane from its neutral position. Now turn loose of the elevator stick and what happens? The plane goes back to its neutral position and enters the dive again. It doesn't matter what position you put the plane in. When you release the controls, it will go back to its neutral position.

This reaction has an effect on how you have to move the controls to trim the plane. What you must do is put the plane in level flight with the control stick and then move the trim lever to hold it there. That sounds simple enough, but let's look at why it works and what the effect is if you don't do it that way.

There is a tendency among students to use the trim levers like the control sticks. They tend to fly the plane to level flight by moving them. Then they wonder why the plane won't maintain that position. Consider the plane that has a slight diving tendency. How would you correct this plane to level flight? You would pull back on the stick-up control until the plane got to level flight. Then you would release the stick. This last part is the key, "you would release the stick." This neutralizes the controls. Now let's consider putting the plane in level flight with the trim levers. You pull back on the trim levers and this causes the plane to nose up to level flight. But when the plane gets to level flight, it keeps on going and enters a climb *because the trim levers are not self-centering*. The amount of up trim you put in to get the nose to climb will always be too much. It's like putting in up control with the main control stick and not releasing it. You are bound to enter a climb. Remember that the trims *change* a neutral position and the control sticks *move the plane about* the neutral position.

Getting back to the plane in a dive, how should you trim it for level flight? The correct procedure is:

—Put in up control to move the plane to the position you want to hold, in this case, level flight.

—Adjust the neutral position by putting in up trim until the plane holds this position. If, during the process of trimming, the plane has moved from its level flight position, fly it back to level flight again and retrim. This same procedure works for all controls of the plane (with the aileron and rudder as well as the elevator).

PREFLIGHT BRIEFINGS

In addition to briefing the student thoroughly before his first flight, you should give him a short briefing before every flight. This preflight briefing contains several items. His understanding of them will make the flight go smoother and make it more meaningful for him.

- You should review his progress from previous flights. This need only be a brief statement, but it can be more if you feel he needs it. For example, if your student consistantly made a glaring error, you would remind him of this and explain in detail how it should be done properly.
- Tell him what he is going to do on the flight. This gives him a chance to think about the specific maneuver or item to be practiced. It also gives him a chance to ask any questions he might have *before* you get him up in the air and flying. He might not be sure what you want him to do or how to do it. Getting a clear understanding of this before the flight will save fuel and time. Telling him what you want him to accomplish also gives him a goal—something to shoot at. This is extremely important. You might know he is making progress, but if he has tangible

goal, even small easy-to-reach ones, he will also know and feel that he is making progress.

- Tell him how long you expect him to fly the plane. This is necessary at first when he is unable to fly out a whole tank of fuel. Saturation is completely natural and expected, but the student might feel that he is getting saturated and beginning to overcontrol too early. A brief statement like the following is adequate: "We'll go up and do some more turns to continue your familiarization with the plane. You'll be flying for a couple of minutes. You might get nervous after this time and I'll take control. You can rest a minute or two and give it a try again."

After the student is able to fly out a full tank, it will be understood that he will fly the entire time and it won't be necessary to tell him every time.

- Remind the student of how you will take control if he gets into serious trouble. Again, this is necessary only at first when he is prone to getting into trouble. No matter what way you do it, make sure he understands. The last thing you or he needs is for him to freeze up and not relinquish the transmitter.

After the student's plane, engine and radio have been preflighted, the plane is tested and the student has had his preflight briefing, you are ready to give him some actual practice. The real, hands-on training starts from this point, in four phases; familiarization, figure 8s, low approaches, and landing.

Familiarization

The first phase of learning to fly R/C is getting familiar with the plane and how the controls respond in the air. During this phase the student learns to use the controls to steer the plane. More specifically, he learns to make a turn and at the latter part of the phase he learns to takeoff his plane.

The length of this phase, as with the other phases, will vary according to the ability of the student. Do not expect that you will be able to familiarize your student in, for example, three flights. Some will be quick learners and be able to do figure 8s on the first or second flight. This is especially true for students who have full-scale aircraft experience.

Other students will be nervous and "all thumbs" during the first half dozen or so flights. To attempt to teach figure 8 training during this period would, for this student, be a waste of time. Generally speaking, as soon as you feel that the student can safely maneuver the plane to a specific location—in line with the runway—it is safe to begin figure 8s.

LEARNING OUTCOMES

There are several specific things that the student should learn in this phase. The first is how the controls move the plane; the elevator for pitch control, the ailerons for roll control, the rudder for yaw and the throttle for power control. He should also learn what physical factors these controls affect. That is, how a change in pitch by the elevator can also change altitude and airspeed and how a power change with the throttle also affects altitude as well as airspeed. This interplay between the throttle and elevator should be thoroughly explained and you should continue to emphasize it in later phases (especially in the low approach phase).

The student should also learn to make a turn. Don't insist that he be able to make a turn that is exactly level, but he should know the use of aileron to set the bank and elevator to control altitude.

Next, he should learn to place the plane in a specific area. Before he starts figure 8s he has to be able to maneuver the plane to a spot generally in line with an extension of the runway centerline. This will require that he is able to steer the plane and control altitude within reasonable limits.

The student should have a basic understanding of the effects of wind on a plane. At this stage, he only needs a rudimentary knowledge of wind effects, but he should recognize what is happening to his plane in the wind. Learning to correct more specifically for the wind will come in a later phase.

It is a good idea to brief the student on the phase learning objectives as well as the specifics he needs to practice and learn on each flight. After he is aware of these learning outcomes, you should demonstrate each of them to him.

INSTRUCTOR DEMONSTRATION

As with all demonstrations, you should show the student the objectives for the familiarization phase twice. The first time with the student watching the plane and again with the student watching your hands on the controls. Show him how the controls function and then let him try them. Talk him through the same control inputs—up and down for the elevator, left and right bank for the aileron (or rudder, for a three-channel plane), and left and right yaw with the rudder. You might have to take the plane in between these maneuvers to reposition it for the student as he probably won't be able to do it. Forcing him at this point to try to position the plane will cause him to concentrate on that rather than on how the controls work.

Pitch-Airspeed Demonstration

You should demonstrate the interplay between pitch control and airspeed as well as that between throttle and altitude. Set the plane up in level flight in front of you and the student. Start at a farily low altitude so that your demonstration won't go out of sight. Raise the nose to about a 30-degree angle and hold it there. Allow the airspeed to bleed off. Explain to the student that from a constant speed, level flight condition, he can't gain altitude without losing airspeed. It might not be noticeable with a small altitude change, but it happens.

While you're demonstrating this, you should also indicate how to recover from a steep, nose-high attitude like the one you have just demonstrated. Show him how he can merely release the controls and let the plane fly an arc until the nose gets low and the speed increases in the dive.

Another way to recover is to roll into a steep bank and allow the plane to slice downward. This is the most effective way for an experienced student. The rank beginner might use this type of recovery and go from one problem situation to another (a nose-low spiral).

It should be emphasized that the steep bank recovery from a nose-high altitude is a rapid recovery, and consequently, the student must expect to have to roll out from the bank quickly and then add up elevator to level off.

Throttle-Altitude Demonstration

To demonstrate the throttle-altitude-airspeed coupling, set the plane up at medium power in level flight. You will do this once for a high-throttle climb demonstration and again for the low-throttle descent demo. From level flight at medium power, increase the throttle to full power. Keep the wings level, but don't make any elevator changes.

As the speed increases, the plane will begin to climb. On some high wing trainers that have a powerful engine, this might be a rapid climb or nose-up attitude due to the large difference between the wing position and thrust line. If this is true, be sure that the student tries and fully understands this. It could happen on a go-around from a low approach and put him in an uncomfortably steep nose-high attitude at a low altitude. You'll need to tailor his instruction to his own specific plane-engine combination, but in any case he will need to learn his plane's reactions.

For the reduced throttle demonstration, set up again in level flight at medium power. Reduce the power to idle. As the airspeed decreases, the plane will enter a descent. Point out that this is what happens when you reduce the power for landing. This is also a good time, if you haven't already done it, to see if his plane needs down thrust.

If he has a trainer that is somewhat overpowered, it might tend to pitch downward severely when power is reduced. This is normally due to the necessity of carrying down trim in level flight to control the tendency to climb caused by the high-power engine. If this happens, explain it to the student and tell him that he will need some down thrust to alleviate the situation. You'll probably have to help him get the down thrust in and retrim the plane.

Often all it takes to correct the thrust line is a couple of washers placed behind the top two bolts on a radial engine mount or under the two back engine mounting lugs. If the nose is cowled and adding down thrust will cause a major rework of the nose, the student will have to be taught to add some up trim (or hold a lot of back stick) during low approaches and landings.

Wind Effects Demonstration

For this demonstration you'll need a windy day. You can show your student what will happen even if it is calm, but a good wind makes the demonstration very graphic. The first thing to show the student is an upwind and a downwind pass. Explain to him that the airspeed is the same and what he is seeing is the ground speed (which is the airspeed plus or minus the speed of the wind). A full throttle pass shows up the speed differential, but it is important that he also understand the effect at low throttle.

Reduce power to where the plane will just hold level flight and fly into the wind. Have the student notice how very slowly the plane is going and also show him how sloppy the controls are. Now turn the plane to a downwind heading and emphasize that you haven't touched the throttle. Point out that even though the plane is faster, the controls are still sloppy because the airspeed is the same.

Next, try to slow down to the same ground speed you had when you were going into the wind. The plane will probably stall. Point out to the student that he must be very careful on windy days not to be fooled into too slow an airspeed while going downwind. This is especially true in the landing pattern.

The next wind effect demonstration should be tracking in a crosswind. Set the plane up so that it is coming toward you with a crosswind. Adjust the crab angle so the plane tracks toward you and point out to the student how the plane is angled off one way (into the wind), but is flying another direction. He might need to use this later in figure 8s and low approaches.

TURNS

The most important maneuver of the familiarization phase is the turn. The others, when the student practices them, show him how his plane reacts to certain changes or in certain situations. The turn is something he must do, not in certain situations only, but every time he flies.

The key to teaching a turn is to emphasize and demonstrate every plane, R/C or full-scale, does not turn like a boat or a car. It has to bank. You should show him that the roll control stick (aileron stick) is essentially a rate control. The more you move the stick, the faster the plane banks. A very small stick displacement gives a very slow roll into the bank, while a large stick displacement gives a very fast roll in (or roll out). Also point out that the rolling motion stops when he releases the stick.

Set the plane up in level flight with medium power and demonstrate a bank. Do not use any up elevator. This shows how the nose drops as vertical lift is lost. Next, show him a correct turn, setting the bank first, then using up elevator to hold altitude. As you did before, have him watch the plane the first time, then your use of the control sticks. Push the aileron to establish a bank, release, then add up elevator.

The roll out is next and this is where he starts to learn how to fly toward himself. As you demonstrate a roll out, tell him to watch the wings of the plane. The first roll out should be with the plane going away so that the controls are directional. The right stick gives a right roll (of course it always does, but when the plane is coming toward you, right stick gives an *apparent* left roll or non-directional steering). Suppose the plane is in a left bank. Tell the student, "The right wing of the plane is *high*. I move the stick to the right to lower it." He will probably catch on to this very quickly as it is similar to steering any other vehicle. You are in a left turn and you want to go straight, so you turn or move the steering device, wheel, stick or whatever, to the right.

Next comes the demonstration of a roll out with the plane coming toward you (the hard one). As the plane comes around the turn toward you, point out that one wing is low and the other is high. Tell him not to think of a right or left wing, but to look for which side of the fuselage the low wing appears on. You might have to circle two or three times for him to see this.

Most students will try to figure out which wing is low when what you really want them to do is to look at the plane and recognize which side the low wing is on. Tell him that to roll out he moves the stick toward the same side the low wing is on. He doesn't even have to think left or right. *He should just look from the nose to the low wing and move the stick that direction*. Another way for him to remember is to tell him to *prop up the low wing with the stick*.

Telling your students to steer backwards is not a good idea. This requires him to think of the directional way to steer and then reverse it. It takes too long and requires extra concentration when he should be learning to roll out correctly by instinct.

STUDENT PRACTICE

Up to this point, you have demonstrated several items and have probably let the student try most or all of them. The main thing he needs to practice in this phase is the turn. With the turn he can learn to place his plane where he wants it. When he can do this, he is ready for figure 8s.

When the student first begins to practice, you will need to stand by his left side and hold on to the upper corner of his transmitter with your left hand. Keep your right hand poised to take over when he gets into trouble. If you are left-handed, like I am, you would modify your position to keep your left hand free to take control.

As the student practices turns, do not overdo the instruction. He still will not be able to listen to you and concentrate on the plane at the same time. When he gets to the roll out point, a quick, "directional," or "stick to the low wing," as appropriate, will do fine.

Errors

There are several errors that can be made in turns. The most prevalent is overcontrolling. This just takes experience to overcome or slower ailerons. Students who overcontrol excessively and have a hard time overcoming it are probably going to be slow learners. They are usually nervous types and you can look for them to make big mistakes when they get near the ground in other phases. Be extra cautious with them.

Another error is using the wrong amount of elevator—either too much or too little. Too much gives a climbing turn, while too little—or forgetting the elevator completely—gives a dive. Do no expect a level turn too soon. The fact that he remembers the elevator and does not stall out or get into a spiral is pretty good at first. It just takes time to learn the sequence and the timing of the inputs needed to make a good, level turn.

Of course, the error everyone makes is using the wrong aileron to roll out with the plane flying toward the pilot. Teach the student to put the stick to the low wing. If his hand went the wrong way and the bank increases, he should immediately release the aileron and move it the other way to correct. You should be ready to instantly take over if he gets the plane in too bad a situation.

INSTRUCTOR TECHNIQUES

Several teaching techniques have already been mentioned in this section, and in previous chapters, but a review of some specifics is in order.

Feedback

Give the student instant feedback on his progress. Do it with everything he does. This can not be emphasized too much. Tell him something with every move of the stick. "Good," "OK," "Wrong way," are good examples. This is especially true at first when he has no basis for judging his own progress. If he makes small errors, a quick word is an adequate correction.

On the other hand, when he makes a large error, it usually means that he does not understand the maneuver. Take control, explain it again and demonstrate. Do not ever try to make a large explanation or explain aerodynamics to him while he is flying. It will go "in one ear and out the other." If it is important enough to talk about in detail, it is important enough to deserve his undivided attention.

Saturation

Always, but especially at first, look out for saturation. When the student really begins to make mistakes, he has had enough for a while. Saturation can be hard to catch if you haven't looked for it before. If you ever get the feeling that the student is trying too hard, that's it. Generally, if he has flown pretty well for a while, and then regresses, he is getting to his saturation point.

You might notice that if you fly on weekends only, his saturation point comes quicker on Saturday than on Sunday. The whole key is to let him learn at his own rate and don't let him overdo it. Most of the crashes I've seen students make came after they should no longer have been flying. They were tense and they were overcontrolling the planes.

HELICOPTER FAMILIARIZATION

Teaching helicopter flying is an altogether different process from teaching the flight of a conventional R/C plane. While the student with the conventional plane learns his flying high up in the air at first, the helicopter student starts out down low and then progresses later to higher flying. A helicopter student is taught to rise to a low altitude, a few inches to a foot, then let back down to the ground. Only when he can hover will he be taught to fly at a higher altitude.

Learning to hover is a difficult task that can be likened to balancing two marbles—one on top of the other. During a hover, the helicopter is actually sitting on top of a bubble of air. It is inherently *unstable* during this time and you must make continual control inputs to correct for the helicopter's movement. How different this is from a conventional plane that is inherently stable and will fly itself "hands off" for some time.

Only an expert R/C helicopter flier should attempt to teach R/C helicopter flight. It helps considerably if the student knows how to fly a conventional plane. Except for the throttle, most of the stick movements produce the same result in either type aircraft.

Figure-8s

The figure 8 phase is the key phase to learning to fly R/C. This is where the student learns how to fly toward himself and learns it well enough to do it without thinking about it first. He must steer toward himself instinctively before he can be allowed to get the plane near the ground. To take him low sooner than this would be courting disaster.

This important phase is also very repetitious, and it is hence boring at times. When your student begins to get tired of the repetition and practice you can teach him some simple, easy acrobatics. One of the later chapters describes four acrobatic maneuvers, the loop, aileron roll, split-S, and immelmann, that can be performed with most trainers. These will not only break up the repetition, but are also instructive in other ways. Besides, he will like them.

At sometime during this phase you should also teach him to takeoff. The takeoff, a maneuver which seems very important to the layman, is usually an afterthought in R/C instruction. The reason is that it is easy. Present-day trainers, with high-lift wings, tricycle landing gear and excess power make getting into the air a snap.

Takeoffs with low power, conventional gear (tail dragger) planes can be a real challenge. You must carefully apply power and watch for the imminent noseover if you use the throttle too quickly. You have to steer by using rudder to counteract the change in engine torque with power change. Once the tail wheel is off the ground, you steer until the plane reaches lift off speed. Then ease in some up elevator for takeoff.

Constrast this with the takeoff of a tricycle gear trainer. The student lines up with the runway, adds full power, makes one or two small corrections, then pulls in some up elevator and is airborne. It is just so much easier with modern, powerful tricycle gear trainers.

Do not rush the figure 8 phase. There is a lot to learn and a lot of practice needed. Let him go at his own pace. Make sure he is competent before you transition to low approaches.

LEARNING OUTCOMES

The student should learn several things from the figure 8 maneuver. First and foremost, he will learn to steer and fly toward himself from both his right and his left. This is an absolute necessity in R/C flying if you aren't going to fly in a continuous circle around yourself. Flying toward yourself is not only important because you have to bring the plane back once you have flown it out some distance, it is necessary for landing.

One of the most important factors in landing is judging and adjusting the sink ratio before you touch down. You can do this best when the plane is right out in front of you, so most of us land there. This landing location dictates that you must fly toward yourself on final approach to get the plane to the landing position. And you must do it from either side, depending on wind direction.

The next things the student learns from figure 8s are precision left and right turns. This means a couple of things. He must learn to estimate the bank angle necessary to fly his plane from its location to a point over the runway. If he is displaced too far out from the runway, he must decide to make two turns with a short crosswind leg in between. He will have to learn to compensate for wind, either blowing him away from or toward the runway, during the turn or turns. He must know all of this from either a right or a left turn.

From the figure 8 the student will learn to judge his roll out so that his plane is aligned with the runway. This learning outcome is coupled to, but not quite the same as the previous one. Just because he can place the plane over the runway in a turn doesn't necessarily mean that he has mastered how to roll out coming toward himself in line with the runway. He will tend to turn too much or too little at first and will need practice to actually be able to roll out correctly.

The last thing the student should learn in this phase is how to make a good, safe takeoff. He should be able to taxi out, having started his own engine of course, line up, takeoff and steer generally down the center of the runway. He should also be able to do this from his left or right side.

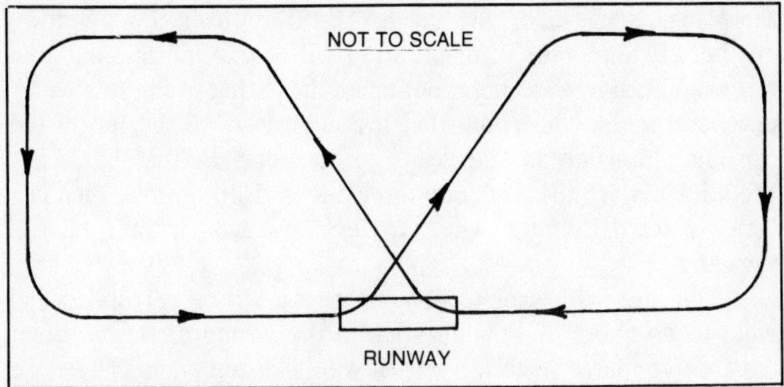

Fig. 10-1. The figure 8 maneuver.

INSTRUCTOR DEMONSTRATION

Look at the figure 8 shown in Fig. 10-1. You need to emphasize the points I stressed. Don't feel that you can show your student this illustration and expect him to be able to do a figure 8. You will probably have to demonstrate it several times before he can get it down. Remember, at first he will be working hard just trying to keep the plane somewhere near the runway and won't be able to concentrate on the actual maneuver.

The first main part of the figure 8 is a leg parallel to the runway. Point out that if he is too close, his turn will have to be very steep or he will overshoot. If he is too far out, he might lose orientation in the turn or have to make an excessively long crosswind leg.

The second part of the maneuver is a turn, or two turns, toward the runway. This is followed by a roll out in line with the runway. Point out where the second of the two turns should be started and how much bank must be used to put his roll out in line with the runway. If he is going to use one large turn, show him how little bank it will take and also how to vary or "play" the bank to get the roll out in the right place. A "stick toward the low wing" reminder might also be necessary here. Emphasize that he should not just roll the plane into a bank and hope it makes it around in line with the runway. He must continually make small changes and corrections to fly the plane where he wants it to go. If the wind is blowing, explain how he should compensate for it.

After you have rolled out and the plane is coming toward you, demonstrate some steering corrections. This might take a few reruns because by the time you make much of an explanation the plane will be over your head. Throttling back to slow down can help extend your demonstration. Of course, do this one into the wind. You need to point out again the "stick to the low wing" procedure. Also show him that if the plane is to the left of the runway centerline and he wants to correct back, he should put the stick toward the direction the plane is drifting, left, then use "stick toward the low wing" to level the wings after he has turned.

You also will want to demonstrate a wrong correction and what to do about it. Put the stick in the wrong direction, point out that you have gone the wrong way and immediately reverse the stick. Use more deflection than you did at first. It can go something like this: "Notice that the plane is going over to the left and we want to correct back. Suppose I correct the wrong way. What would I do? Watch the plane. Oops, wrong way. I immediately reverse the stick. See how the plane corrects now?" Make sure the student understands this and hammer it in during practice.

When the plane approaches close enough so that you are looking up about 45 degrees, it is time to turn away from the runway. You might want to go ahead and fly straight overhead once just to show him what a difficult position it puts him in. It is extremely hard to judge the plane's pitch and bank attitude, as well as the altitude, when it's straight overhead. Also, tell him that as it passes he will be looking up and turning around. Doing this can induce disorientation and cause some people to lose their balance. When all is said and done, it's better to make it a rule never to fly overhead—turn off first.

After you turn from the runway heading, fly out to the same displacement from the runway as you did for the other leg, turn parallel to it, and demonstrate the turn to final from the other end of the runway. Explain to him that the figure 8 is the most efficient way for him to practice turns to runway heading from both directions as well as flying toward himself.

One more thing you need to demonstrate, or actually to point out, is the appearance of altitude change with the change in the distance that the plane is from you. Take the plane out a considerable distance, then turn and fly down the runway toward yourself. Tell the student to watch the plane and see if it doesn't appear to be climbing as it gets closer. You should be maintaining altitude, of course. Now do the reverse. Fly at a constant altitude going away and have him notice that the plane appears to be in a shallow descent. This realization will be very imporant to him as he begins to fly down the runway during his practice flights.

After you demonstrate figure 8s on one or two flights, show him a takeoff. It's best to do it this way to avoid giving him too much to assimilate on any one flight. When he understands the figure 8 and is doing most of the flying during his flights, show him a take off or two and then let him try it.

Demonstrate the taxi out and show him how you line up with the runway. The student will be steering toward himself for part of the takeoff roll. In the case of a student learning with a two-stick transmitter, this will be done with his non-dominant hand. You need to show him a takeoff that is slightly different from your usual one. For the first part of the takeoff roll, as shown in Fig. 10-2, you only use partial power (about one half throttle).

Once the plane passes in front of you and the steering becomes directional, add throttle up to full power and steer until you have takeoff speed. See Fig. 10-2 again. As you are steering, hold a little up elevator and at takeoff speed the plane will lift off. Tell the student that he should climb straight ahead until he is at a good, safe height before he attempts a turn.

This takeoff scenario is set up this way for several reasons. You could have him stand behind the plane at the end of the runway so he will have only directional steering to worry about. This works fine for the first few takeoffs, but only if you have the luxury of flying when no one else is flying and you can safely stand out at the end of the runway. You will eventually have to let him learn a takeoff standing at the site of the runway. Doing

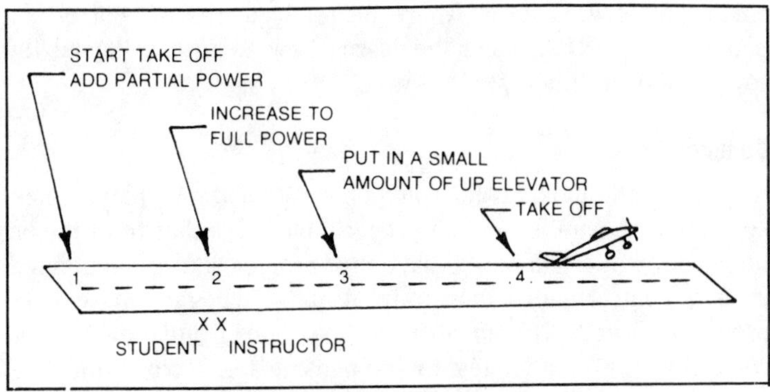

Fig. 10-2. Power application during beginning takeoff.

it this way to start with eliminates his having to learn two takeoff methods.

The slower, first part of the takeoff roll, the portion before the plane gets to a point directly opposite to where he is standing, makes it easier for him to steer and make corrections. This is especially true for two-stick fliers. The single-stickers won't have much trouble because they use their "good" hand for steering on the ground. The slower speed also means that smaller corrections will be needed or that he will be able to notice the need for a correction before the plane gets too far off the centerline.

Stress the straight ahead climb to a safe altitude. He'll be nervous and you don't want him slapping the stick around (overcontrolling) until he is good and high. It will give him a chance to relax a moment, collect his wits and think about the next thing he has to do—make a turn. Once he is airborne, safe and headed to the flying area, have him set up for some more figure 8 practice.

STUDENT PRACTICE

After you demonstrate, give the student the plane and talk him through the first couple of figure 8s. These should be at a very safe altitude (at least a couple of mistakes high). He should be high enough so that he can make a mistake, then make another mistake trying to correct the first one, and still be high enough for you to take control, yank in full up (or whatever is needed) and comfortably clear the ground. You can expect him to be very sloppy at first. You might not get a recognizable figure 8 and you might have to demonstrate several times. He will need a number of flights of figure 8 practice before he is proficient. Keep him at it. This is where he really learns to control his plane and fly R/C. When he learns how to turn well and fly toward himself, the rest is easy.

Common Errors

Be on the look out for common errors and give him a quick correction. A parallel leg not properly placed, either too wide or too close, will cause him to have turn problems. You might have to take control and demonstrate again so that he can see the proper position. He can also get into a bad situation by not relocating the parallel leg to compensate for a crosswind. He should locate farther out if the wind is blowing the plane toward the runway. Locate closer if the wind is blowing the plane away from the runway or fly a longer crosswind leg.

Another common error is using a constant turn rate. For example, 30 degrees of bank no matter where the plane comes out. This is caused purely by lack of experience and practice. He is still trying to make a turn and is not yet able to handle the additional chore of varying the turn to place the plane where he wants it. You might use phrases like: "Don't let the plane fly you, you fly it," and "Make the plane go where you want it to go." These will remind him to try to place the plane in line with the runway.

On the subject of making mistakes, always tell the student that you expect him to make mistakes. Errors are a part of learning. When he corrects for the error, he learns that it was a wrong control or decision so that the next time he will have a greater probability of doing it properly.

Do not under any circumstances reinforce his errors. If you tell him to turn right and fly to the south, for instance, and he starts a turn to the left, don't let him complete it. Have him reverse the controls and turn right, even if it puts the plane in a poor location for the next maneuver. Letting him complete the left turn reinforces the wrong response and will greatly slow his progress. He will be sloppy at first, seesawing the controls back and forth to compensate for wrong inputs, but he will be learning and learning rapidly.

Another error found in this phase is the same turn error you probably saw in the familiarization phase—improper altitude control in the turn. There is either too much up elevator for the bank, resulting in a climb, or too little—giving a dive. Tell your student that when he puts in the up elevator he should look specifically at the *nose* of the plane. He should look at the nose and judge accordingly. Nose up, release some up elevator; nose down, pull in some more up.

The turn is not the only place where he can have altitude problems. You will recall the demonstration of the appearance of climbing when the plane is coming toward you. Most students have a tendency to keep the plane in an attitude that *looks* level to them. They erroneously think that doing this will keep the plane level. This attitude that looks level to them, however, is usually a shallow dive. It seems to the student that if the plane appears to be climbing coming toward him, then nudging in a little down elevator will level it. This is fine until he buzzes over your head at low altitude.

The only correction for this error is a reminder not to dive (or a reminder to climb if he's begun descend) and lots of experience. Generally speaking, as the plane flies toward the student he should see some of the bottom of the plane at first and more and more of it as the plane gets closer. If he sees only a head on view, then the plane is coming straight at him. Directly, as in aimed at him in a dive. This is a very common error, so expect it and don't be too worried about it.

Low Figure 8 Practice

As the student gets better on his steering and no longer makes the big error (the one that would get him inverted) you can have him lower the altitude. You should have him practice at a lower and lower altitude until he is at the altitude that he will fly the traffic pattern for his low approaches. Go step by step and let him get comfortable at each slightly lower altitude before you take him lower.

When he first starts flying lower, look for some of his old errors to crop up again. This is normal and will always occur during his stress situations like flying closer to the ground. He will, however, quickly overcome this regression and be ready for even lower altitude practice.

INSTRUCTOR TECHNIQUES

I cannot stress too much going at the student's rate. Pushing him quickly through figure 8s is a common failure of many instructors. It only causes problems and perhaps a crash later on when the student gets closer to the ground. Granted, it is not very exciting for the instructor to watch figure 8 practice, but it is the meat of learning to fly R/C. You might break up the monotony with acrobatics, but do not rush the learning process.

Feedback

Be sure you are continuing to give the student feedback on a regular basis. With every maneuver—turn, roll out, correction, etc.—give him a pat on the head or a correction. Don't just sit back silently and let him practice. There will be a tendency to do this, but you must give immediate feedback and correction if he is to learn rapidly.

Remember not to overdo the correction when he is flying the plane. Just a quick word is all he can absorb. Examples are:

"good," "you overshot," "you're diving," "you turned too close." These are quick and easy and give the student an instant grade on his performance so that he can try for the same quality on his next try or strive to upgrade it. Also, if he does need a longer correction or explanation, you should take control of the plane while you make it. Give him a chance to listen to you without worrying about flying the plane.

The Preflight Briefing

You should continue to give a preflight briefing before each flight during the figure 8 phase. This should be done to set a tangible goal for the student which will give him something to try for on that particular flight. The goal might be very simple, like practicing rolling out of the turn in line with the runway, or more complex, perhaps a low altitude figure 8 with a smooth, constant altitude throughout the maneuver. Tell him what you want him to practice, what you expect and introduce anything new you want to have him learn at this time.

Another important part of the preflight briefing is the progress review. A progress review is a means of letting the student, who often can't judge how well he's doing, know how the instructor feels about his progress. It can be brief. An example might go something like this: "Last flight you practiced figure 8s. Your set up downwind was good, but your turns tended to be too tight and you usually undershot the runway. This time I want you to really concentrate on the turn rate. Vary the bank, move the stick. Don't worry about making it look pretty, fly the plane around in line with the runway. Try a shallower bank to start with, then steepen it toward the end, if necessary. Your steering down the runway has been good. Keep it up. And remember, stick toward the low wing."

Another progress review you should give the student is a review after his last flight of the day and especially if it is the last flight of the weekend. Your student will no doubt be doing some ground flying or thinking his way through the maneuvers at home. A review of what he needs to work on will give some direction to his thoughts. Ground flying can be especially helpful when he is trying to learn to fly toward himself and steer backwards.

While I'm on the topic of ground flying, one technique that the student can use to help in this is steering on the ground with the aileron stick. I recommend this only in extreme cases because there can be a bad side effect. For cases where the student is having a real, persistent problem learning to steer, he can practice at home with a quick mod. Have him plug the servo connector from the rudder-nosewheel steering servo into the aileron connector on the receiver. This allows him to control the nosewheel with the aileron stick. He can now taxi to the end of his driveway or a good way out in a shopping center parking lot turn and taxi toward himself. He should imagine that the plane is flying and that he is trying to steer it down the runway centerline.

You can already see the bad side effect. He is practicing steering on the ground with the wrong control. This is about the same as practicing a mistake. In an extreme case, I have had this technique work and the benefits more than outweighed the wrong taxi practice. For a three-channel plane, of course, you won't have to change the servo connections because the plane doesn't have ailerons. And there won't be any control differences in taxiing.

Saturation

You might not think that the student can get saturated at this stage, but he can. Actually, any time he is learning new and complex material he can get saturated and need a break. This is especially true with those students who showed an early grasp of R/C flight during the familiarization phase and progressed to figure 8s after only a few flights. Common symptoms are overcontrolling late in the flight or making an error on something he has gotten right several times before. Again, this occurs late in the flight or after several flights in a day.

Your student's next phase of training will be low approaches. After he is fully proficient in figure 8s at traffic pattern altitude, and you are confident that he won't make any gross errors, you can move him on to this next important phase.

Low Approaches

Many instructors rush the student into landing without teaching them a proper low approach and go around. Flight instructors would shrink in horror at the thought of allowing the student to bounce a real plane on the ground from his first approach. This, however, all too common in R/C flying. What many R/C instructors don't remember is that the key to a good landing is a good approach. If the student can make a good approach to within a couple of feet of the ground, he can easily make a good touchdown. The solution to the problem of teaching the student to land is to *not* stress the touchdown, but to stress very much the approach. You must emphasize at first that he will learn a low approach and a go around. In the next phase, he will learn to land from a good approach and still go around from a poor one.

There are some differences in this phase that the instructor should stress. One is that the student will be flying the plane near the ground for the first time. This will be scary for him at first because by now he realizes his flying limitations and knows that he is capable of a wrong move that will spell disaster.

The second difference is that a new control is used; the throttle. The addition of the throttle to the scenario means that his other hand—the left for right handed people—must be used. It doesn't seem like much, but for many people it can be trying until they learn. Compare it to learning to drive a clutch car and shift gears. When you were first learning, you had trouble synchronizing your foot with your hand in the shifting.

The use of the throttle, or more specifically a reduction in power, also means that the plane will descend and the student must control the descent rate. Unlike the earlier phases in which the student made the turn and generally tried to maintain level flight, now he must make a turn while controlling the descent to place the plane at a certain altitude. All of these make this a difficult phase.

LEARNING OUTCOMES

The major learning goals of this phase are to become proficient in low approaches and go arounds. This statement, however, does not adequately cover what the student will really gain during the low approach phase. What the student has to learn is not so much individual maneuvers, but the integration of several small tasks into a series action—a low approach and go around. Specifically, he must learn to fly to a point at a certain altitude and judge the wing placement. He must then reduce power an appropriate amount, turn, judge the turn to place the plane in line with the runway taking into consideration the wind again (hopefully he has learned this during figure 8s), then roll out in line with the runway.

During the turn he must control the descent rate to end up at a certain altitude. Next, he must steer towards himself while adjusting the plane's descent rate with the elevator and power, if necessary, still compensating for the wind. He must watch the speed of the plane and "play" the power to keep the plane from getting too slow and stalling as he flies down the runway. All of this is just to bring the plane to the end of the runway at a very low altitude. Then he must add power, pull up, and complete the go around.

You are probably thinking that an approach isn't that hard. It isn't, really, once you know how to do it. Think of the first time you tried to parallel park a car compared to how easily you do it now. Go back and read over the items you have to do during a low approach. You'll find that you do every one of them every time you land. There are a lot of them to incorporate and that is why the student will be awkward at first.

INSTRUCTOR DEMONSTRATION

Prior to any flight demonstration, you should thoroughly brief the student. This is particularly true for the low approach and go around because it is a long maneuver with many parts and not very many spaces for explanation. Show him Fig. 11-1 and explain it. You'll first want to show him a simple low approach and go around. You might even want to call it a high approach. It is essentially a figure 8 with a power reduction, then a power addition for the go around.

Show the student the correct altitude and displacement from the runway to fly his plane downwind. Point out the location of the turn point. You might mention that this turn point is for the specific wind you have today and that you will brief him on how to compensate for other winds. At the turn point, reduce to about half power, turn, and let the plane descend. At this time you are only trying to get the student accustomed to using the extra control, the throttle, and to fly a descending turn. As you descend, allow the airspeed to bleed off so that you can maintain a safe height while flying toward yourself. Remind him that he will be steering just as he did in figure 8s, but that the control response might be slower due to the lower airspeed.

When the plane gets nearly even with where you are standing, you should demonstrate a go around. Smoothly add power and raise the nose. Caution him about slamming the power in. On some planes, especially the higher powered ones, it can cause a torque roll, placing him in a very bad situation. This point, with the power applied and the nose up, is where many students try to steer and make a mistake.

This is a point of high stress, especially after a poor approach, and invariably the point where regression and incorrect steering occur. Tell him not to steer. Demonstrate this by letting the plane's natural stability work. Say to him, "I have added power and raised the nose. Now I just hold everything and let the plane fly." Tell him to pause, take a deep breath, and wait until the plane is past him and the steering is directional again before making any large corrections. He can, of course, make minor, stick-to-the-low-wing type corrections, but he should avoid any large inputs unless the safety of people or the

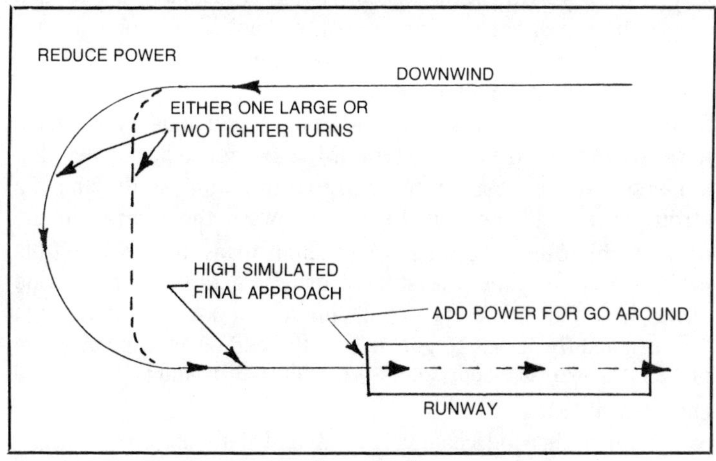

Fig. 11-1. Initial low approach and go around.

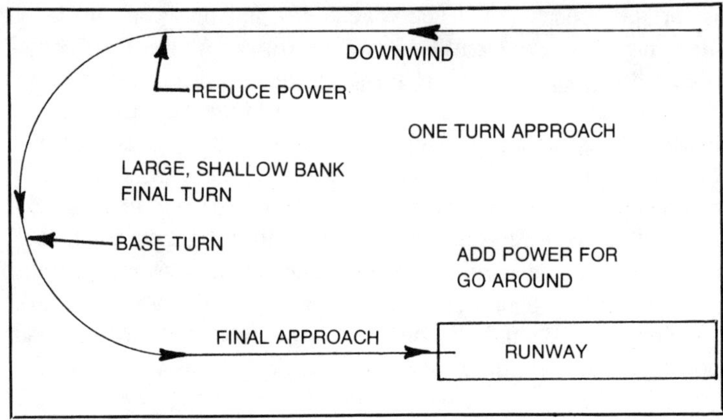

Fig. 11-2. Landing approach patterns.

plane is involved. You will, of course, be standing right next to him and give him instructions in a low, calm voice.

After the student has the simple low approach pretty well mastered, you'll have to demonstrate a true low approach and go around. This demonstration should include a reduction of power to bring the plane to final approach speed and then a demonstration of how to modulate the power to get the plane to the end of the runway. You should also demonstrate again the go around from this low approach.

During this demonstration, you need to think about whether you will teach a one-turn or a two-turn approach. See Figs. 11-2 and 11-3 for what I mean. Essentially, it is maneuvering to final approach with either one large, shallow banked turn or with two 90-degree turns with a base leg in between.

The student might have had exposure to both during the figure 8 phase, because the different crosswinds might have necessitated the use of each type. My experience has shown that students have an easier time with two turns unless they have a strong crosswind blowing the plane toward the runway in the turn. In this case, one-turn is just about mandatory. During his early low approaches, the student usually sets up on downwind pretty wide out, so he ends up having to roll out halfway through the turn and fly across to get over to the end of the runway. This makes it a two-turn approach, so I don't fight it and just go ahead and teach it that way.

With each wind change, you should demonstrate the maneuver. A very strong headwind will require an early turn point and more power on final apporach. This situation might cause the student to have to go around, but the crosswind is what usually causes crashes. There are two crosswind situations and each one creates its own special problems.

A crosswind blowing the plane away from the student, that is, one that blows on your back as you face the runway, causes a headwind on the base leg of the turn to final. In effect, the wind tried to blow the plane back and keep it from getting to the runway. When you demonstrate a low approach from this type of crosswind, set up close to the runway, turn, then add power as necessary while the plane comes around into the wind on the base leg. Reduce the power as the plane approaches runway heading and angle, or crab down final as you did during a figure 8 in a crosswind.

The crosswind blowing the plane toward the student is the more dangerous one. This situation normally calls for a one-turn approach unless you set up extremely wide. Bear in mind that I am referring to strong crosswinds. This type of wind causes overshoots and the steeper turn used to compensate for it can lead to a stall and snap roll. Without the steep turn, the plane will overhsoot and end up flying over or behind the pits. This is a definite safety hazard.

For your demonstration of a low approach with a wind blowing the plane toward the runway, set up wide or displaced a large distance out from the runway. Reduce power to idle and roll into a steep bank. After you pass the halfway point in the turn, start reducing the bank. Play it against the wind drift to

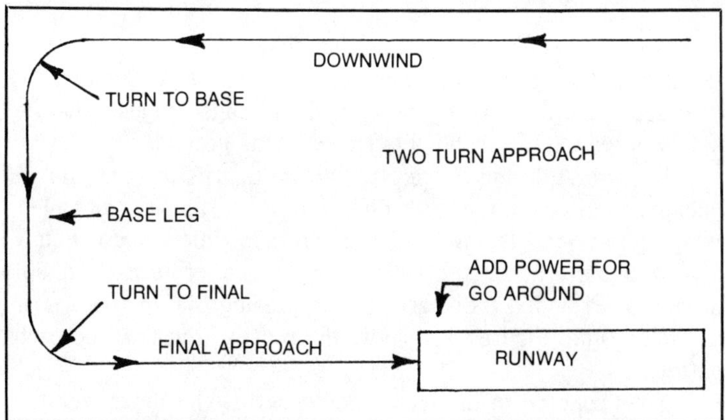

Fig. 11-3. Landing approach patterns.

roll out in line with the runway. Compensate for the crosswind on final as well.

You can see that this phase will take many demonstrations. Take your student step by step through the low approach and go around. You'll have to catch the wind demonstrations as you can when the wind is right. If there is no other activity at your field, you might be able to demonstrate one type of crosswind approach from one side of the runway, then go to the other side of the runway and demonstrate an approach with the opposite crosswind.

STUDENT PRACTICE

You should break up the student's practice into two parts. Let him first learn the simple approach, then progress him to the one like an actual landing approach as he gets used to operating near the ground.

Early Practice

His early practice will be on the simple low approach. The first of these can be like a figure 8 with a single power reduction. You will have to talk him through the first several tries. Be sure that you talk him through the go arounds as this will be his most panicky time. Remember he should:

—Add power.
—Raise the nose.
—Hold everything and let the plane fly.
—Pause, take a deep breath, and wait until the plane flies past him.
—Begin making steering corrections.

It will also be a good idea to give him a reminder while he is on final approach. A "stick to the low wing," might be just what he needs to remind him as he gets closer to the ground.

Be careful during this early practice that he does not do all his approaches from the same direction. For example, from a left turn. If the wind is low, you can do a modified figure 8 low approach pattern for practicing both types of turns and approaches. Provided there aren't others using the approaches at the same time. Figure 11-4 shows the route of this low approach pattern.

Your concern in this area should be that he never gets so used to practicing all his approaches from one direction or the other. Later, when he's flying by himself and is confronted with

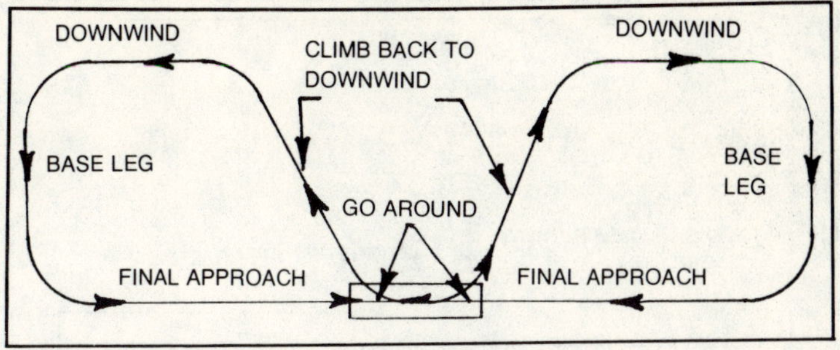

Fig. 11-4. Figure 8 style low approach practice pattern.

a different wind, he would probably get confused and crash the plane.

In some parts of the country where the fields are crowded and the wind stays from the same direction most of the time, it will be hard to find a time to demonstrate and let the student practice from both directions. In an area like this, try to find a time when the wind is low—usually in the evening just before dark—and let the student practice low approaches using the other turn direction even if you have to accept a slight tail wind on final approach.

Advanced Practice

When the student can perform the simple low approach and go around adequately, have him begin to reduce the power more and more until his speed is approaching a good final approach speed. This point comes when he can steer toward himself well and control the descent enough to divert part of his attention to throttle control. You will have to demonstrate and talk him through the power changes. Watch for regression as he concentrates on power control to the exclusion of steering and descent rate control. You will probably want to start these high and gradually work him lower and lower until he approaches the end of the runway.

Do not forget the go around during this advanced practice. As he can handle it, allow him to make very small steering corrections during the go around. If he shows regression, however, go back to the "hold what you have and let her fly" type of go around.

Common Errors

Because there are many parts to a low approach and go around, there are many errors. Many of these are the same ones

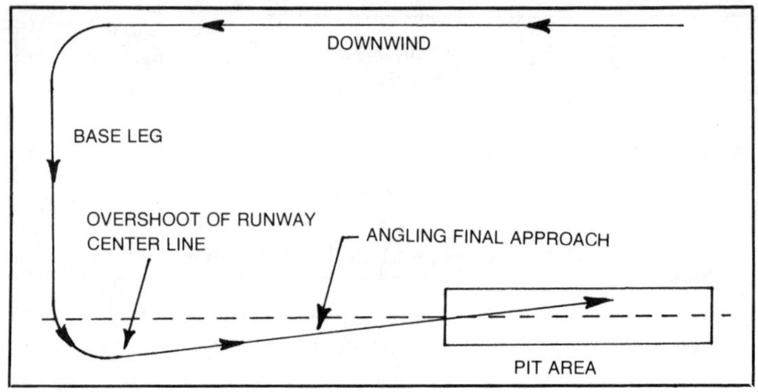

Fig. 11-5. Overshoot of runway.

that you will have seen in earlier phases. I will start from the first part of the maneuver, go completely through it and note the errors.

An improper set up on down wind is the first major error. The student's altitude or his displacement can be wrong. If there is a crosswind, he might be using the normal displacement. This might be too close or too far. It depends on the wind direction. This calls for you to take the plane and demonstrate the correct location. If he is fairly proficient and just has not seen a certain crosswind, all that might be needed is to tell him of the proper location of the down wind leg.

Next, he can have improper altitude control in the turn. His turn to final should be a shallow descent. You might see climbing turns with the plane losing airspeed and approaching a stall and also a diving turn where the student has just rolled into the turn without any backstick. Have him watch the nose of the plane and use the elevator stick to control the descent rate.

A third error is a wrong turn rate. I mentioned this in the figure 8 phase, but without going into the consequences. A turn too shallow or delaying the second turn (the one that lines him up with the runway), will cause an overshoot. This is not too great a concern unless the overshoot is considerable.

Take a look at Fig. 11-5 and I will explain. After an overshoot the student will invariably line the plane up with the end of the runway. This puts the flight path away from the pit area—a safe direction. There is also another factor to be considered. The student knows he is close to the unsafe area—the pits. This causes him to be overly cautious and prone to go around. Contrast this situation with an undershoot condition.

When the student makes his final turn too tight, all too common at first, he will undershoot the runway centerline and have an angling final (Fig. 11-6). In this case, the student feels, in his own mind, that he can still correct for his error. This is where the trouble starts. Look at the final approach in Fig. 11-6. It is aimed straight at the student, his instructor and the pit area where other fliers and spectators will be. With a student in control who might at any time make a wrong input, you have a real safety hazard. This situation calls for a go around and a new set up along with an explanation by the instructor (take control for this one) on turn rate and line up on final.

If the safety problem weren't enough, look at what the student would have to do to correct an undershot approach. Suppose he flies his plane on the angling final approach to the end of the runway. This is point A in Fig. 11-5. Now he has to make a turn in the correct direction to line up with the runway. Add to this the fact that the turn is usually at a very low altitude, a place of high stress for the student, and therefore a place where he is likely to make a mistake.

Here he is, the plane is coming straight at him, he is controlling descent, he is low, and he has to try and make a turn. It's too much for a novice. There is no use in having him try to recover from this type of approach. This teaches him that he can make a poor approach and survive it rather than that he should go around and set up a good one. During the landing phase, this type of approach will result in scraped wing tips, bent nose gear, cartwheels and worse. Have him go around.

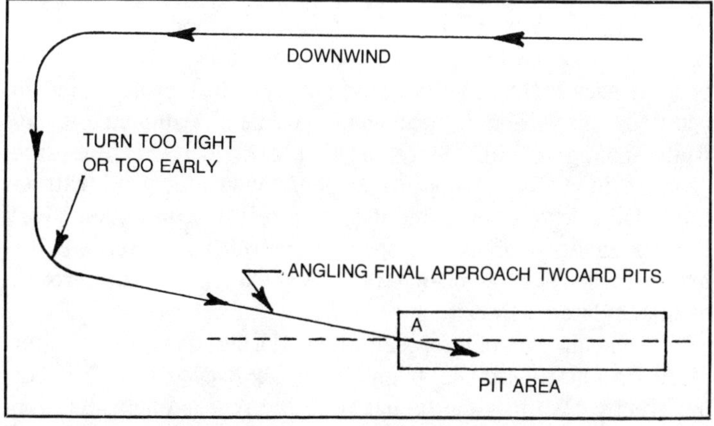

Fig. 11-6. Undershoot of runway and angling final approach.

Fig. 11-7. Using the wing-stab gap to fix the plane's attitude on final approach. A large gap indicates very nose-high attitude.

INSTRUCTOR TECHNIQUES

The main instructor techniques, feedback and reinforcement, saturation, and error correction, have been detailed several times so I will only touch on them briefly. The key item to remember when instructing this phase is that the low approach is a very complex maneuver. There is a myriad of things for the student to integrate: position, altitude, wind, turn rate, descent rate, steering direction, and others. Do not rush him and do not thing he will gain proficiency faster if he gets a few on the ground no matter how bad they look. Stick to the low approach and go around until he has mastered them. Go at his rate and not yours. Advance him on his proficiency and not on how many flights he has. Forcing him to land before he is ready will only delay him while he rebuilds his plane.

Continue with your preflight briefings and the progress checks. As stated before, these give the student an accessable goal for each flight and a gauge of how well he's progressing. In addition, you will often uncover the source of a student's errors while talking to him before or after a flight. Sometimes the problem might be a simple misunderstanding of your instructions. Other times you'll find it to be a real misconception about the maneuver or about the specific control inputs needed. It's better to discover a misunderstanding like this on the ground instead of later in the air.

Keep an eye out for saturation during this phase. After three or four flights he might begin to overcontrol or steer incorrectly. At this time he has probably reached his saturation point and is ready to stop for the day. Be careful about overdoing

Fig. 11-8. A small gap indicates close to the proper angle.

it in this phase, because he is down low and he can get into a situation in which the plane is too low for you to take over and recover.

Continue to give the student regular and immediate feedback as you have in the past. This reinforces his flying and points out his errors so that he can try to correct them on his next maneuver. Remember, and this is important because the low approach and go around are so complex, take control for a long correction and use demonstration if there is any question in his mind.

In the area of teaching hints, there is one that can be used if the student has trouble flying a final approach. This is not usually the case, but you will run into it if you instruct long enough. The problem is not being able to judge and maintain a fairly constant sink rate from roll out on final to the end of the runway.

Fig. 11-9. A Stabalizer hidden by the wing indicates nose-low attitude.

In this case, what the student lacks is a good mental picture of what the plane should look like in the proper descent. If you do run across this, you might find that it is the same student that displayed the minor perceptual difficulties which were covered in an earlier chapter.

What you will need to do to cure his problem is to give him some visual references on the plane. I have found that using the distance or space between the wing and the stabilizer when the plane is coming toward you as an attitude indicator works fairly well. Take a look at Fig. 11-6 and 11-7 and 11-8. Notice that for a high wing trainer type plane, the lower the nose the smaller the space you can see between the wing and tail. At an even lower attitude, the stab is completely hidden by the wing. This works just the reverse for a low wing plane. The lower the nose, the more space you see between the wing and stab.

To use this aid, what you should do is to land his plane and watch for the relative position of the wing and tail when you are at the proper pitch attitude on final approach. On many trainers I have flown, the stab needs to be just under the wing, but you'll have to make your own check on this one. Once you have it figured out, explain to the student that he should hold that attitude with the elevator stick and adjust the descent rate and landing point with small throttle changes.

This method of measuring attitude gives the student something specific to look at until he gets a feel for the overall picture of the plane during final approach. It also gives you a way to give him more specific feedback on the quality of his approaches. Quick corrections like, "you've got too much space," or "nose too low, the tail's hidden," tell him something concrete. However "your final approach wasn't too good," doesn't convey the specific information as well.

Watch your student and judge his progress carefully. When he can make a good low approach and go around, you and he both will know that it is time for him to get on with the culmination of R/C flight training—the actual touchdown. Then you can begin to teach landings.

Landing

Landing is the successful conclusion to a good approach. The student has come a long way. He has learned to steer, to make a low approach and go around, and perhaps a little acrobatics, but he can't really say that he can fly until he can land. A *solo* is what it is called; taking off, flying around and then landing by himself. Do not think that just because he has made one or two solo landings that he is safe to fly by himself in all conditions. He will need plenty of instruction during his landing practice phase until he is proficient. You might recall that during the familiarization phase you started off instructing him just a little during a flight and then increased it as he could handle it. During the landing phase the opposite happens. You start off with maximum instruction as he makes his first touchdowns and then taper off as he gets better and better. Soon he'll be on his own.

LEARNING OUTCOMES

In this phase, the student learns to flare the plane at the correct altitude and to make a smooth touchdown. By flare, and it is sometimes called a *roundout* in full-scale flight training, I mean to change the attitude of the plane with the elevator to break the descent of the final approach. The plane's attitude is changed from the nose-low descent attitude to a nose-high landing attitude. The student then learns to hold this attitude, or vary it slightly depending on the situation, until the plane touches down smoothly.

All this will take some effort on the part of the student because he has to continue to make aileron (or rudder) steering corrections while he is using the elevator control on the same stick to flare the plane. This is more difficult than it appears at first. You'll probably notice that the student will make a couple of nice landings at first, then get worse and then, after some more practice, get consistently good. This happens because his first few landings will come only from a near perfect approach, judged with your help, where the plane just about lands itself. Later he will try to land from an approach that is not so good and the landings will suffer. But as he gains more experience from continued practice, he will get better and better.

INSTRUCTOR DEMONSTRATION

The flare and touchdown demonstration goes rather quickly. Because it does, it causes a problem. Trying to talk, or instruct and fly at the same time is difficult at best unless you are specifically trained to do it—as military pilot training instructors are. During the actual landing it is extremely difficult.

Realizing this, give your student a thorough briefing on what you are going to do beforehand. Then you can take the plane up, fly an approach and demonstrate the flare and touchdown. It also helps if you've explained the technique a few times when you've done the landings during the earlier phases. You could have gotten him started by talking him through the landings you made during the last part of final approaches and given him an idea of what proper attitude and airspeed look like.

To do the actual demonstration, set the plane up on a good approach to the end of the runway. At about 5 to 6 feet in the air, cut the power to idle if it is not already there and start easing in the up elevator. Plan your elevator input so that the plane will descend to a height of about 2 to 3 feet before it levels off.

Have the student watch the plane first and then demonstrate it again so that he can watch your hands on the controls and see about how much stick movement is needed. Because the plane is now level at idle power, the airspeed will bleed off and the plane will start to descend again. Now add a little more up to attain a nose high attitude and let the plane settle to the ground.

There is not much time to demonstrate, but there is a lot to do. You need to brief your student thoroughly on what part of the plane to watch and when to make the control changes. At the flare, tell him to watch the fuselage and the angle it makes with level flight. The plane should be about level while it is several feet high. At this point he should watch the altitude of the plane. When it begins to descend again, the student should ease in a little more up elevator. He should now be looking for a nose-up

Fig. 12-1. The proper landing attitude.

attitude, but still descending. This is the landing attitude as shown in Fig. 12-1. You might point out that all planes, from the Boeing 747 down to the smallest R/C model, land this way.

After landing, you should demonstrate a touch-and-go. Release the up elevator, add power and takeoff again. Many times, the ability of a student to make a touch-and-go is contingent upon the length of the runway and the distance down from the end of it that he landed. Naturally, on a short runway, he might not have enough runway distance left to make a safe takeoff. Remember that his takeoffs will be longer than yours. On a long runway, there should be no problem and touch-and-go's should be the rule after he gains proficiency.

STUDENT PRACTICE

The student's practice of a landing from a particular approach must depend on the quality of that low approach. If he makes a good approach to within a few feet of the ground, he should land. He should go around from a poor approach. Keep this in mind during the latter stages of his low approach practice. Brief him on how to flare and touch down.

When he gets a really good, nearly perfect approach, have him cut the power to idle and land. You can easily talk him through it from a good approach where little or no steering correction have to be made. At the flare point tell him, "add a little up," then, "good," when he levels. "Hold it, hold it," helps him as the plane gradually slows. Then, "up, up," as needed to get the nose up for landing. He will probably make a nice landing. At that point you should give him a rousing, "Way to go!"

Have him do his first few landings this way. Coach him through it after a good approach. At this point, he will probably only be making a landing every six approaches or so. That's fine. It is very good, in fact, because it not only builds his confidence, it teaches him to land only from a good approach and to remember to go around after a bad one.

As he gains proficiency, let him begin to assess the approach and make his own decision on whether to land or not. Reduce the coaching during the flare and begin to let him judge his own touchdown. His proficiency will more than likely show a drop. This is perfectly natural and he will get better as he practices more and gains more experience in landing.

Common Errors

There are several specific errors that can be made during the landing flare and touchdown. By far the largest number of them are caused by simple inexperience on the part of the pilot. For some of them, an improperly set up airplane can be at fault. The incorrect set up might not be noticed by the instructor due to his proficiency and ability to compensate for it. This is especially true on an easy-to-fly trainer. However, it might be a dramatic problem for a student. I will cover these in detail as I get to them.

The first error you'll probably notice is that the student will concentrate on making the flare and touchdown and forget to steer. The plane might drift off the runway over the grass, but it will be making a perfect touchdown. Forgetting to steer during the flare is entirely due to a lack of experience. The student does not know how to flare and touchdown well enough to be able to perform these two while also keeping the plane line up with the runway. Explain the error to him and be sure to advise him that it is a perfectly natural error. Keep him practicing.

Right after you correct your student for not steering during the flare, he will concentrate on the steering. But he will probably release the up elevator he is holding to keep the plane in the landing attitude and the plane will drop for a nose-first landing and perhaps a broken prop. Here again is lack of experience showing.

Many students alternate between these two errors until they finally learn. The culprit is the design of the radio set with the sticks spring loaded to center. This is the only practical way to fly, but it does cause this minor landing problem for beginning fliers. When the student concentrates on the roll control, he will at first unconsciously release a little pressure in the elevator direction on the stick and the plane will drop. All you can do is to keep reminding him of it in preflight and post-flight briefings and let him practice.

A third error is flaring too high. This usually occurs after a hard landing when the student is a little bit afraid of the ground. It can lead to a very slow speed condition and a stall with perhaps a crash as the final result. A flare that is much too high should call for an immediate addition of power and a go around. Those that are just a little high can possibly be salvaged by a small addition of power and reflaring. In 99 percent of the cases, however, I recommend a go around. When the student is first learning to land, it is asking a lot of him to make the power correction.

Teaching him the correct flare altitude is the problem. His idea of the proper flare altitude is higher than it should be. Give him a demonstration of the correct height. This is one time where a demonstration of his error might be beneficial. Show him the correct altitude, 2 to 3 feet high, and then immediately fly one like he did. Point out the difference. Let him try it again, but talk him through it. Tell him, "Don't flare yet, hold it. Now a little up," etc. Start your verbal directions well before the flare point and continue to talk him right through it. Don't forget a "good" after he does it, even if you did coach him all the way down. This reinforces his mental picture of the correct point.

Another error is not flaring at all. For this one you have to determine if he is actually not moving the stick to flare, if he is moving the stick and it is not enough to move the plane, or if his timing is off. The first cause, not moving the stick or just driving the plane into the ground, is caused by rushing the student.

He is still trying so hard on the final approach that he cannot even think about landing. This student needs a lot more low approach practice. Cases like this are usually caused by the instructor rushing the student and not going at his rate. It can also be caused by the student rushing himself and the instructor.

Sometimes the student might be competing with another student to see who can solo first or he might just be impatient to get out on his own. Watch out for this and restrain the student. Keep him at the best rate for his particular abilities.

Another cause for this error—where the student tries to flare, but doesn't get a reaction from the plane—is probably a control or CG problem. It might simply be that the plane just doesn't have enough elevator control. Try moving the clevis in on the control horn and see if that doesn't help.

On the other hand, it might be that the plane needs a CG adjustment. Many trainers that were designed for a light .19- to

.35-sized engine end up with a heavy .40 in the nose. The instructor can land this plane, possibly needing full up elevator, without even noticing how much control he is using. Experienced fliers tend to make the plane perform using whatever control is necessary without thinking too much about the amount.

A student, on the other hand, needs some extra control to correct for the mistakes he will invariably make. You cannot expect him to use full up to lane. He'll come in with the nose too low one time, will not have enough up, and end up landing hard or breaking the nose of the plane. Try moving the CG back to correct this nose-heavy tendency in the plane.

Check his plans and recheck the actual CG of the plane. A couple of stick-on weights will move the CG back and you can give it a test and trim flight. Doing one of these two minor "fixes" will correct virtually every case of low response. A final caution, though, the plane will fly differently—especially for the student. Be sure to let him get the feel of it before you go back to low approaches and landings.

Still another landing error is *ballooning*. Ballooning occurs when the student puts in too much up during the flare. This causes the airplane not to level off, but to "balloon" into a climb. Then the plane loses airspeed and descends or stalls or the student releases up and the plane descends. See Fig. 12-2. Usually the descents are too fast and the result is a hard landing. Ballooning can be the result of inexperience that causes the student to be nervous and too quick on the controls. In that case, the student needs to practice low approaches some more.

Another cause of ballooning is nervousness brought on by a crash or a hard landing on a previous flight. It is understandable that after a problem that the sutdent will be nervous. It might last only a short time or it might be more pronounced. In either case, you need to build his confidence to get him to be able to relax as he flies. Talk him through a low approach or two and when he has a really good one, talk him through the flare and touchdown. More practice and more successful practice is once again the key.

All of these have been reasons for ballooning and suggestions as to what to teach the student to correct the tendency. How about what to do immediately when it happens? The best thing for anything more than a very mild balloon is to add power and go around. You must be the judge on this. Many instructors have a tendency to let the student try to fly out of a balloon and go ahead and land. I don't think this is a good practice because it can result in a hard, nose-first landing and damage to the plane. The student will do better in the long run with respect to learning and keeping his trainer in one piece if he makes a go around and tries again.

Bouncing is another landing error and it is one of those that can be caused by the student or by the plane. A bounce can be any size. Little hops of a few inches happen all the time. We all bounce a little some time and don't think a thing of it. Then there are *bounces*. I mean the bounce or bounces following a really bad landing that puts the plane back up in the air high enough for it to be damaged when it comes down. This bounce is the kind I'll detail.

One cause of a bad bounce is a hard landing. This can be the result of not flaring, flaring too high or ballooning and then dropping in. Bounces caused by one of these errors can be eliminated by curing the specific error (as discussed earlier). As with a balloon, go around if the engine is still running. It might not be if the bounce was hard enough to break the prop and stop the engine. With the engine not running the student is forced to fly it through the best way he can.

Get the nose down to retain the airspeed. Then try to flare again. This is about the best that can be done. In any case, the student should not hold the up elevator. This will result in a stall and probably a wing drop—with disasterous results. It is anticlimactic to say, "avoid a hard landing and a bounce," because everyone tries. The best advice is for the student to go around on this one if he can and to get more experience.

Bouncing also results from a nose gear-first landing. You can just about be guaranteed that if the nose gear—which is forward of the CG—touches first, you are going to get the nose of the plane bouncing back into the air. Many times this can

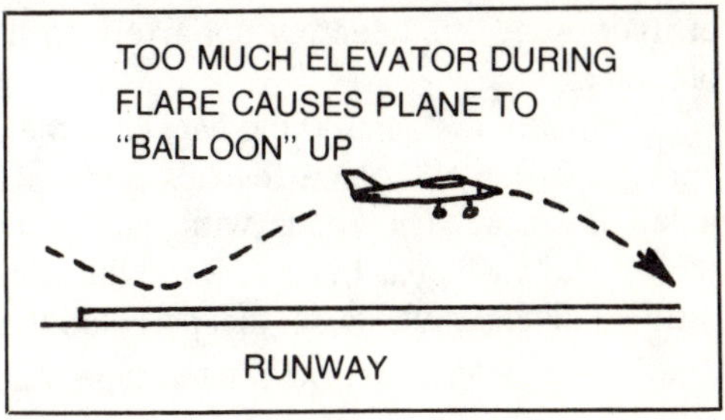

Fig. 12-2. The balloon.

result in a series of bounces or hops while the student vainly tries to correct, but is too slow on the controls. This series of nose gear bounces is called *porpoising* or a *porpoise*.

In a full-scale aircraft, a porpoise is an extremely dangerous event that can destroy a plane and injure the pilot and passengers. Pilots are taught to correct for a porpoise by holding a small amount of up elevator and going around. This is also sound advice for R/C pilots.

But let's go a little farther into it. To cure a porpoising tendency in a student, you must first find out what causes it. Is he just not flaring enough? Keep a close eye on the angle of the fuselage just before he touches down. He might be inadvertently releasing some of the up elevator. This will cause the nose to drop and the nose gear will hit first. If this is the case, the student needs a briefing emphasizing the need to hold the elevator control and watch the angle of the fuselage as the plane settles in.

The other reason the student might land nose gear first is that the nose gear is too long. A similar situation can result if the main gear is too springy. Naturally, you would not knowingly set up a plane with the nose gear too long.

However, this can happen. Let me explain. Most high wing trainers have the main gear made out of 5/32 wire mounted in the fuselage. The wire, as shown in Fig. 12-3, angles outward and downward so that the wheels are several inches apart. For most fliers, this type of gear is quite adequate. But for students who do not make soft landings, it is not.

After a few weeks of firm student landings, or a lesser time of hard ones, the landing gear becomes little by little flattened out (as shown by the dotted lines in Fig. 12-3). This flattening or squashing down of the main gear lowers the rear of the plane. This makes the nose gear too long in relation to the now shortened main gear. The longer nose gear has a tendency to touch first unless the plane is in a pronounced nose-high landing attitude—one a student is not likely to have. The result is a porpoise.

Virtually the same thing happens when the main gear is too springy. When the plane touches down a little bit on the hard side, the main gear bends with only a small amount of resistance. The nose gear touches while the plane is still in a nose-up attitude. The result, again, is a porpoise or a bounce.

The cure for this gear-related type of landing error is to get

Fig. 12-3. Wire landing gear.

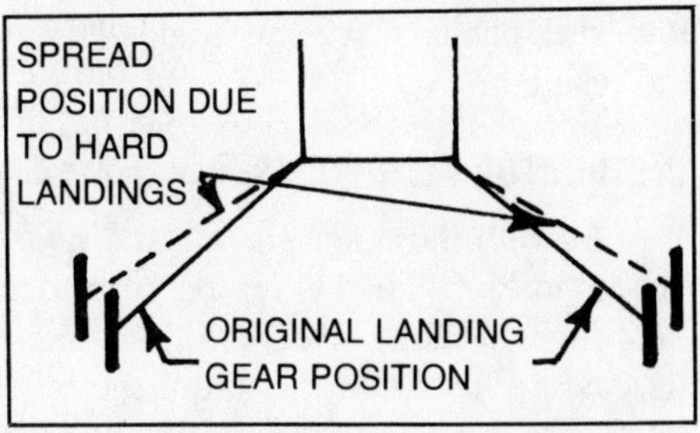

the main wheels in the correct position and keep them there. Notice that I said *wheels*. Bending the 5/32 wire gear legs back down will only work for a short while (until another firm landing flattens them again).

There are two solutions. One is a change of landing gear, the other is a modification of the student's present gear. Changing to a dural aluminum gear will definitely cure the problem. This type of landing gear—made from a stiff, tempered aluminum—resists bending and has just the right amount of spring.

It might, however, require a rework of the lower fuselage of the plane for the addition of a suitable gear mount and might not be the best way to go. The easiest way to correct the problem in a trainer the student is already flying is to add a spreader bar or wire between the wire gear to keep them from spreading out and becoming flattened.

On the landing gear, you can see that a small wire (three-thirty-seconds or even one-sixteenth is sufficient) has been soldered between the two main gear legs. This spreader wire keeps the main gear from becoming flattened. Have the student bend the main gear back to its original shape. Then wrap and solder the small gauge spreader wire in place. Be sure the ends are wrapped well with some copper or soft iron wire. A plain solder joint won't take the strain.

You might have a little trouble convincing the student that he needs a stiffer main gear. As a matter of fact, you might be a little skeptical yourself. The old saying, "Don't knock it till you've tried it," applies here.

Look at it this way. A low-wing plane has only the torsion bar effect of the gear to absorb the landing shock. Fliers make good landings with low-wing planes every day. Don't think the gear will be too stiff. Adding the spreader bar only changes the trainer gear to one that has shock absorbing action like that of a low-wing plane. Have the student try it. You'll be surprised at the results.

INSTRUCTOR TECHNIQUES

As with the other phases, the same instructional techniques are important. To review, be sure to conduct a preflight and a post-flight briefing. Because the student will be landing, it will be easy to have him taxi the plane off the runway and keep the engine idling while you critique his landing. After the quick briefing, he can taxi back out and take off. If he is doing touch-and-go's and only needs a quick comment that is fine. But after the last one, give him a rundown on his progress.

Never forget feedback and reinforcement. At this stage, you might be prone to simply let him practice. Don't fall into the he's-getting-too-good-for-a-correction trap. If he still needs you to stand with him, he still needs feedback. Even if you just say, "good, good, good," all the way through the pattern and landing, you are telling him something. You're probably telling him that he's just about ready for a higher performance plane and will need you to test and trim it for him.

I emphasize again to go at his rate. Be careful, especially at the first of this phase, not to rush him into landing. Be on the lookout for signs of inexperience such as not steering or not flaring. Make him land only from a good approach and go around from a poor one.

This has a twofold effect. It forces him to concentrate on making a good approach, which is the key to a good landing, and it gets him in the habit of going around if anything goes wrong. This habit of going around can save him many times in the future. As a matter of fact, I can say positively that the best immediate correction for any landing error is to go around.

Let me give you one more rule. Stay with your student until he has real proficiency. Do not get him through a few passable landings and then drop him. Make sure that he can really land his plane in most wind conditions. There is a lot of time and several hundred dollars invested in an R/C plane. Be sure the student will not destroy it through an error you should have caught and corrected.

Once your student can land, the whole world of R/C flight is open to him. There are two things, however, that are as inevitable as death and taxes; the crash and the second airplane.

Simple Acrobatics

Much of the R/C flight instruction course is repetition and practice. This is especially true in the figure 8 phase. During this time, the student will probably reach a noticeable plateau in his learning and might become bored. He might still be making mistakes in his steering, so you will not want to bring him down for low approaches yet. What you can do at this time is teach him some acrobatics that any trainer can perform.

Teaching acrobatics to the student at this stage can do several things for him. First, of course, they break up the monotony and repetition of practice. Second, it teaches the student how to handle his plane better in different situations and at different attitudes. This builds his confidence in himself and in his plane and equipment. Third, it's just fun to do acrobatics and it will certainly build his enthusiasm. This can actually help his other practice, because it gives him an accomplishment at a time when he might feel concerned about his slow progress in his phase practice.

The acrobatics I recommend teaching to the student at this stage of learning are the loop, the aileron roll, the split S, and the Immelmann. These are easy and within the capability of most trainers. Three-channel trainers, especially those which are the slow moving, old timer types, might not be able to do the roll or might have wings that are not strong enough to do the other maneuvers. You will have to make a careful check of the trainer for safety. Checking the wing in particular for strength. Another area to check is the wing mount. Whether is it dowels for rubber band wing hold down or tapped blocks for bolts, it will be under much more stress during acrobatics than it was before. If the trainer uses rubber bands, as most do, you might want to add a few more just to be on the safe side.

INSTRUCTOR TECHNIQUES

The instructor techniques for teaching acrobatics are basically the same as those you used in the phase training. Brief the student first and then demonstrate the maneuver. Let him try it. Reinforce his good performance and correcting his errors when he shows poor or sloppy maneuvers.

Preflight Briefing

You should thoroughly discuss the maneuver and how to do it. The details for each one will be given later. Limit the new maneuvers you teach him to one per flight. These maneuvers might seem easy to you, but remember, this is the first time he has ever had his plane intentionally upside down. Don't push him. The best way to use the acrobatic maneuvers is to brief him on them, then let him do his regular figure 8 or low approach practice for a few minutes before you let him try it. After another few minutes of acrobatics, go back back to his regular practice before it's time to land. This breaks up the practice and gives him something to look forward to.

During the briefing, have him take the transmitter and practice the stick movements he will be going through. You might want to get the frequency pin and turn on the transmitter and plane to let him see what the controls will be doing. Make sure he is thoroughly familiar with the maneuver before he tries it in the air.

Demonstrating the Maneuver

Demonstrate the maneuver before you let him try it. You will actually be demonstrating more than the maneuver itself. You will also be showing him how to position the plane and set up to enter the maneuver.

Earlier I mentioned the additional benefits from acrobatics over and above the actual learning of the maneuver. It is easy to see that he is also learning to handle the plane at full power rather than at a reduced setting and he is learning to position the plane on a heading and altitude. While this might be second nature to the instructor, it is very difficult for an inexperienced student. Remember, you have been teaching him to fly down the runway like he will have to for a landing. Now he must fly to a different position and then fly the plane on a course parallel to the runway to set up for acrobatics.

You should always demonstrate the maneuver at least twice. First, fly through the maneuver with the student watching the plane. Explain each control input as you do it. Be careful that you don't forget to demonstrate how to set the plane up to enter the maneuver. For the second demonstration, have your student watch the transmitter and how you move the sticks. This is very important. It is one thing to show him how the sticks move when the plane is on the ground and another to let him watch you move the sticks while you actually do the maneuver. He will get a better idea of the timing of the control inputs and how far the sticks actually have to move. He knows that if he moves the sticks exactly like you moved them, the plane will perform the maneuver.

STUDENT PRACTICE

After you demonstrate the maneuver twice for the student, give him the transmitter and let him try it. Talk him through the set up and the maneuver the first few times until he gets the mechanics down. Then let him try it by himself. Limit his acrobatic practice so that he doesn't get tired of it. Use it to break up the other phase practice. It is particularly helpful to use it during a learning plateau or period when the student seems to be a little bored with his normal practice flights.

Reinforcement and Error Correction

After he had completed the maneuver for the first time, even if he botches it, give him a pat on the head. A comment like, "not bad for the first time," or "pretty good," will really make him feel great. This is what he needs at this time. Later you can give him more objective criticism, but the first time is always an occasion for praise.

As with the maneuvers in phase training, give the student immediate and frequent reinforcement of good performance and an immediate comment on poor flying. This is particularly true if he is getting through the maneuver, but just not doing it well. For example, not tracking through a loop properly. "You drifted right," might be an appropriate comment.

Try not to overcorrect. Remember that this is a beginner you are teaching acrobatics to and not a person getting ready for a pattern contest. You'll also need to keep in mind the limitations of the student's plane. A trainer naturally will not perform acrobatics as well as a plane designed specifically for that purpose. A good way to judge your student's acrobatics is to use the quality of the maneuver when you do it with his plane as the standard.

If you have to make a long correction or explanation during the maneuver, take control of the plane. The student is probably not yet at stage where he can simultaneously fly and listen to your explanation.

Another time you will want to take control is in case of excessive nervousness. Sometimes just doing his first acrobatic maneuver will make the student nervous. You might notice erratic flying, regression and fast breathing. Be on the look out for any of these symptoms and immediately take control of the plane if you notice them. As the student gets used to doing acrobatics, he will get over this nervousness.

THE MANEUVERS

These four maneuvers, loop, aileron rool, split-S, and Immelmann, are ones that just about any trainer can perform. The step-by-step method for performing each one will be discussed first, followed by common errors you might encounter during teaching the maneuver and how to correct them.

Loop

The loop is the easiest maneuver to teach. All the student has to do is hold full up and most planes will loop. You should, of course, do one with the student's plane first to see how it performs. Some planes may need a dive to build up enough speed to loop—even at full power.

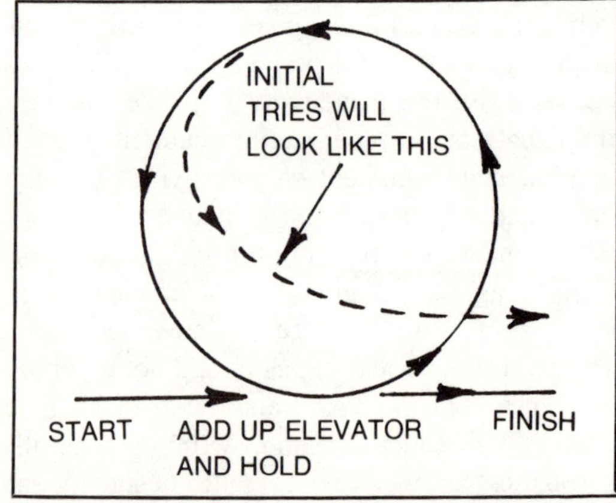

Fig. 13-1. The loop.

The steps in the maneuver (Fig. 13-1) are as follows:

- Advance the throttle to full power.
- Put the plane on a course parallel to the runway and in a position so that it will fly in front of you a comfortable distance away. The altitude should be a "mistake high" or high enough so that you can grab the plane, pull full up and save it.
- When the plane is in front of you, smoothly put in full up elevator and hold it until the plane completes the loop.

Common Errors. There are two main errors common to the loop: releasing the up control and not keeping the wings level (causing poor tracking). Releasing the up control at the wrong time will cause the plane to fail to complete the loop. If he releases on the up side, the plane will continue in a climb until it runs out of airspeed. It will then stall and fall.

If the up control is released on the down side, the plane will end up in a screaming dive. In either case, take control and correct the plane to level flight. The second error, not keeping the wings level, can be caused by either the pilot or the plane.

The student pilot can cause it by inadvertently putting in a slight amount of aileron control along with full up elevator. If this is the case, just remind him to be very careful not to deflect the ailerons when he puts in elevator.

The student can also cause a poor loop by entering it with the plane in a slight bank. This is caused by him not having the correct "picture" of what the plane looks like in level flight. Of course, it might be the student's plane that causes poor tracking through loops. Some trainers are prone to "pulling off" instead of tracking true. Try one yourself to get an idea of how the plane performs.

Most errors caused by the pilot can be corrected as he gains experience and learns the maneuver. If the plane is the culprit, teaching the student to correct with ailerons as the plane tracks through the loop is the answer.

Aileron Roll

The next maneuver to teach the student is the aileron roll. Of course, you will need to try one with his trainer to see how fast the plane rolls and whether it actually can do it, but virtually every aileron trainer will roll.

The steps in the maneuver (Fig. 13-2) are as follows:

- Advance the throttle to full power.

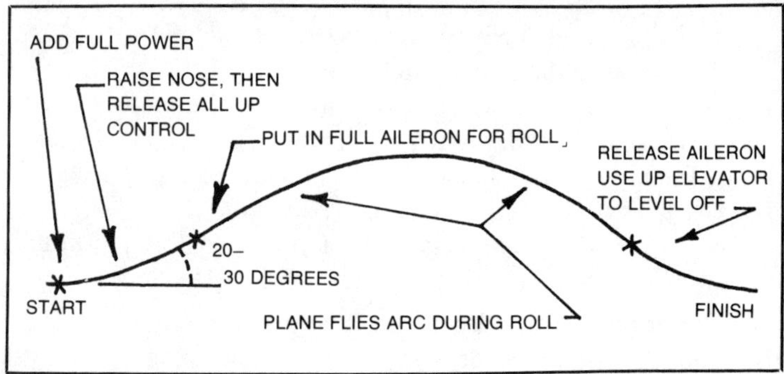

Fig. 13-2. Aileron roll.

- Line the plane up just as you did for the loop.
- As the plane passes in front of you, put in a small amount of up elevator to cause the plane to enter a gentle climb of about 30 degrees. When you reach that climb angle, completely release the stick.
- After releasing the stick and letting it center, put in full aileron control and hold it until the plane completes the roll. Then release the aileron stick.
- At the completion of the roll, the plane will probably be in a dive. The student will have to be ready to put in a little up elevator to correct the plane back to level flight.

Common Errors. There are three common student errors to watch for in teaching the roll: barrel rolling, a screaming dive, and not finishing the maneuver. The first two are caused by not releasing the up control prior to rolling. They can also be caused by inadvertently putting in up control during the maneuver, but this is essentially the same thing.

If the student holds a slight amount of up and begins the roll, the plane will barrel roll. This is not too much of a problem. Most trainers tend to barrel roll a bit anyway. Just remind him to release all the up before he rolls. The more severe problem is when he holds a large amount of up control. Once the plane gets inverted with gravity to help, the nose will drop rapidly and he will end up in a steep inverted dive.

As soon as you see him getting into this situation, take the plane and recover it. Let the student calm down and then demonstrate with him watching your hands on the control sticks. Emphasize doing it "by the numbers" and releasing the stick before applying aileron to roll.

The third error, not finishing the roll, sounds trivial. But some students will tend to hold the aileron stick over for a certain length of time, then release it, no matter whether the roll is finished or not. This rarely happens past the first few tries, but when it does, the plane is usually inverted and the student might panic and do anything. Take control and emphasize that the student should concentrate on watching the plane and not release the aileron stick until the plane is right side up.

Split S

The split S is a turn around maneuver that can be very useful to the student as he progresses. It allows him to reverse course without changing his distance out from the runway centerline as he would with a simple turn. I've yet to meet a student who didn't fall in love with a split S turn around once he learned it. You don't have to keep the plane level like in a turn and that is another reason students like it so much.

The steps in the maneuver (Fig. 13-3) are as follows:

- Advance the throttle to full power.
- Line the plane up for entry into the maneuver. This should be in a line parallel to the runway and passing in front of yourself.
- After the plane passes in front of you, add a slight amount of up elevator to raise the nose about 5 to 20 degrees. When you reach this angle, completely release the stick.
- After the stick centers, put in ful laileron. Hold it until the plane is inverted. Then release the stick.
- With the plane inverted, put in up elevator and hold it until the plane half-loops back around to level flight.

Common Errors. Frequency problems that you should watch for are not getting the wings level inverted and putting in down control instead of up. The roll to inverted flight might take a little practice before he gets it right. Failure to have the wings level before putting in up control will cause the plane to pull off to one side or the other. This is a very common error and he will learn to correct and do a pretty good maneuver very quickly. The best learning he can get from the maneuver, however, is how to make a correction while he is going through it.

As he holds up elevator to pull through, he makes small aileron corrections to insure that he is heading in the proper

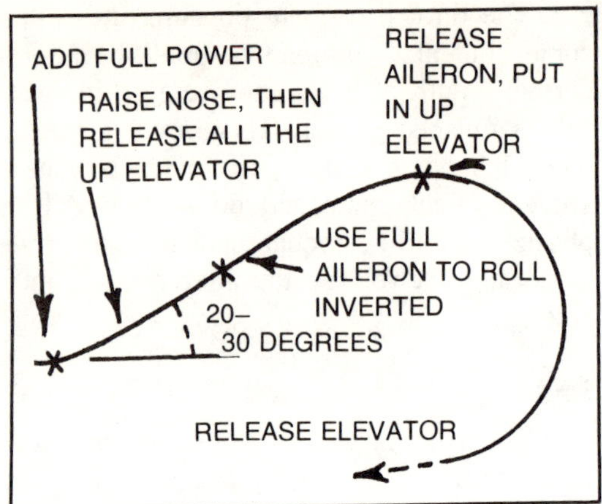

Fig. 13-3. Split S.

direction when the maneuver is finished. It is best to try to teach them this only after he is fairly comfortable with a basic split S.

The other error that is common when the student is first learning the split S is to use the down elevator instead of the up elevator. For some reason, many students will get confused after they release the stick when the plane is upside down. They will push in down control. It tends to take you by surprise the first time you see it if you aren't looking for it. Generally speaking, all you need to do is to rebrief and demonstrate the maneuver. Make sure when you do that the student has an understanding of how a plane reacts to control when it is inverted.

Immelmann

The Immelmann is another turn around maneuver. It is a maneuver that allows you to gain altitude in the turn around rather than lose it as you do in a split S. The maneuver was named for its originator, Max Immelmann, a German WWI ace who used it as an escape maneuver after an attack. He would dive on the enemy plane and gain speed in the process. After firing, he would pull up into a half-loop and then roll over when he reached the inverted position. This put him much higher and going the oppostie direction from his former prey—essentially immune from a counter attack.

The steps in the maneuver (Fig. 13-4) are as follows:

- Advance the throttle to full power.
- Position the airplane the same as for a split S (parallel to the runway and in front of yourself).

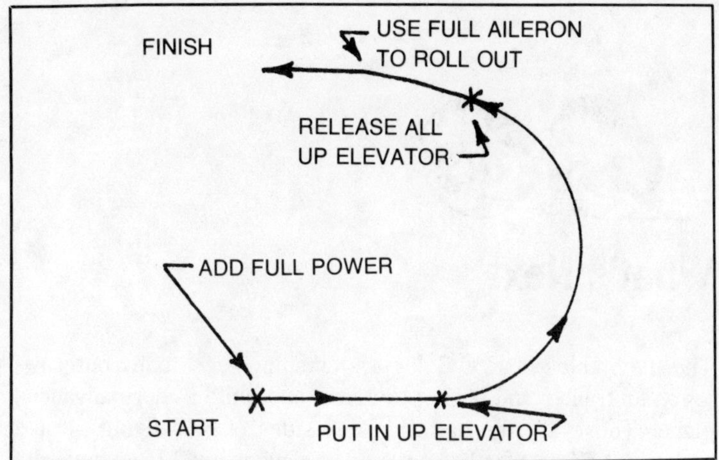

Fig. 13-4. Immellmann.

- Put in up elevator just as you did for a loop.
- Just as you get to the highest point of the loop, where the plane is inverted, release the up control.
- Immediately after releasing the controls, put in full aileron to roll the plane right side up.
- At the completion of the roll out, the plane will probably be slow and in a shallow dive. Use small corrections to bring it back to level flight.

Common Errors. Very few errors occur in the Immelmann after the first few tries. The student might forget to roll out and just do a loop. This happens because he has already learned the loop and has a feel for the control movements and timing for it. When he starts an Immelmann, his hand feels loop controls and he can't think quickly enough to release the controls when it is time to roll. A more common error is a spiral diving roll out. This is caused by not releasing the up elevator before applying aileron control to roll. It is easily recognized, so be ready to take control if you notice it. Demonstrate with the student watching your hands on the controls. It might take a few tries for the student to get the timing and control inputs down.

These four acrobatic maneuvers should keep the student enthused and occupied during the more repetitious portion of his training. As he progresses, and if his plane is capable, don't hesitate to teach him other acrobatic maneuvers that you know. They are not only fun, they will teach him a lot more about handling a plane than just the maneuver itself.

What's Next

The inevitables in R/C flying are crashing, eventually outgrowing your trainer and having to select and build a more advanced plane. These are the bad and good sides of R/C flying. I have never met a flier who has not torn up a plane and I have met only a few who stopped with their first trainer.

THE CRASH

Ask a few light plane pilots how often they perform acrobatics. Most will say they never do any. Most R/C'ers can't wait to learn acrobatics. When they master the simple maneuvers, they want to learn the more complex and more dangerous ones. And if this isn't enough, as the R/C pilot gains profiency he tends to fly under worse and worse weather conditions. Rather than miss a day of flying, the enthusiast decides that he can "handle" the crosswind and is off into the wind. Both of these inducements, as well as plain old inexperience, can lead to a crash.

A crash that destroys a plane, and perhaps a radio and engine, is a traumatic experience even for a proficient pilot. It does not, however, set the experienced pilot back in his flying (other than the fact that he has to build a new plane).

With a student, a crash can cause pyschological damage that the instructor must watch out for and help to repair before the student will be able to continue learning to fly. Some students are crushed and demoralized. Maybe they are flying on a limited budget and the expense of a new plane and radio repair staggers them.

There are many who will crash at a plateau point in their learning. They might feel that the crash is an indication that they can't learn. Others will simply regress and have a very difficult time passing the level of proficiency they reached before the crash.

All of these are detrimental to the student's progress in R/C. They can, however, be mitigated by proper analysis and corrective action by the instructor. The first thing to do is to analyze the reason for the crash. Determine what caused it and how to insure that it does not happen again. Next, you should assess the damage to the plane, radio and engine to decide if and how quickly it can be fixed. The instructor should also assess the damage done to the student's confidence and to the continuity of his flight instruction program.

Analyze The Reason For The Crash

Generally speaking, student mishaps can be put into three categories: radio failure, structural failure and student error. Sometimes it will be hard to tell which one you are dealing with. Was the crash during the funny looking maneuver caused by radio problems or was it the student correcting the wrong way? Radio trouble can be intermittent. It might occur only during a high vibration or g condition. The structural failure might have been masked by crash damage. You will have to do your best in the determination of the most likely reason.

If you decide that the reason was radio failure, insist that the student have the set fixed. It is a good idea to have the radio set inspected in any event after a crash. Some damage might have been incurred as a result of impact with the ground. You should test and range check the radio. If anything doesn't work just right, get it looked at. I also recommend that, if the plane crashed hard, the crystal in the receiver be replaced. More intermittent radio problems are cuased by cracked crystals than any other reason. Considering the cost of crystal replacement compared to the cost of a new plane if the intermittent condition shows up again to cause a second crash, it is just not worth it to take a chance. It has been said that a crystal can last through an earthquake or break if you look at it wrong. I recommend that you replace it if the plane has crashed hard.

The second reason for a crash is structural failure. This is becoming more common as larger engines are put into old style trainers that were designed for less power and speed. It is good to see old stand-bys like the Falcon 56 redesigned with stronger wings. Failure can also happen to a part that has been damaged before and not noticed of perhaps fixed improperly.

This is a good reason for the instructor to make a close inspection of the plane after a hard landing or minor crash and after any repairs. Your student might not know what is important in the repair or how strong he should make it.

For example, a hard, nose gear-first landing might damage or break loose the firewall to which both the nose gear and the engine are mounted. The student might repair it with a glue other than epoxy and not use any bracing next to the fuselage sides. A repair like this might end up coming loose after a few flights.

One area in particular to check after a minor ding, especially one that involved a cartwheel or the wing touching the ground, is the wing spars. These or the leading and trailing edge are areas that might crack and the damage might be hidden from immediate view by the covering. Flex the wing and look for spots that appear to be broken underneath. Do this for the tail, too, and don't forget the underside of the wing or the tail-fuselage joint.

If you decide it was a structural failure that caused a bad crash, try to figure out what caused the failure. If the wing broke, you need to take a look at the student's construction techniques or at the strength of the wood that comes in the kit compared to the power and use the plane gets. For example, some trainers simply weren't designed to take the stress of a quick, tight loop. If a control surface came off, look at the others. It is likely that the hinges were not installed securely enough or were not pinned. Give the hinges a try to see if they will come out. If they do, give your student some instructions on installing them before he repairs them or builds a new plane.

Student error can arise a hundred different ways. It can also be partially the fault of the instructor. Students will tend to get into trouble in bad wind conditions or other high stress situations, where they are not quick enough to make corrections and end up in a crash. This is a type of crash that is avoidable if you are careful to let your student fly only under managable weather conditions and within his capabilities.

Flying in only good weather is difficult. Students generally want to fly all the time. Holding them back is difficult after they progress a bit. The other problem, letting the student exceed his capabilities, comes from pushing the student or letting him go at a rate quicker than is justified by his progress.

You must go at his rate. Letting him fly low approaches or landings before he is ready will induce errors and perhaps a crash. You must be patient if you intend to instruct properly.

This does not mean that you take a year to teach someone to fly R/C. It means you must carefully judge and not exceed the student's level of ability. As an example, you would not wait until the student is as proficient as you are in figure 8s before you begin low approaches. As soon as you feel 90 percent confident that he will not make a gross error and get the plane in an unrecoverable position, begin the early "high approaches." Keep his progress and abilities in mind so that you do not rush him into a situation that will result in a crash.

Assess The Damage

When the student looks at his broken trainer—his creation of many hours of hard work—laying in splinters and pieces, he will more than likely want to take a couple of weeks off and then start on a new plane. Don't let him be too hasty in his judgement. First look the damage over with an eye on repair.

Repairing is virtually always the best route to go with a trainer. Certainly a pattern flier with a competition quality plane that has to be carefully balanced must take into consideration the weight and location of the repair as he decides whether or not to rebuild it.

The beginner and sport flier, on the other hand, don't have to be so particular and should always consider repair except when the plane is an extreme basket case. Five-minute epoxy and fiberglass work wonders on seemingly unrepairable wrecks. Actually, the only time I *don't* consider repair is when the wood has become so fuel soaked that epoxy glue won't stick to it.

Many times only half a plane will be damaged. The fuselage might be demolished, but the wing and possibly the tail, might be relatively free from damage. In this case, think about making a new fuselage. Use as many parts—tail, bulkheads and hardware—from the old one as possible. I have found the lightweight poplar three-ply wood called *LitePly* is an excellent material for a quick, strong fuselage. LitePly is available from hobby shops and discount houses in both 36-inch and 48-inch lengths. Using LitePly and quick setting 5-minute epoxy, a new fuselage can be framed very quickly.

If the wing happens to be damaged, but the fuselage isn't, the problem might be even simpler to correct. Wings tend to be easier to fix than they appear. New ribs can be made. Spars and leading and trailing edges can be spliced much quicker than a whole wing can be built. Generally, only one side of the wing will be damaged with the damage concentrated on the outboard side. You usually will not have to rebuild the center section, dihedral, and control hook-up.

This saves a lot of time and gets the plane ready in a hurry. Of course, if the wing is completely destroyed you are faced with replacing it. Many manufacturers sell replacement wing kits for their planes. Wing kits are relatively inexpensive. They usually run about one-third the price of a full kit. In addition to the kit manufacturer's wing kit, foam wing cores are available from several companies or possibly from someone in your club who makes them. These are quick and easy to construct and can be a real time saver.

Learning Problems Caused By The Crash

A crash and a destroyed trainer can result in many problems aside from the financial loss—which is a great concern to many students. The main problems the instructor is concerned with are the loss of self-confidence by the student and the loss of continuity in training.

Some students accept a crash philosophically and others are severely shaken. Most are somewhere in between. In any case, most students will suffer a large loss of confidence in their ability to fly R/C. You need to work on rebuilding the student's confidence and enthusiasm.

While still at the crash site you have analyzed the crash and assessed the damage. Discuss it completely with the student. Give him your impression of the cause of the accident and the possibilities for repair. Be as encouraging as you can. Be sure to have the student save *all* the parts of the wreck in case it can be repaired.

In a day or two, give him a call and go over the incident. You'll need to give him a pep talk to bolster his confidence. Tell him how many other club members crashed while they were learning. You might even relate one of your own mishaps. This is the time for the "you can't quit now" pat on the head. He'll probably need it.

During your pep talks, go over how the plane can be repaired (if it can). You might even want to give him a hand in getting the rebuilding started. Keep in mind that he will not have all the knowledge of repair techniques or know all the tricks of the trade that you've amassed over the years. You can take a look at a damaged plane and know immediately where to start. He looks at it and sees a hopeless case. Get him started in the right direction on the repairs.

The best thing you can do to restore his self-confidence is to get his plane back into the air as quickly as possible. It's like getting back on the horse after you've been bucked off. That's the big reason why repair is so much more desirable than building a new model. If the student knows that he can get back into the air in a week or two, his enthusiasm will return along with some vestige of his original self-confidence.

Getting your student's plane back into the air as quickly as possible minimizes the other problem caused by a crash—loss of continuity in training. Nothing can be worse than to have the student progress to a certian level of proficiency, crash, and then have to start the learning process virtually all over again because of a long lay off.

It's like trying to learn to ride a bicycle. If you try for a while, but never quite learn to balance and then stop practicing for a few months, you are still going to have to essentially learn from scratch all over again when you start again. Lack of continuity in training due to a crash or other reason can just about double the learning time required.

Bear in mind when your student does get back out to the field for instruction that he is likely to be nervous and gun-shy at first. It's often a good idea to step back a phase, say from low approaches to figures 8s, to let him settle down and regain his confidence for a flight or two. Before you know it, he'll be coming along as well as ever and be ready before you know it to go on to selecting and building his second plane.

THE SECOND PLANE

Like potato chips, it's hard to stop with just one R/C plane. Trainers get so beat up during the learning process that they look like they've been through a war. (Some might say they have.) The hard landings and small crunches take their toll so that the life of a trainer just about corresponds to the time required to learn how to fly. A trainer is also very limited in its acrobatic potential. This is especially true after it has been banged up and repaired a couple of times. For these reasons, but also for the simple reason that there are dozens of planes out there waiting for the interested modeler, virtually every R/C flier will be working on a second plane by the time he is learning to land.

When your student is ready to move on up to his second plane, he will still not be able to successfully fly all of the planes on the market. This is especially true if he learned on a three-channel trainer. Even if his trainer had ailerons, he needs a second plane that still has some of the forgiving traits of a trainer. The plane can certainly have more acrobatic potential, but it should also be easy to land, fairly stall resistant and not too fast. You might call it an intermediate plane, but you will have to look hard to find many planes that are advertised as such.

Most R/C fliers, no matter what their abilities are, tend to want a scale or a contest-proven plane. May be they've been in love with Corsairs all their lives and go right out and buy one to step up to after their basic trainer. Or maybe all the high powered advertising got to them with promises that they'd fly like a champion with a certain design.

The student's own wish for a "neat" looking plane, along with the flurry of advertising in the model world, make it very hard for the novice, student to make a good choice for his second plane. All too many make a wrong choice, perhaps a plane that lands too hot, and regret it.

Take a look underneath the advertising prose and see which planes fill the bill as good second planes. First, for those who learned on a three-channel plane, the best second plane is one of the trainers with ailerons. The three-channel student has learned on an ultra-stable plane that does most of the work for him. He still must learn to handle a plane with ailerons, so he should build one of these type trainers and then go through an abreviated version of the R/C Flight Instruction program again. Once he has mastered this plane, he is ready for the planes I'll discuss now.

In an earlier chapter, I recommended a .40- or a .60-sized engine. I did so because the large majority of planes are made for these size engines. If your engine is in this size range, you'll have a much larger selection to choose from. In the .40-size engine, the Skylark is an excellent second plane. It is made by the same manufacturer that makes the Falcon 56. For all practical purposes, it is a low-wing version of the famous and successful Falcon trainer. Another good intermediate is the Contender. It comes in both .40 and .60 sizes. Both have been used by show teams to put on acrobatic performances under all types of conditions. They are forgiving, easy to fly planes with a lot of potential. Show teams also use the Sig Kougar. It has a bit higher landing speed than the Contender, but is a fine choice.

Also in the .40 size is the Super Kaos. This is an easy plane to fly with contest acrobatic potential. It's bigger brother, the Kaos, is my recommendation for the second plane in the .60 size. The regular Kaos (as opposed to the Super Kaos 60) is inexpensive for a .60-sized plane. It is light and easy to build and it has a relatively slow landing speed. Overall it is a great performer. Another .40-sized plane is the Saker. It is a light, high-performance sport plane that any flier could handle.

Although they are not low wingers, which most fliers want for a second plane, there are three planes I'd like to add to the list. The Strikemaster, the Sweet Stick and the Ugly Stick are all shoulder wing planes, but they can be high-performance ones. The Strikemaster is a sport plane detailed to look like a shoulder wing jet fighter.

The styling is such that you don't think of it in the high-wing category. The performance lives up to the looks. The other planes, the Sweet Stick and the Ugly Stick, were listed in the trainer category. Many R/C'ers have enjoyed learning to fly on them. They do, however, also have the strength and performance ability to make great second planes. You'll more than likely see several of them around your club.

It is not uncommon for even competitors to keep a Stick plane around for fun flying. Both planes are strong enough to be grossly overpowered. In some clubs .60-powered Sweet Sticks that can climb straight up are common.

Of course, there are other planes that make good second planes. The things to keep in mind are that the plane should be relatively stable, easy to land and forgiving to some extent. Asking around the club will get you the names of the planes your club members recommend as second planes. It will also get a novice flier an idea of what he probably shouldn't tackle yet.

When the student graduates from his trainer, most instructors consider him finished with flight training. Well, he is and he isn't. He will still need you. Give him a hand trimming and check him out on his second (and even his third and fourth) plane. Stand by him until he is thoroughly familiar with the new plane's performance. He is just getting started in the fast growing and challenging sport/hobby of radio controlled airplane flying. You've helped him along this far. Stick with him just a bit longer until you've turned him into a full-fledged pilot. Good luck and happy landings.

Index

Edited by Steven Bolt